Beginning C# 2005 Databases

From Novice to Professional

James Huddleston, Ranga Raghuram,
Syed Fahad Gilani, Jacob Hammer Pedersen,
and Jon Reid

Apress®

Beginning C# 2005 Databases: From Novice to Professional

Copyright © 2006 by James Huddleston, Ranga Raghuram, Syed Fahad Gilani, Jacob Hammer Pedersen, and Jon Reid

ISBN-13 (pbk): 978-1-59509-777-4

ISBN-10 (pbk): 1-59059-777-X

Printed and bound in the United States of America 9 8 7 6 5 4 3 2 1

Lead Editor: Jonathan Hassell
Technical Reviewer: Vidya Vrat Agarwal
Editorial Board: Steve Anglin, Ewan Buckingham, Gary Cornell, Jason Gilmore, Jonathan Gennick, Jonathan Hassell, James Huddleston, Chris Mills, Matthew Moodie, Dominic Shakeshaft, Jim Sumser, Keir Thomas, Matt Wade
Project Manager: Elizabeth Seymour
Copy Edit Manager: Nicole Flores
Copy Editors: Nicole Abramowitz, Liz Welch
Assistant Production Director: Kari Brooks-Copony
Production Editor: Janet Vail
Compositor: Linda Weidemann, Wolf Creek Press
Proofreader: April Eddy
Indexer: Kevin Broccoli/Broccoli Information Management
Cover Designer: Kurt Krames
Manufacturing Director: Tom Debolski

Distributed to the book trade worldwide by Springer-Verlag New York, Inc., 233 Spring Street, 6th Floor, New York, NY 10013. Phone 1-800-SPRINGER, fax 201-348-4505, e-mail orders-ny@springer-sbm.com, or visit http://www.springeronline.com.

For information on translations, please contact Apress directly at 2560 Ninth Street, Suite 219, Berkeley, CA 94710. Phone 510-549-5930, fax 510-549-5939, e-mail info@apress.com, or visit http://www.apress.com.

The source code for this book is available to readers at http://www.apress.com in the Source Code/ Download section.

To Jared, Quinn, and Tess
I love you.
—Jim Huddleston

Contents at a Glance

Contents

About the Author

■JIM HUDDLESTON worked with computers, primarily as a database designer and developer, for more than 30 years before becoming an Apress editor in 2006. He has a bachelor's degree in Latin and Greek from the University of Pennsylvania and a juris doctor degree from the University of Pittsburgh. Author also of *Beginning VB 2005 Databases: From Novice to Professional*, Jim still finds databases an endlessly fascinating area of study. But, what he currently finds most interesting in computing is F#, which is almost as intriguing as his life-long hobby, translating ancient Greek and Latin epic poetry.

His translations of Homer's *Odyssey* and the pseudo-Hesiodic *Shield of Heracles* are available at The Chicago Homer (http://www.library.northwestern.edu/homer/). His translation of the last and longest Greek epic poem, the *Dionysiaca* of Nonnus, will start to appear online in early 2007. You can reach Jim via his classical blog, http://onamissionunaccomplished.blogspot.com/, or at james.huddleston@apress.com.

About the Technical Reviewer

VIDYA VRAT AGARWAL holds Microsoft Certified Trainer (MCT), Microsoft Certified Solution Developer (MCSD) for Microsoft .NET, Microsoft Certified Application Developer (MCAD) for .NET, and MCSD certifications and is a Life Member of the Computer Society of India (CSI). He started working on .NET with its first beta release. He is currently a Senior Subject Matter Expert—Microsoft for Lionbridge in Mumbai, India, where he lives with his beloved wife and lovely daughter Vamika (nicknamed Pearly). Vidya believes that nothing will turn into a reality without them. Besides authoring articles for Programmers Heaven (http://www.programmersheaven.com/) and tech reviewing for Apress, he blogs at http://dotnetpassion.blogspot.com/.

Acknowledgments

First, I'd like to thank Ewan Buckingham of Apress for convincing me to revise this book now rather than wait until all the goodies for C# 3.0 and ADO.NET 3.0 come sometime in the future. SQL Server 2005 and LINQ are both exciting topics that deserve current coverage, and I've tried to do them justice in a way that will keep this book fresh and valuable for readers for quite a while.

Second, I'd like to thank my tech reviewer, Vidya Vrat Agarwal, for his thorough and careful work on both the manuscript and code. His extraordinary professionalism and dedication made this book a better one. Of course, any errors that remain are entirely my responsibility, not his. Thanks so much, Vidya.

Third, I want to thank my editor, Jonathan Hassell, project manager, Elizabeth Seymour, and production editor, Janet Vail. All made this endeavor far less of an effort than it otherwise could have been. Thanks too to my copy editors, Nicole Abramowitz and Liz Welch, whose trained eyes saved me from a variety of inelegancies and inadvertencies and who were invariably polite in pointing out even the most embarrassing glitches. All of you make Apress the warm and pleasant place for authors that it truly is.

A variety of people contributed encouragement and support. Thank you, Amy Abrams, Nicholas Andrea, Laurie Apgar, Tiffany Armstrong, Elizabeth A. Baker, Wesley R. Bowman, W. Truxton Boyce, Robert Chodoroff, Liam Patrick Clerkin, Wydell Conley, Chip Deaton, Rebecca Doeltz, Melissa Dupre, Elrod S. Ferreira, Justin Finucan, Francoise Friedlaender, David Gaines, Milo Gibbons, Lania Herman, Sarah James, Jackie Jones, Renee L. Kane, Elizabeth Keelan, Cary Kerrigan, Gil Lachance, Jeff Lee, Joel Lipman, Darren R. Lloyd, Ron Maguire, Jason B. Majewski, Rosemarie Naguski, Edna Ocampo, Susan Paul, Jax Pierson, Paul Preiss, John Reda, Helen Rei, Eric Robson, Michael P. Small, Teri Small, Michael Thompson, Susan Tussey, James Tuzun, and Paul Yip.

Finally, special thanks to very special people for extra-special help: Roy Beatty, Michael Green, Judith Lane Gregory, David Moffitt, Joseph Rickert, Yi Soon-Shin, and Yi Ui-Min.

James Huddleston

Introduction

Every program manipulates data. Most real-world programs use data stored in relational databases, so every C# programmer needs to know how to access relational data. This book explains how to do this in C#, with ADO.NET and Language-Integrated Query (LINQ), against SQL Server 2005. The same principles and techniques apply to C# programming against other relational database management systems, such as DB2, MySQL, Oracle, and PostgreSQL, so what you learn here is valuable whatever database you use.

Who Is This Book For?

This book is for anyone interested in how to access relational data with C#. Only a bit of experience with C# is assumed, and no prior experience with relational database or the relational database language SQL is required. We cover all fundamentals carefully and in an order we believe leads easily from one topic to another, building knowledge and experience as you progress through the book. So, chapters are best read in sequence.

What Does This Book Cover?

This book covers all the fundamentals of relational databases and ADO.NET that every C# programmer needs to know and understand. These concepts and techniques are the foundation for all database programming. Even if you never learn anything else, by the end of the book you'll be able to handle the vast majority of real-world database applications in a professional way. The chapters progress as follows.

Getting Started

The first three chapters set things up for our later work. Chapter 1 explains how to download and install our tools (all free from Microsoft). Chapter 2 gives you some practice with them as we configure a few things. Chapter 3 is a primer on Transact-SQL (T-SQL), SQL Server's dialect of the standard database language, SQL.

Learning ADO.NET Basics

Chapters 4 through 8 describe the essential features of ADO.NET, the interface between C# programs and databases. Each major feature is explained with example programs that you can use as the basis for your own programs, whatever part of ADO.NET you need.

Building Windows Applications

Chapter 9 covers data binding, mapping database data to graphical user interface controls. We provide simple Windows Forms examples, but the principles are equally applicable to ASP.NET Web controls.

Learning More About SQL and Relational Databases

Chapters 10 through 12 delve more deeply into relational database concepts and techniques, from designing and creating tables, to more advanced queries and data manipulation, to a full chapter on writing stored procedures in T-SQL.

Using Advanced Features

Chapters 13 through 15 cover exception handling, transactions, and ADO.NET events.

Using Special Data Types

Chapter 16 explains how to handle large data objects, such as images and documents. Chapter 17 covers the new XML data type and other features for conveniently using XML with T-SQL. It carefully explains some techniques that even experienced T-SQL users puzzle over and demonstrates their power.

Introducing LINQ

Chapter 18 is an exciting one. It describes how to use Language-Integrated Query (LINQ), Microsoft's new technology for accessing any kind of data. LINQ is easy to use and is the future direction of ADO.NET and .NET database programming.

What Do You Need to Use This Book?

Windows XP Professional (or any other operating system that can run SQL Server 2005 Express), 512MB of memory, and a couple spare gigs of disk space, so you can download and install the tools in Chapter 1. After that, just the willingness to read closely and the patience to actually perform the steps we carefully describe for building C# database applications and using SQL. Nothing teaches better than hands-on practice, and that's what our code is designed to provide.

How to Download the Sample Code

All the source code is available in the Source Code/Download section at http://www.apress.com.

CHAPTER 1

■ ■ ■

Getting Our Tools

In this book, you'll learn how to access relational databases with C#. Our primary development tools will be Microsoft Visual C# 2005 Express Edition (VCSE) and Microsoft SQL Server 2005 Express Edition (SSE), since they're free, powerful, and designed to work well together.

VCSE is an integrated development environment (IDE) that provides a subset of Visual Studio 2005 functionality for building C# applications.

SSE is the relational database subset of SQL Server 2005 that provides virtually all the online transaction processing (OLTP) capabilities of SQL Server 2005, supports databases up to 4GB (and up to 32,767 databases per SSE instance), and can handle hundreds of concurrent users. SSE doesn't include SQL Server's data warehousing and Integration Services components. It also doesn't include Business Intelligence components for online analytical processing (OLAP) and data mining, because they're based on SQL Server's Analysis Services server that is completely distinct from its relational database engine.

SSE is also completely distinct from its predecessor, Microsoft SQL Server Desktop Engine (MSDE), which was a subset of SQL Server 2000. MSDE databases cannot be used with SSE, but they can be upgraded to SSE databases.

Let's start by learning how to obtain and install our tools.

Note We'll also use LINQ in Chapter 8, but you can wait until then to install it, since it's not needed if you're not interested in LINQ.

In this chapter, we'll cover:

- Installing VCSE and SSE

- Installing SQL Server Management Studio Express Edition (SSMSE)

- Installing SQL Server 2005 Books Online (BOL)

- Installing the Northwind sample database

Installing VCSE and SSE

VCSE and SSE can be downloaded and installed separately, but since SSE can be installed as part of VCSE installation, let's do it that way. VCSE can be downloaded from `http://msdn.microsoft.com/vcsharp/downloads/2005/`. Go there and click Download Visual C# 2005 Express.

■Note .NET Framework 2.0 is required for all Express software. We assume you already have it installed and won't cover its installation here. If you don't have it, it's available for free at `http://msdn.microsoft.com/netframework/downloads/updates/default.aspx`.

To install VCSE and SSE:

1. Create a folder for downloads. We use `C:\bcs2005db\install`, but you can use whatever folder you prefer.

2. On the VCSE Overview page, click Download Now. On the Download Now! page, carefully read the "1. Uninstall beta versions" item and make sure you comply with it, then click Download. A File Download - Security Warning window appears (see Figure 1-1). You can either run or save the `vcssetup.exe` file. We'll save it, by clicking Save and then specifying our download folder.

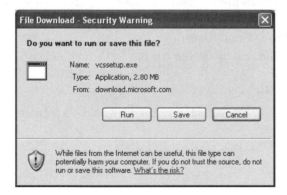

Figure 1-1. *VCSE download confirmation*

3. Run `vcssetup.exe`, which starts the VCSE installation process. When the File Download - Security Warning window appears, click Run. A few message boxes appear, then the Welcome window appears (see Figure 1-2). If you want to, check the check box, then click Next.

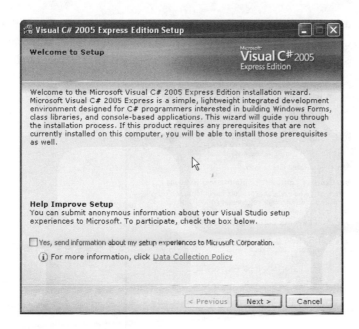

Figure 1-2. *VCSE Welcome*

4. The End-User License Agreement window appears (see Figure 1-3). Check the check box to accept the license, then click Next.

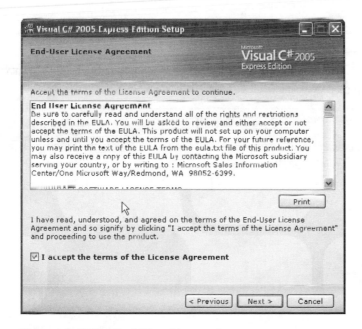

Figure 1-3. *VCSE End-User License Agreement*

5. When the Installation Options window appears (see Figure 1-4), check *only* the second check box, for SSE. (You can check both, but the MSDN Express Library is quite large, isn't essential for this book, and can be installed later.) Then click Next.

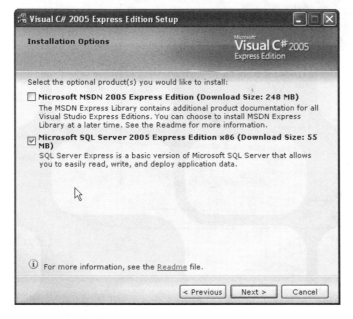

Figure 1-4. *VCSE Installation Options*

■**Note** Though we don't need it for this book, we encourage you to eventually install the MSDN Express Library. It's full of additional documentation and samples that are well worth the time it takes to download it, if you have about 1GB of disk space to hold it when it's installed.

---

6. The Destination Folder window appears (see Figure 1-5). You can't change the destination, so just click Install.

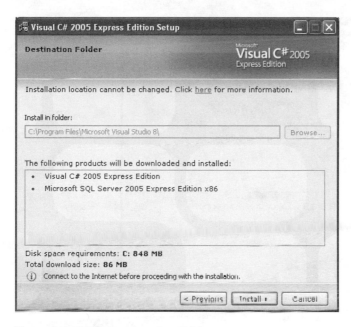

Figure 1-5. *VCSE Destination Folder*

7. The Download and Install Progress window appears (see Figure 1-6). It first reports the progress of the file downloads (about 30MB for VCSE and 56MB for SSE), then reports on their installation. Wait patiently for the Setup Complete window to appear (see Figure 1-7).

8. You can register your copy of VCSE by clicking Register Now, but this is optional and can be done later, so we won't cover it here. Whether or not you register, click Exit to end the installation.

Both VCSE and SSE are now installed (in fact, an SSE *instance* should now be running), but you need a few other things before you can use them for this book.

■**Note** When you install SSE as part of VCSE installation, an *instance* of SSE named *localhost* SQLEXPRESS is created. For example, our instance is named JQT\SQLEXPRESS, since our machine is named JQT. An SSE instance is a *database server* (i.e., a program that provides SSE database services). Multiple SSE instances can run simultaneously on the same machine, and each instance can have multiple databases associated with it.

Figure 1-6. *VCSE Download and Install Progress*

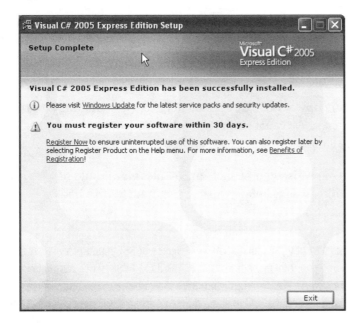

Figure 1-7. *VCSE Setup Complete*

Installing SSMSE

SSMSE is the primary tool for administering SSE databases. Let's install it next. To install SSMSE:

1. Go to `http://msdn.microsoft.com/vstudio/express/sql/download/` (the MSSE download page) and scroll down to "3. Download and install." Click Download under SQL Server Management Studio Express. When the File Download - Security Warning window appears, either click Run or click Save and specify your install folder. (We're saving `SQLServer2005_SSMSEE.msi` in `C:\bcs2005db\install`.)

2. If you saved the file, run `SQLServer2005_SSMSEE.msi`, which starts the VCSE installation process. When the Open File Security Warning window appears, click Run. A message box is followed by the Welcome window (see Figure 1-8). Click Next.

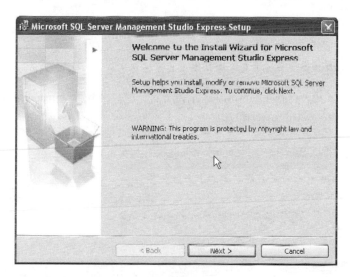

Figure 1-8. *SSMSE Install Wizard Welcome*

3. In the next window, accept the license agreement, then click Next.

4. In the next window, fill in your information, then click Next.

5. When the Feature Selection window (see Figure 1-9) appears, click Next.

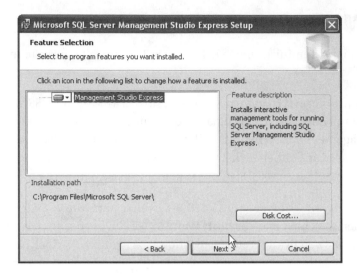

Figure 1-9. *SSMSE Feature Selection*

6. When the next window appears, click Install.

7. A progress window appears (see Figure 1-10), and is followed by a window that reports successful installation (see Figure 1-11). Click Finish.

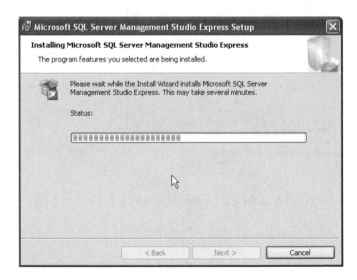

Figure 1-10. *SSMSE progress window*

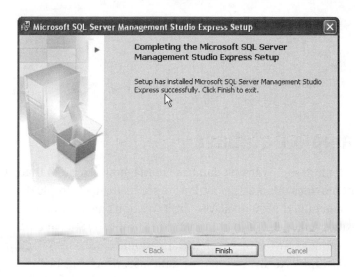

Figure 1-11. *SSMSE setup completion*

SSMSE is now installed.

Installing the SQL Server Documentation

The SSE documentation is part of BOL. To install BOL:

1. Go to the SQL Server 2005 Books Online download page, http://www.microsoft. com/technet/prodtechnol/sql/2005/downloads/books.mspx. Click Go.

2. On the next page, click Download.

3. When the File Download - Security Warning window appears, either click Run or click Save and specify your install folder. (We're saving SqlServer2K5_BOL_Apr2006_ v2.msi in C:\bcs2005db\install.)

4. If you saved the file, run SQLServer2005_ BOL_Apr2006_v2.msi, which starts the BOL installation process. When the Open File - Security Warning window appears, click Run. A message box is quickly followed by the Welcome window. Click Next.

5. In the next window, accept the license agreement, then click Next.

6. In the next window, fill in your information, then click Next.

7. When the Feature Selection window appears, click Next.

8. When the next window appears, click Install.

Microsoft SQL Server 2005 Books Online is now installed.

Installing a Sample Database

SQL Server 2005 is a much more sophisticated database management system than SQL Server 2000, so Microsoft provides much larger and more sophisticated sample databases—AdventureWorks and AdventureWorksDW—for it. We don't need sample data of this quantity or complexity. (In fact, only AdventureWorks is usable by SSE, and navigating it isn't easy for those without some experience with relational databases.) For our purposes, the smaller and simpler Northwind sample database, which has been part of SQL Server forever, is more appropriate.

■**Note** The AdventureWorks and AdventureWorksDW sample databases are available for download at `http://www.microsoft.com/downloads/details.aspx?familyid=E719ECF7-9F46-4312-AF89-6AD8702E4E6E&displaylang=en`.

We'll install Northwind in three steps: downloading the creation script, creating the sample database, and uninstalling the creation script. We'll back up the sample database in Chapter 2.

Installing the Northwind Creation Script

To install the script that creates the Northwind sample database:

1. Go to `http://www.microsoft.com/downloads/details.aspx?FamilyID=06616212-0356-46a0-8da2-eebc53a68034&DisplayLang=en` and download `SQL2000SampleDb.msi`. When the File Download - Security Warning window appears, either click Run or click Save and specify your install folder. (We're saving `SQL2000SampleDb.msi` in `C:\bcs2005db\install`.)

2. If you saved the file, run `SQL2000SampleDb.msi`, which starts the installation process. When the Open File - Security Warning window appears, click Run. A message box is followed by the Welcome window (see Figure 1-12). Click Next.

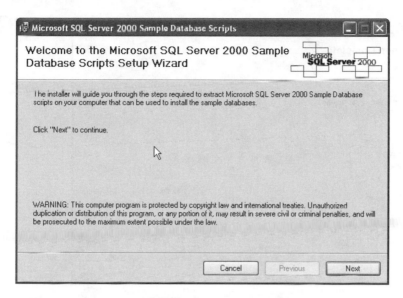

Figure 1-12. *Northwind Installation script's Setup Wizard Welcome*

3. When the License Agreement window appears, click the I Agree radio button. When the Next button is enabled, click it.

4. When the Choose Installation Options window appears, click Next.

5. When the Confirm Installation window appears, click Next.

6. A progress window briefly appears, followed by the Installation Complete window. The installation files have been extracted to (no, we're not kidding) C:\SQL Server 2000 Sample Databases (see Figure 1-13). Note that the sample databases haven't yet been created. Only the script files that create them have been "installed." Click Close.

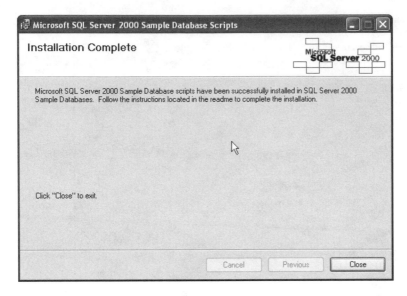

Figure 1-13. *Northwind installation script's Installation Complete*

Creating the Northwind Sample Database

We need to run a Transact-SQL (T-SQL) script to create the Northwind database. We'll do that with the SQL Server command-line utility sqlcmd.

To create the Northwind sample database:

1. Open a command prompt, and then go to whatever directory contains the instnwnd.sql file (for convenience, we copied it from C:\SQL Server 2000 Sample Databases to C:\bcs2005db\install, but that's not necessary).

2. Enter the following command, making sure to use -S, not -s. This should produce the output in Figure 1-14:

```
sqlcmd -S .\sqlexpress -i instnwnd.sql
```

■**Tip** Code snippets like this are available in the code download, in the snippets.txt file for a chapter. For example, this snippet is in C:\bcs2005db\code\Chapter01\snippets.txt.

```
bcs2005db                                                           _ □ ×
c:\bcs2005db\install>sqlcmd -S .\sqlexpress -i instnwnd.sql
Changed database context to 'master'.
Changed database context to 'Northwind'.

c:\bcs2005db\install>
```

Figure 1-14. *Creating the Northwind database*

This command executes the sqlcmd program, invoking it with two options. The first option, -S .\sqlexpress, tells sqlcmd to connect to the SQLEXPRESS instance of SSE on the local machine (represented by .). The second option, -i instnwnd.sql, tells sqlcmd to read the file instnwnd.sql and execute the T-SQL in it.

■**Caution** sqlcmd cannot connect to SSE unless the SSE instance is running. A Windows service named MSSQL$SQLEXPRESS should have been created when you installed SSE, and it should have been started automatically, so the SQLEXPRESS instance should already be running. If sqlcmd complains that it can't connect, you can start the service from a command prompt with the command net start mssql$sqlexpress.

The Northwind sample database has now been created. Let's access it to make sure. We'll use sqlcmd interactively.

1. At the command prompt, enter the following command, which runs sqlcmd and connects to the SQLEXPRESS instance (see Figure 1-15):

```
sqlcmd -S .\sqlexpress
```

```
SQLCMD                                                              _ □ ×
c:\bcs2005db\install>sqlcmd -S .\sqlexpress
1>
```

Figure 1-15. *Connecting to* .\SQLEXPRESS *with* sqlcmd

2. At the sqlcmd prompt (1>), enter the following T-SQL:

```
use northwind
select count(*) from employees
go
```

The first two lines are T-SQL statements. USE specifies the database to query. SELECT asks for the number of rows in the Employees table. GO is not a T-SQL statement but rather a sqlcmd command that signals the end of the T-SQL statements to process. The result, that there are nine rows in Employees, is shown in Figure 1-16.

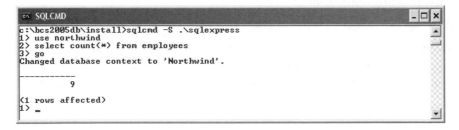

Figure 1-16. *Running a simple query against the Northwind database*

3. Enter the sqlcmd command quit to exit sqlcmd. See Figure 1-17.

```
c:\bcs2005db\install>sqlcmd -S .\sqlexpress
1> use northwind
2> select count(*) from employees
3> go
Changed database context to 'Northwind'.

-----------
          9

(1 rows affected)
1> quit

c:\bcs2005db\install>_
```

Figure 1-17. *Exiting sqlcmd*

■**Note** We don't cover sqlcmd further, since we submit SQL with SSMSE, but we recommend you play with it. It's the latest command-line tool for SQL Server, superseding the earlier osql and isql tools, and it's still a very valuable tool for database administrators and programmers.

Uninstalling the Northwind Creation Script

When you installed the creation script, the installer created not only a folder but also an application, Microsoft SQL Server 2000 Sample Database Scripts. You don't need this anymore, so you can remove it with Add or Remove Programs from the Control Panel.

Summary

In this chapter, you installed Visual C# 2005 Express, SQL Server 2005 Express, SQL Server Management Studio Express, SQL Server Books Online, and the sample Northwind database. You used `sqlcmd` to create and query the Northwind database.

Now that you have the tools, let's get acquainted with them.

■ ■ ■

CHAPTER 2

Getting to Know Our Tools

Now that you've installed the tools you'll use in this book, we'll show you just enough about them so you can use them easily to do the things you need to do the rest of the way.

Our goal isn't to provide tutorials on any of the tools. We'll focus on SSMSE, since we assume you have no familiarity with it. We'll show you just a few things about VCSE, since we assume you know C# and have either used Visual Studio or even VCSE for programming. (If you haven't, Chapter 4 gives detailed enough instructions on building our first C# examples in VCSE that you should be able to use VCSE without any problems. We intentionally keep our programs very simple and avoid exploiting VCSE features just in case you're new to using the Microsoft IDEs.)

In this chapter, we'll cover:

- Using SSMSE

- Configuring VCSE

- Using BOL

Note There are two SSE configuration GUI tools—SQL Server Configuration Manager and SQL Server Surface Area Configuration—that we don't need to use for this book, since all our programs run locally against the SQLEXPRESS server. If you plan to use SSE for things like ASP.NET applications, you'll need to use these tools to enable SSE to accept remote connections.

Using SSMSE

SSMSE is the new GUI interface for SQL Server 2005. It combines the features of earlier SQL Server GUI tools to make database administration and T-SQL development possible from a single interface. We use it in this book primarily to submit T-SQL, but we'll also look briefly here at its Object Explorer so we can view and manage database objects.

Let's take a quick tour of SSMSE:

1. To open SSMSE, click Start ➤ All Programs ➤ Microsoft SQL Server 2005 ➤ SQL
   Server Management Studio Express. You should see the window as in Figure 2-1.
   Click Connect.

Figure 2-1. *Opening SSMSE*

2. The Object Explorer and tabbed Summary windows will appear, and you should
   be connected to your SSE instance. You should see a screen as in Figure 2-2. The
   top node in Object Explorer should be your SSE instance, and the Summary
   tabbed window should display folder icons for the five other nodes in Object
   Explorer. Expand the Databases node in Object Explorer.

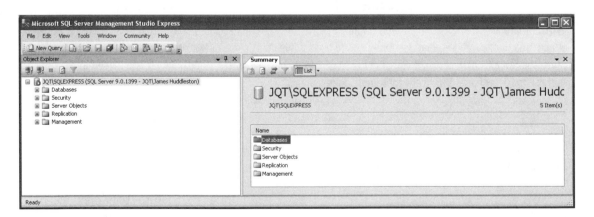

Figure 2-2. *SSMSE Object Explorer and Summary*

3. There should be two nodes under Databases: System Databases and Northwind. Expand the System Databases node and you'll see the screen in Figure 2-3. SSE has four system databases. The *master* database records global information for the SSE instance. The *model* database is the basis for new databases. The *msdb* database supports job and alert features beyond the scope of this book. The *tempdb* database holds temporary tables and other database objects, either generated automatically by SSE or created explicitly by you. The temporary database is re-created each time the SSE instance is started, so objects in it do not persist after SSE is shut down.

Figure 2-3. *System Databases*

4. Click the New Query button above Object Explorer. You'll see the screen in Figure 2-4. A tabbed edit window appears and overlays the Summary window. Look at the bottom of the window. The status bar indicates you're connected to the master database. By default, you connect to the master when you connect to an instance. Any SQL you submit will be run against the database you're currently connected to. Click the X at the top right of the window to close it.

5. Click the Northwind node in Object Explorer, then click New Query. You'll get a new SQL edit window, as in Figure 2-5. The status bar shows you're connected to Northwind instead of master. Note also that the name of the window has changed. SSMSE provides a default name for the file you can optionally save your SQL in and increments its number each time you open a new edit window.

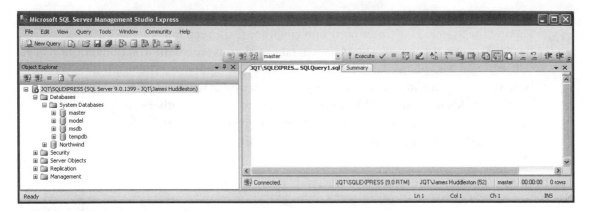

Figure 2-4. *SQL edit window*

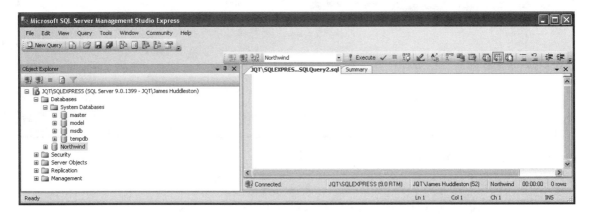

Figure 2-5. *SQL edit window connected to Northwind*

6. Enter the simple query `select * from employees` and click the Execute button. You'll see the screen in Figure 2-6. SSMSE displays a grid of the result set in the Results window. It also reports the number of rows in the result set in the status bar. Error and informational messages are provided in the Messages window. There are no errors, but if you click the Messages tab, as shown in Figure 2-6, you'll see the message "(9 rows() affected)," confirming the status bar information.

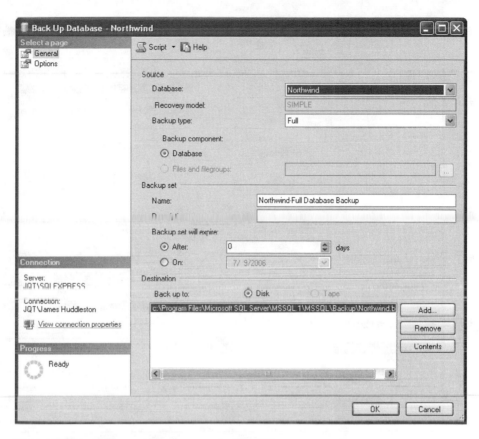

Figure 2-6. *Executing a simple query in SSMSE*

7. Though you clicked New Query to get there, the SQL edit window isn't limited to just queries. You can execute virtually any T-SQL statement from it, so before you go any further, you should back up the Northwind database, so you can restore it if you need to. Right-click the Northwind node in Object Explorer, click Tasks ➤ Backup… . You'll see the window in Figure 2-7.

8. Accept all the default values. SSMSE does a full backup of the Northwind database, creating a "backup set" for you that will not expire. The backup will be stored in the Northwind.bak file in the default SSE backup folder. Click OK, and you'll see the Progress indicator go from Ready to Executing and spin a bit. A message box will appear (see Figure 2-8) to inform you the backup succeeded. Click OK. The Northwind database is now backed up. You'll see how to restore it soon.

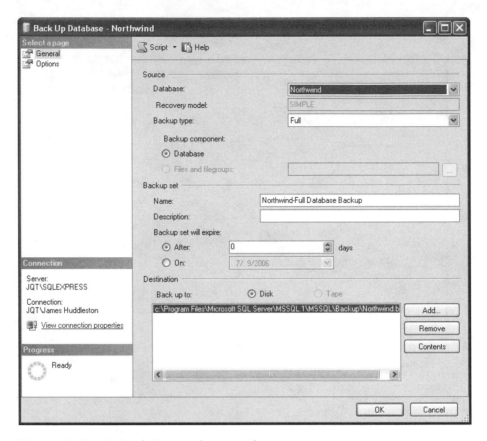

Figure 2-7. *SSMSE Back Up Database window*

Figure 2-8. *SSMSE database backed-up message*

9. Now, expand the Northwind node in Object Explorer, expand its Tables node, right-click dbo.Employees, and click Open Table. You'll see the screen in Figure 2-9. SSMSE again displays a grid of all the rows and columns in the Employees table. It also adds a tab for an autohidden Properties window to the right of the grid. We don't care about the properties, so we won't open it, but it

shows that SSMSE supports Auto Hide (as well as many other Visual Studio features for configuring your working environment). You're positioned in the first row and column of the grid, and the status bar alerts you that the cell is read-only (because the column is an IDENTITY column and SSE populates if for you), but you can change table data from the grid. For example, if you moved to the LastName column, the alert would disappear and you could modify the value. For some tables (but not Employees), if you use the last row, you can insert a new row. You can also delete rows. But, **BE CAREFUL**! Any changes, except for deletions, will be made in the database **without prompting you for confirmation**. Horizontal and vertical scrollbars appear appropriately, and buttons and a text box in the status bar also let you navigate through table rows.

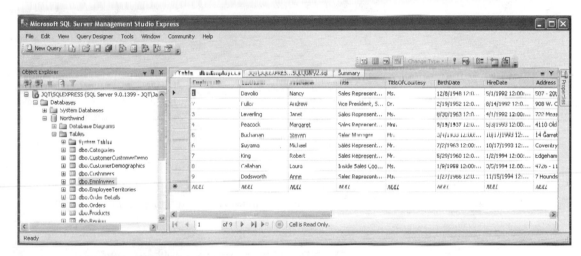

Figure 2-9. *Displaying table contents with Object Explorer*

10. Close the window and expand the dbo.Employees node. You'll see the screen in Figure 2-10. All the Employees columns are listed as nodes and labeled with their data type and nullability. Primary keys and foreign keys are indicated by "PK" and "FK," respectively.

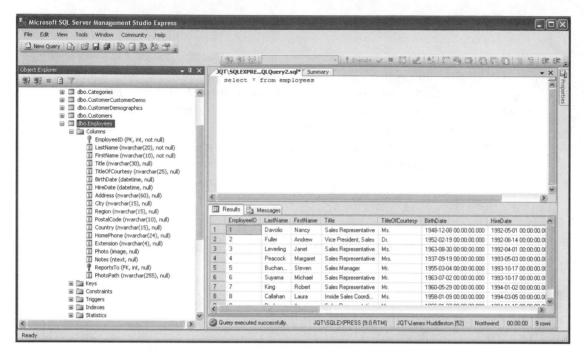

Figure 2-10. *Displaying table columns with Object Explorer*

11. Double-click the EmployeeID node, and you'll get a complete list of its properties, as in Figure 2-11. Close the window by clicking OK, Cancel, or just the **X** icon.

12. Contract the Northwind Tables node (simply to make the Object Explorer tree smaller), and expand the Programmability node. You'll see the screen in Figure 2-12. You'll use the Stored Procedures node in Chapter 12, and we'll cover how to use it there. (Note that you can also create and manage user-defined functions and database triggers from Object Explorer, though we won't cover them in this book.) Now, go up to the Database Diagrams node and try to expand it. The plus sign disappears because no diagrams exist.

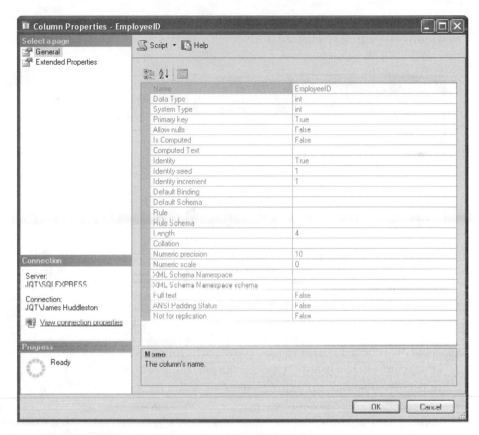

Figure 2-11. *Displaying column properties with Object Explorer*

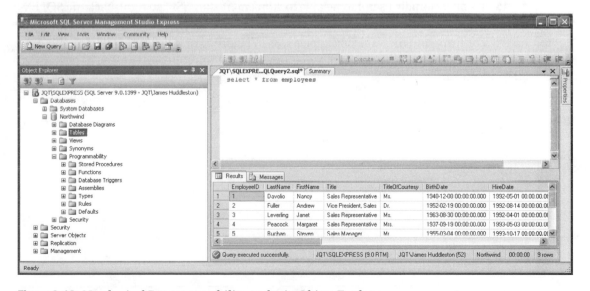

Figure 2-12. *Northwind Programmability nodes in Object Explorer*

13. Right-click Database Diagrams and click New Database Diagram. The Add Table window appears (see Figure 2-13).

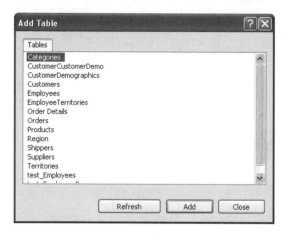

Figure 2-13. *Selecting tables for a database diagram*

14. Click Customers, hold down Ctrl as you click Orders, then click Add. The Add Table window remains open, so you can add more tables, but these are enough for this demonstration, so click Close. A diagram, showing the tables, their columns, and the relationship between the tables, appears in its own window, as in Figure 2-14. Close the diagram window, and click Yes when prompted to save the changes. Accept the default name, and click OK in the Choose Name window.

15. It's occasionally useful to be able to stop and restart SSE, so right-click the SQLEXPRESS instance node (the top node in Object Explorer) and click Stop. A confirmation message box appears, as in Figure 2-15. Click Yes to stop the MSSQL$SQLEXPRESS service that runs the SQLEXPRESS instance.

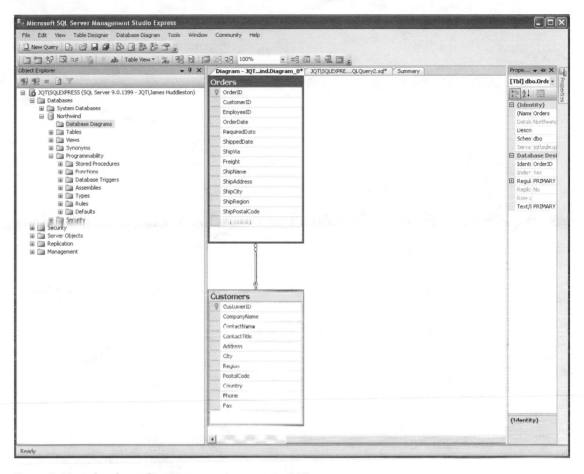

Figure 2-14. *A database diagram*

Figure 2-15. *Stopping an SSE instance*

16. Now try to execute the query in the SQL edit window (or try anything to access the instance, if you've already shut the window). There will be no Results window, and the Messages window will report an error, as in Figure 2-16.

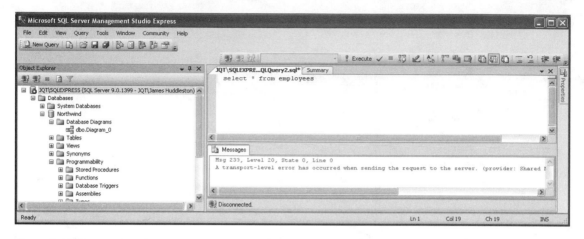

Figure 2-16. *Error on trying to query a stopped SSE instance*

17. To start SQLEXPRESS, right-click the instance node in Object Explorer, click Start, and click Yes in the confirmation message box. Click the Northwind node and retry the query. It should work fine.

18. To restore the Northwind database, right-click the Northwind node in Object Explorer, than click Tasks ➤ Restore ➤ Database… . You'll see the window in Figure 2-17.

19. Click OK and you'll get the message box in Figure 2-18. You can't restore the Northwind database, because the kind of restore you're doing requires exclusive access, and SSMSE is currently connected to Northwind through the query. Click OK to close the message box, then close the SQL edit window (click No when prompted to save it).

20. Click OK again in the Restore Database window. You should get the message box shown in Figure 2-19. To see that the database has been restored, try to expand the Database Diagrams node under Northwind. You saved a diagram earlier, but once again the plus sign disappears, since the database diagram was stored in Northwind in step 14, but you backed up the database in steps 7 and 8, so you've restored Northwind to a state before the diagram was saved. The same holds true for any data in any SSE database.

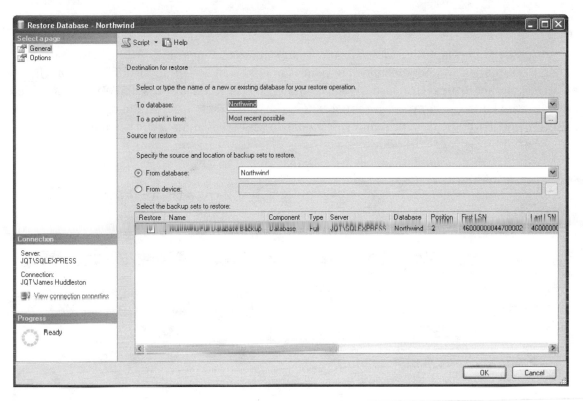

Figure 2-17. *Restoring the Northwind database*

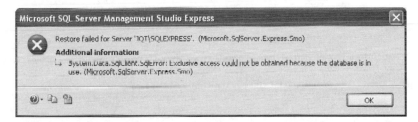

Figure 2-18. *Restore-failure message box*

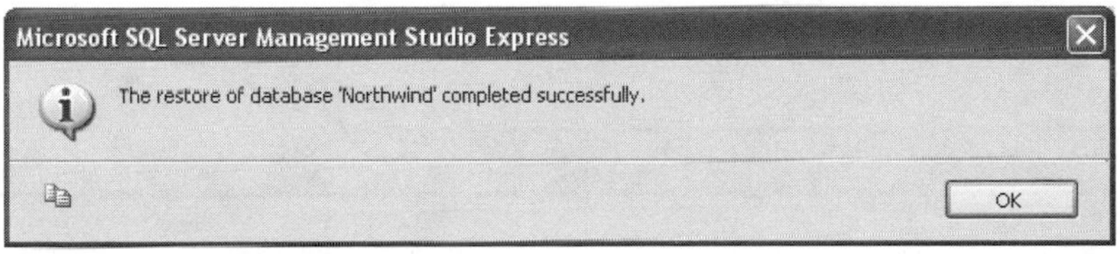

Figure 2-19. *Message box stating the Northwind database is restored*

Configuring VCSE

VCSE offers a significant subset of Visual Studio 2005 functionality, limited to C# programming and not including templates for building ASP.NET applications (for which another Express IDE, Visual Web Developer 2005 Express, is available). We assume since you know C# that you have some experience with either Visual Studio or VCSE, so we'll only cover the specific things you should do with VCSE to make the examples in this book easiest to work with.

Let's do these few simple things with VCSE:

1. To open VCSE, click Start ➤ All Programs ➤ Microsoft Visual C# 2005 Express Edition. You should see the screen shown in Figure 2-20.

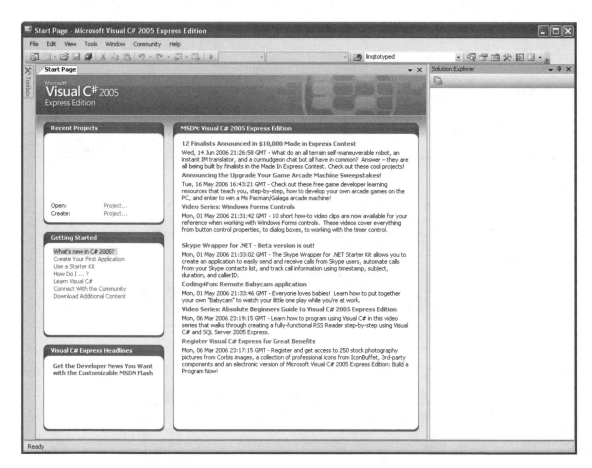

Figure 2-20. *Opening VCSE*

2. VCSE is a highly configurable IDE that each user typically adapts to personal preferences. We use it in a rather vanilla way and don't at all try to exploit its many features that can significantly enhance developer productivity, because what seems the best way to one user may seem the worst way to another. But, we do customize the configuration a bit, because we want to control how we indent code and where we store our VCSE solutions. You don't have to do this, but here's what we did, if you'd like to be consistent. Click Tools ➤ Options… to open the window, as in Figure 2-21.

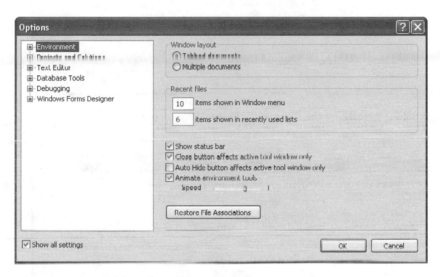

Figure 2-21. *Opening VCSE Options*

3. Check the "Show all settings" check box, then expand the Projects and Solutions node. Click the General node and change the "Visual Studio projects location" to C:\bcs2005db\solutions, as in Figure 2-22.

4. Expand the Text Editor node. Expand the All Languages node and click the Tabs node. Make the information consistent with Figure 2-23. This changes tabs and indentations to three spaces. Click OK.

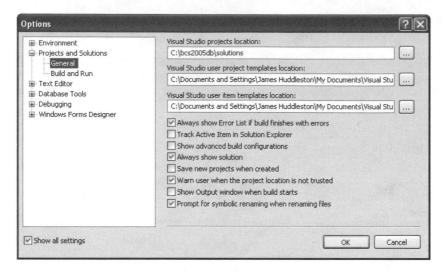

Figure 2-22. *Changing the default folder for VCSE projects*

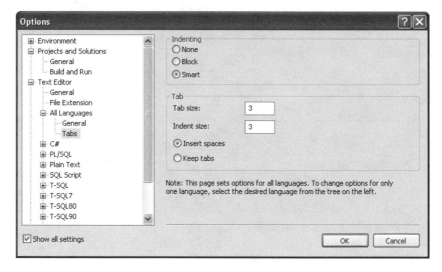

Figure 2-23. *Setting VCSE tabs and indentations*

5. You'll need a connection to the SSE Northwind database, so let's create one. Click View ➤ Other Windows ➤ Database Explorer to open Database Explorer (which is very similar to SSMSE's Object Explorer). Notice in Figure 2-24 that there are no Data Connections nodes.

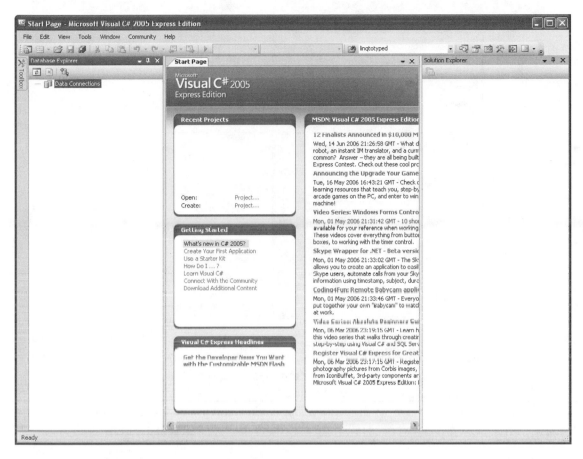

Figure 2-24. *Database Explorer with no connections*

6. Right-click the Data Connections node and click Add Connection… . The Add
    Connection window appears, as in Figure 2-25. Note that the data source is a
    SQL Server database file and will be accessed through SqlClient (the .NET data
    provider for SQL Server, to be covered in Chapter 4). The connection will use
    Windows Authentication, meaning any user who can log in to the server machine
    can connect to the Northwind database.

Figure 2-25. *Add Connection*

7. You need to specify a database to connect to. Browse to the Northwind database in `C:\Program Files\Microsoft SQL Server\MSSQL.1\MSSQL\Data\northwnd.mdf`, and select it. Then click Test Connection. A message box should appear telling you "Test connection succeeded." Click OK to close it. Click OK to save the connection. A northwnd.mdf node will appear in Database Explorer. Expand the node, and you'll see nodes in Figure 2-26 that are very similar to the ones in Figure 2-14 for SSMSE.

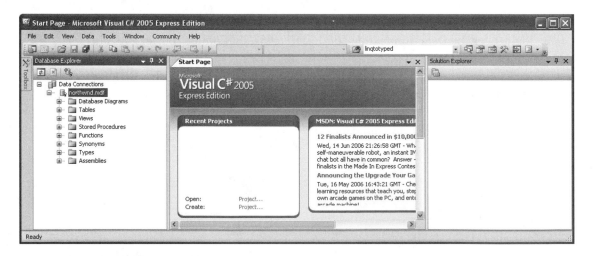

Figure 2-26. *An expanded connection in Database Explorer*

8. Expand the Tables node and right-click the Employees node. You'll see the menu in Figure 2-27. Database Explorer basically offers the same features for database access and management as SSMSE's Object Explorer, but it doesn't offer administration functions for managing instances. VCSE's New Query has a slightly different format from SSMSE's New Query, but it's as powerful. VCSE's Show Table Data has the same format and functionality as SSMSE's Open Table.

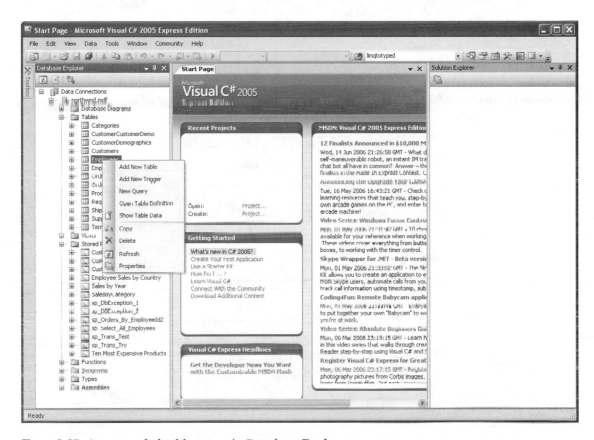

Figure 2-27. *An expanded table menu in Database Explorer*

Using BOL

BOL is the official source of SQL Server documentation. The documentation for SQL Server Express is part of BOL. BOL is a hypertext application that is both a blessing and a bane for SQL Server users. It's an enormously rich source of tutorials as well as reference information, but despite the fact that it's extensively indexed, finding what you need to know can sometimes be quite frustrating.

We'll only point out a few things to help you get started:

1. To open BOL, click Start ➤ All Programs ➤ Microsoft SQL Server 2005 ➤ Documentation and Tutorials ➤ SQL Server Books Online. You should see the screen in Figure 2-28.

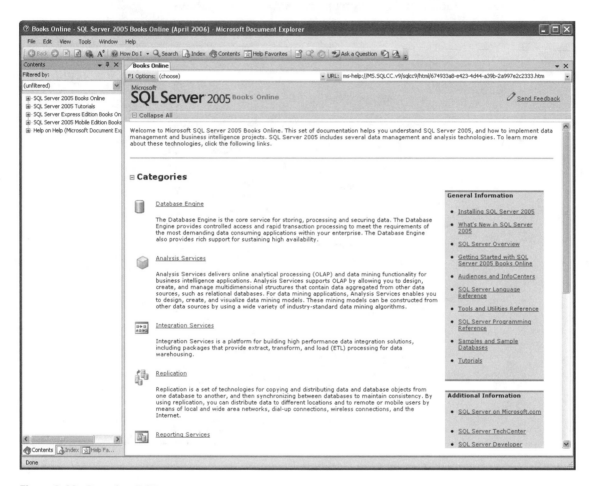

Figure 2-28. *Opening BOL*

2. There are five nodes in the Contents tree. The third one leads to SSE-specific documentation, but unless you plan to use SSE exclusively as a production server, you probably won't find this very useful. What you'll find most useful is the first node, SQL Server 2005 Books Online, so expand it. Then expand the SQL Server Language Reference node and the Transact-SQL Reference node within it. Scroll up to the top, and you'll see a screen as in Figure 2-29. All T-SQL language components are listed alphabetically.

Figure 2-29. *T-SQL Language Reference Table of Contents*

3. Click the Index tab below the Contents tree. You'll see the screen in Figure 2-30. The "Look for:" text box is where you specify what to search for. Above it is a "Filtered by:" drop-down. Click the down arrow and click SQL Server Express, to keep search results to a minimum (since SSE doesn't support most of the other topics in the list).

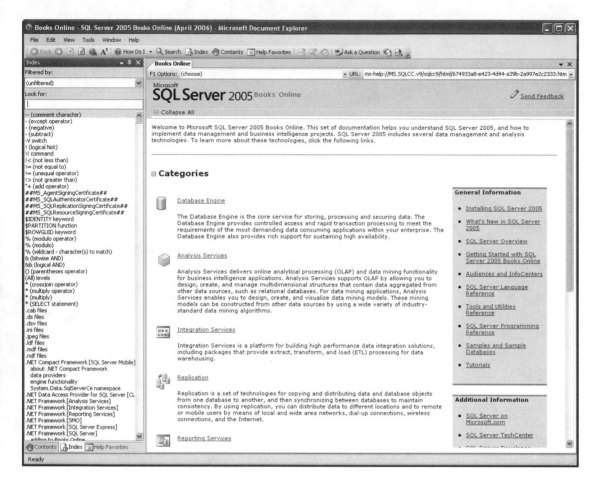

Figure 2-30. *BOL Index*

4. The index redisplays entries as you type, so if you enter "sel" (it's not case sensitive), you'll see the screen in Figure 2-31.

Figure 2-31. *BOL Index entries for "sel"*

5. Click on the "SELECT INTO statement" entry and you'll see an Index Results window at the bottom of the screen offering alternatives to the first topic, which is displayed in the window above it (see Figure 2-32). Filtering helps reduce your having to deal with alternatives that may not be relevant to your needs, but alternatives do frequently occur. Clicking on an entry in the Index Results window displays that topic. Now you're able to search BOL as well as the rest of us. Good luck!

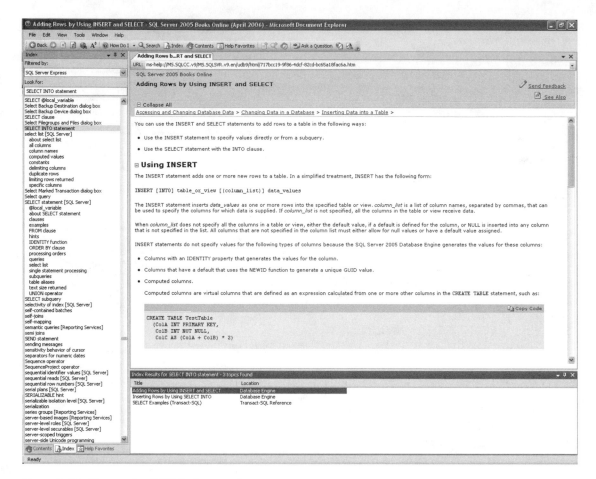

Figure 2-32. *Alternative BOL Index results*

Summary

In this chapter, we covered just enough about SSMSE to get you familiar with the kinds of things you'll do with it later in this book. Among other things, we showed how to execute T-SQL, back up and restore a database, and create database diagrams. We then showed you how to configure a few VCSE options to be consistent with the ones we use in writing our example programs in VCSE. We also showed you the basics of using BOL.

Now that your tools are installed and configured, you can start learning how to do database programming by learning the basics of T-SQL.

HOW TO RECOVER NORTHWIND, WHEN ALL ELSE FAILS

If you need to recover Northwind and can't do it in SSMSE (see Figure 2-17), follow these steps:

1. In SSMSE Object Explorer, right-click the Northwind node and click Delete. The Delete Object window will appear. Check "Close existing connections" and click OK. The Northwind database will be dropped from the SSE instance.

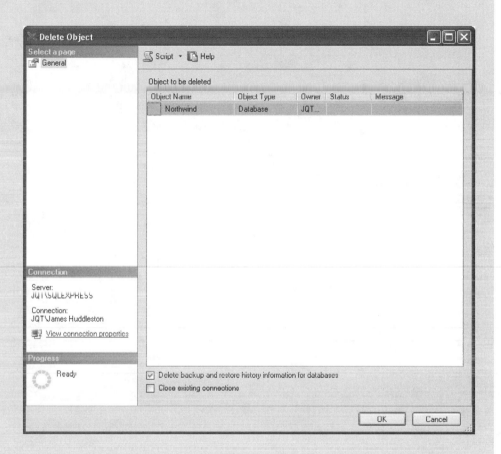

2. Right-click the SSE instance at the top of Object Explorer, click Restart, and click Yes when prompted for confirmation.

3. In `C:\Program Files\Microsoft SQL Server\MSSQL.1\MSSQL\Data`, delete any files starting with northwnd.

4. Re-create the Northwind database by running `instnwnd.sql` with `sqlcmd`, as described in Chapter 1.

■ ■ ■

CHAPTER 3

Introducing SQL

In this chapter, we'll cover the most common elements of SQL that you need to write database programs in C#:

- Queries

- INSERT statements

- UPDATE statements

- DELETE statements

- T-SQL data types

What Is SQL?

If you've ever worked with relational databases, you've probably used SQL. SQL is the international standard database language. You can use SQL to create, retrieve, change, or delete data (and a lot of other things).

The formal definition of SQL comes from the American National Standards Institute (ANSI). It's the same as the international standard specified by the International Organization for Standardization (ISO). T-SQL is the dialect of SQL provided by SQL Server. Since we're using SSE, we'll focus on T-SQL rather than standard SQL, but unless we're discussing a feature not found in standard SQL, we'll refer to both simply as "SQL." We'll use "standard SQL" when referring specifically to the ISO/ANSI version of the language. Each database vendor offers its own implementation of SQL, which conforms at some level to the standard but typically extends it. T-SQL does just that, and some of the SQL used in this book may not work if you try it with a database server other than SQL Server.

■**Tip** Relational database terminology is often confusing. For example, neither the meaning nor the pronunciation of SQL is crystal clear. IBM invented the language back in the 1970s and called it Structured English Query Language (SEQUEL), changing it shortly thereafter to Structured Query Language (SQL) to avoid conflict with another vendor's product. SEQUEL and SQL were both pronounced "sequel." When the ISO/ANSI standard was adopted, it referred to the language simply as "database language SQL" and was silent on whether this was an acronym and how it should be pronounced. Today, two pronunciations are used. In the Microsoft and Oracle worlds (as well as many others), it's pronounced "sequel." In the DB2 and MySQL worlds (among others), it's pronounced "ess cue ell." We'll follow the most reasonable practice. We're working in a Microsoft environment, so we'll pronounce SQL as "sequel."

Retrieving Data

A SQL query retrieves data from a database. Data is stored as *rows* in *tables*. Rows are composed of *columns*. In its simplest form, a query consists of two parts:

- A SELECT list, where the columns to be retrieved are specified

- A FROM clause, where the table or tables to be accessed are specified

■**Tip** We've written SELECT and FROM in capital letters, simply to indicate they're SQL keywords. SQL isn't case sensitive, and keywords are typically written in lowercase in code. In T-SQL, queries are called SELECT statements, but the ISO/ANSI standard clearly distinguishes "queries" from "statements." The distinction is conceptually important. A *query* is an operation on a table that produces a table as a result; *statements* may (or may not) operate on tables and don't produce tables as results. Further, *subqueries* can be used in both queries and statements. So, we'll typically call queries "queries" instead of SELECT statements. Call queries whatever you prefer, but keep in mind that queries are special elements of SQL.

Performing Simple Queries

Using two keywords, SELECT and FROM, here's the simplest possible query that gets all the data from the Employees table:

```
select
    *
from
    employees
```

The asterisk (*) means you want to select all the columns in the table. If you run this query against the Northwind database, you'll get all the rows and columns in the Employees table.

■**Tip** Although most of the SQL you'll see in this book is short and sweet, statements, and especially queries, can be complex and require many lines (in extreme cases, hundreds) of code. Formatting SQL as carefully as you format C# code is an excellent coding practice.

Try It Out: Running a Simple Query

We'll use SSMSE to submit queries, since it's a convenient interface to SQL Server. Here's how to submit a query to retrieve all employee data:

1. Open SSMSE and select the Northwind database (see Figure 3-1).

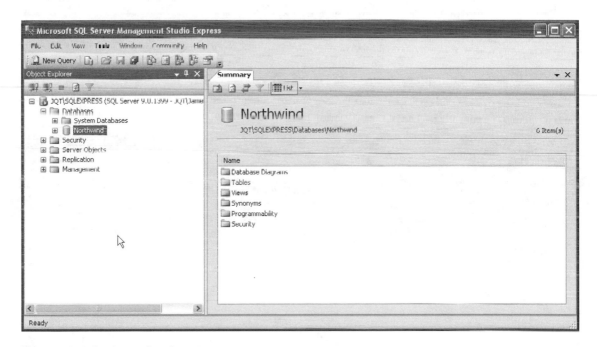

Figure 3-1. *Selecting a database to query*

2. Click New Query. A tabbed window opens, in which you can enter SQL. Note that the status bar below the window shows that you're connected to the Northwind database (see Figure 3-2).

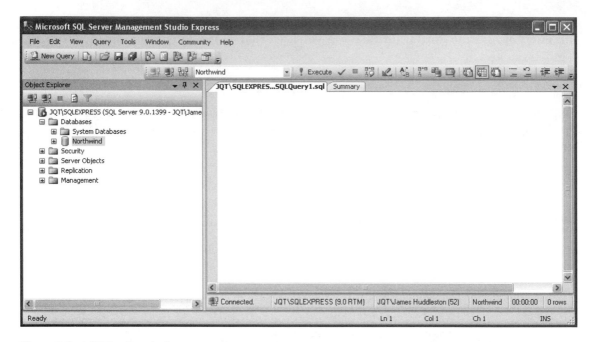

Figure 3-2. *A SQL edit window*

3. Enter the query as shown in Figure 3-3, then click Execute (or press F5 or select Query ➤ Execute).

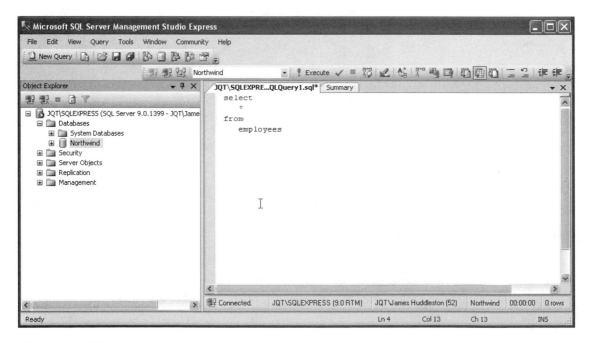

Figure 3-3. *Writing a query*

4. A Results window should open, as in Figure 3-4. Note that the status bar indicates the query was successful and shows how many rows (nine) were retrieved.

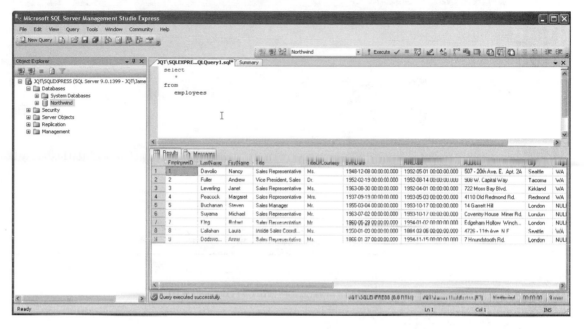

Figure 3-4. *Query Results window*

How It Works

You asked the database to return the data for all columns, which is exactly what has happened. If you scroll to the right, you'll find all the columns in the Employees table.

Most of the time, you should limit queries to only relevant columns. When you select columns you don't need, you waste resources. To select columns explicitly, enter the column names after the SELECT keyword (see Figure 3-5):

```
select
    employeeid,
    firstname,
    lastname
from
    employees
```

This query selects all the rows from the Employees table but only the EmployeeId, FirstName, and LastName columns. (Use the splitter between the query and result windows to expand/contract them.)

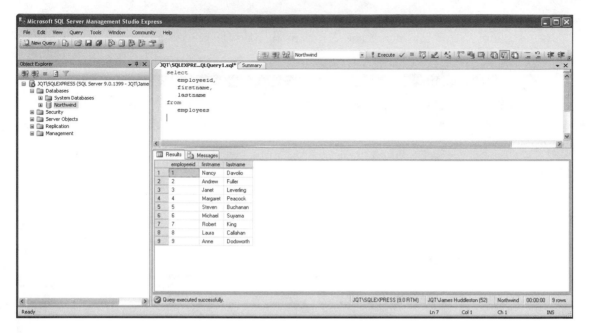

Figure 3-5. *Selecting specific columns*

Using the WHERE Clause

Queries can have WHERE clauses. The WHERE clause allows you to specify criteria for select-ing rows. This clause can be complex, but we'll stick to a simple example for now. The syntax for our example is

```
WHERE <column1> <operator> <column2>
```

where <operator> is a comparison operator (for example, =, <>, >, or <). See Table 3-1, which lists the T-SQL comparison operators.

Try It Out: Refining Your Query

To refine your query:

1. Add the following WHERE clause to the query in Figure 3-5:

   ```
   where
       country = 'USA'
   ```

2. Run the query by pressing F5, and you should see results as in Figure 3-6.

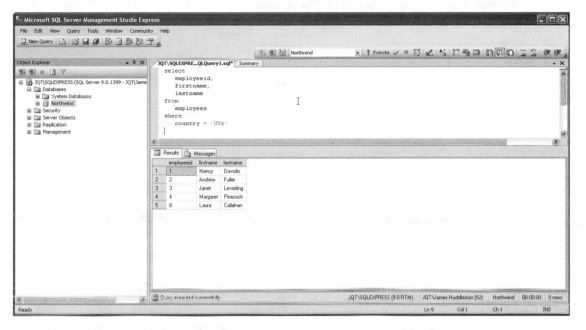

Figure 3-6. *Using a* WHERE *clause*

Caution SQL keywords and table and column names aren't case sensitive, but string literals (enclosed in single quotes) are. So, use 'USA', not 'usa', for this example.

How It Works

The new query means: Return the data for columns EmployeeID, FirstName, and LastName from the Employees table, but only for rows where the Country column equals USA.

Using Comparison Operators in a WHERE Clause

You can use a number of different comparison operators in a WHERE clause (see Table 3-1).

Table 3-1. *Comparison Operators*

Operator	Description	Example
=	Equals	`EmployeeID = 1`
<	Less than	`EmployeeID < 1`
>	Greater than	`EmployeeID > 1`
<=	Less than or equal to	`EmployeeID <= 1`
>=	Greater than or equal to	`EmployeeID >= 1=`
<>,!=	Not equal to	`EmployeeID <> 1`
!<	Not less than	`EmployeeID !< 1`
!>	Not greater than	`EmployeeID !> 1`

■**Tip** As mentioned earlier, every database vendor has its own implementation of SQL. This discussion is specific to T-SQL; for example, standard SQL doesn't have the `!=` operator and calls `<>` the *not equals operator*. In fact, standard SQL calls the expressions in a `WHERE` clause *predicates*; we'll use that term because predicates are either true or false, but other expressions don't have to be. If you work with another version of SQL, please refer to its documentation for specifics.

In addition to these operators, the `LIKE` operator (see Table 3-2) allows you to match patterns in character data. As with all SQL character data, strings must be enclosed in single quotes (`'`).

Table 3-2. *The `LIKE` Operator*

Operator	Description	Example
LIKE	Allows you to specify a pattern	`WHERE Title LIKE 'Sales%'` selects all rows where the `Title` column contains a value that starts with the word *Sales* followed by zero or more characters.

You can use four different wildcards in the pattern (see Table 3-3).

Table 3-3. *Wildcard Characters*

Wildcard	Description
%	Any combination of characters.
_	Any one character. WHERE Title LIKE '_ales' selects all rows where the Title column equals *Aales, aales, Bales, bales,* and so on.
[ ]	A single character within a range [a-d] or set [abcd]. WHERE Title LIKE '[bs]ales' selects all rows where the Title column equals either the word *bales* or *sales*.
[^]	A single character not within a range [^a-d] or set [^abcd].

Sometimes it's useful to select rows where a value is unknown. When no value has been assigned to a column, the column is NULL. (This isn't the same as a column that contains the value 0 or a blank.) To select a row with a column that's NULL, use the IS NULL operator (see Table 3-4).

Table 3-4. *The* IS [NOT] NULL *Operator*

Operator	Description	Example
IS NULL	Allows you to select rows where a column has no value.	WHERE Region IS NULL returns all rows where Region has no value.
IS NOT NULL	Allows you to select rows where a column has a value.	WHERE Region IS NOT NULL returns all rows where Region has a value.

■Note You must use the IS NULL and IS NOT NULL operators (collectively called the *null predicate* in standard SQL) to select or exclude NULL column values, respectively. The following is a valid query but always produces zero rows: SELECT * FROM employees WHERE region = NULL, because nothing "equals" NULL (not even another NULL). If you change - to IS, the query will return rows where regions have no value.

To select values in a range or in a set, you can use the BETWEEN and IN operators (see Table 3-5).

Table 3-5. *The* BETWEEN *and* IN *Operators*

Operator	Description	Example
BETWEEN	True if a value is within a range.	WHERE extension BETWEEN 400 AND 500 returns the rows where Extension is between 400 and 500, inclusive.
IN	True if a value is in a list. The list can be the result of a subquery.	WHERE city IN ('Seattle', 'London') returns the rows where City is either Seattle or London.

Combining Predicates

Quite often you'll need to use more than one predicate to filter your data. You can use the logical operators shown in Table 3-6.

Table 3-6. *SQL Logical Operators*

Operator	Description	Example
AND	Combines two expressions, evaluating the complete expression as true only if both are true.	WHERE (title LIKE 'Sales%' AND lastname ='Peacock')
NOT	Negates a Boolean value.	WHERE NOT (title LIKE 'Sales%' AND lastname = 'Peacock')
OR	Combines two expressions, evaluating the complete expression as true if either is true.	WHERE (title = 'Peacock' OR title = 'King')

When you use these operators, it's often a good idea to use parentheses to clarify the conditions. In complex queries, this may be absolutely necessary.

Sorting Data

After you've filtered the data you want, you can sort the data by one or more columns and in a certain direction. Since tables are unsorted by definition, the order in which rows are retrieved by a query is unpredictable. To impose an ordering, use the ORDER BY clause:

```
ORDER BY <column> [ASC | DESC] {, n}
```

The <column> is the column that should be used to sort the result. The {, n} syntax means you can specify any number of columns separated by commas. The result will be sorted in the order in which you specify the columns.

The following are the two sort directions:

- ASC: Ascending (1, 2, 3, 4, and so on)

- DESC: Descending (10, 9, 8, 7, and so on)

If you omit the ASC or DESC keywords, the sort order defaults to ASC.

Now that you've seen the following basic syntax for queries

```
SELECT <column>
FROM <table>
WHERE <predicate>
ORDER BY <column> ASC | DESC
```

let's use it in an example.

Try It Out: Writing an Enhanced Query

Let's code a query that uses all this. We want to do the following:

- Select all the orders that have been handled by employee 5.

- Select the orders shipped to either France or Brazil.

- Display only OrderID, EmployeeID, CustomerID, OrderDate, and ShipCountry.

- Sort the orders by the destination country and the date the order was placed.

Does this sound complicated? Let's try it:

1. Enter the following query in SSMSE:

```
select
    orderid,
    employeeid,
    customerid,
    orderdate,
    shipcountry
from
    orders
where
    employeeid = 5
    and
    shipcountry in ('Brazil', 'France')
order by
    shipcountry asc,
    orderdate asc
```

2. Click F5, and you should see results as in Figure 3-7.

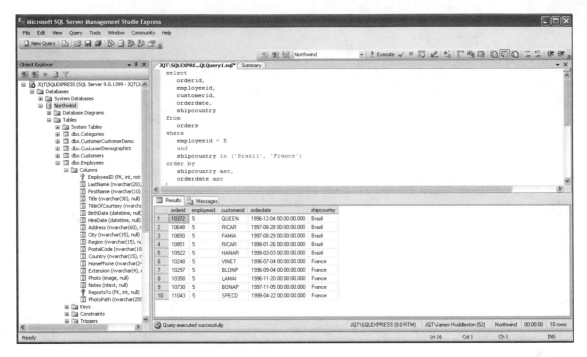

Figure 3-7. *Filtering and sorting data*

How It Works

Let's look at the clauses individually. The SELECT list specifies which columns you want to use:

```
SELECT
    orderid,
    employeeid,
    customerid,
    orderdate,
    shipcountry
```

The FROM clause specifies that you want to use the Orders table:

```
FROM
    orders
```

The WHERE clause is a bit more complicated. It consists of two predicates that individually state the following:

- EmployeeID must be 5.

- ShipCountry must be either Brazil or France.

As these predicates are combined with AND, they both must evaluate to true for a row to be included in the result:

```
WHERE
    employeeid = 5
    AND
    shipcountry IN ('Brazil', 'France')
```

The ORDER BY clause specifies the order in which the rows are sorted. The rows are sorted by ShipCountry first and then by OrderDate:

```
ORDER BY
    shipcountry ASC,
    orderdate ASC
```

Inserting Data

The second important task you need to be able to do is add data (i.e., add rows) to a table. You do this with the INSERT statement. The INSERT statement is much simpler than a query, particularly because the WHERE and ORDER BY clauses have no meaning when inserting data and therefore aren't used.

A basic INSERT statement has these parts:

```
INSERT INTO <table>
(<column1>, <column2>, ..., <columnN>)
VALUES (<value1>, <value2>, ..., <valueN>)
```

Using this syntax, let's add a new row to the Shippers table of the Northwind database. Before you insert it, let's look at the table. In the SSMSE Object Explorer, right-click the Shippers table and click Open Table. The table has three rows, which are displayed in a tabbed window (see Figure 3-8).

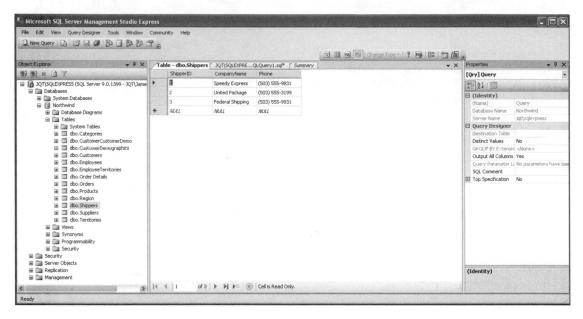

Figure 3-8. *Shippers before adding a row*

The first column, `ShipperID`, is an `IDENTITY` column, and you can't insert values into it explicitly—SSE will make sure a unique value is inserted for you. So, the `INSERT` statement will look like this:

```
insert into shippers
   (
   companyname,
   phone
   )
values ('We Shred Them Before You Get Them', '555-1234')
```

Executing this statement in the query window should produce a Messages window reporting "(1 row(s) affected)." After the insert, return to the Table - dbo.Shippers window, and click the exclamation point to refresh the table display. You'll see that the new row has been added, as Figure 3-9 shows. (To see the full company name, double-click the separator between the CompanyName and Phone columns.)

Be careful to insert data of the correct data type. In this example, both the columns are of character type, so you insert strings. If one of the columns were of integer type, you would insert an integer value instead. We'll describe the SQL data types soon, in the "T-SQL Data Types" section.

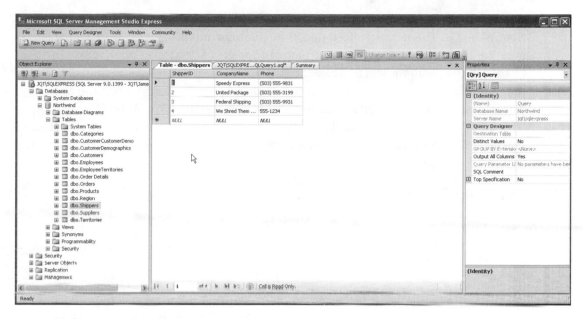

Figure 3-9. *Shippers after adding a row*

Updating Data

The third important task you need to be able to do is change data. You do this with the UPDATE statement. When coding UPDATE statements, you must be careful to include a WHERE clause, or you'll update *all* the rows in a table. So, always code an appropriate WHERE clause, or you won't change the data you intend to change.

■Tip Should you inadvertently change something in the Northwind database, remember that you can restore the database as described in the section "Backing Up and Restoring Northwind" in Chapter 2.

Now that you're aware of the implications of the UPDATE statement, let's take a good look at it. In essence, it's a simple statement that allows you to update values in one or more rows and columns:

```
UPDATE <table>
SET <column1> = <value1>, <column2> = <value2>, ..., <columnN> = <valueN>
WHERE <predicate>
```

As an example, let's imagine that the company you added earlier, We Shred Them Before You Get Them, has realized that, though (unfortunately) accurate, its name isn't good for business, so it's changing its name to Speed of Light Delivery. To make this change in the database, you first need to locate the row to change. More than one company could have the same name, so you shouldn't use the CompanyName column as the key. Instead, look back at Figure 3-9 and note the ShipperID for We Shred Them.

The ShipperID is the primary key (unique identifier for rows) of the Shippers table, so you can use it to locate the one row you want to update. Run the following statement in the query window:

```
update shippers
set
    companyname = 'Speed of Light Delivery'
where
    shipperid = 4
```

This should produce a Messages window reporting "(1 row(s) affected)." Refresh the Table - dbo.Shippers window, and you'll see that CompanyName has changed, as in Figure 3-10.

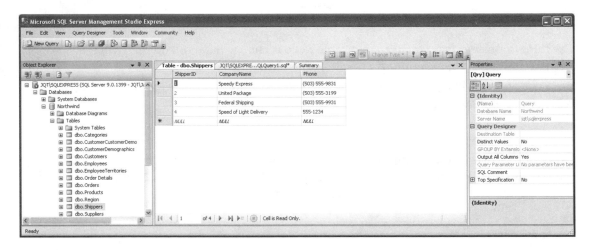

Figure 3-10. *Shippers after updating a row*

When you update more than one column, you code the SET keyword only once. For example, the following statement would change both the name and the phone of the example company:

```
update shippers
set
    companyname = 'Speed of Light Delivery',
    phone = '555-9876'
where
    shipperid = 4
```

Deleting Data

The fourth important task you need to be able to do is remove data. You do this with
the DELETE statement. The DELETE statement has the same implications as the UPDATE
statement. It's all too easy to delete every row (not just the wrong rows) in a table by
forgetting the WHERE clause, so be careful. The DELETE statement removes entire rows, so
it's not necessary (or possible) to specify columns. Its basic syntax is (remember, the
WHERE clause is optional, but without it, *all* rows will be deleted):

```
DELETE FROM <table>
WHERE <predicate>
```

If Speed of Light Delivery finally gives up and goes out of business, you'd need to
remove it from the Shippers table. As with the UPDATE statement, you need to determine
the primary key of the row you want to remove (or recall that it's 4) and use that in the
DELETE statement:

```
delete from shippers
where shipperid = 4
```

This should produce a Messages window reporting "(1 row(s) affected)." Refresh the
Table – dbo.Shippers window, and you'll see that the company has been removed, as in
Figure 3-11.

If you try to delete one of the three other shippers, you'll get a database error.
Shippers may handle many orders, and an order can exist only if assigned to a shipper.
A *foreign-key relationship* exists from Orders to Shippers, and SSE enforces it, prevent-
ing deletion of Shippers rows that are referred to by Orders rows. We'll examine this in
detail in Chapter 11.

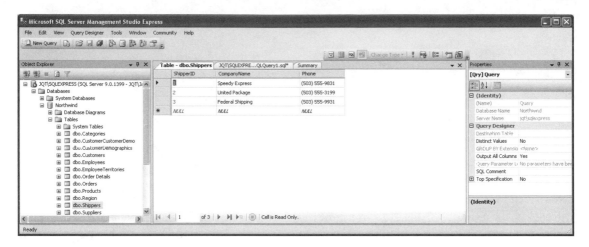

Figure 3-11. *Shippers after deleting a row*

Sometimes you do need to remove every row from a table. In such cases, the TRUNCATE TABLE statement may be preferable to the DELETE statement, since it performs better. The TRUNCATE TABLE statement is faster because it doesn't do any *logging* (saving each row in a log file before deleting it) to support recovery, while DELETE logs every row removed. See BOL for descriptions of both TRUNCATE TABLE and logging.

This concludes our introduction to basic SQL for retrieving, adding, changing, and removing data. Next we'll look at T-SQL data types.

T-SQL Data Types

T-SQL provides a variety of "base" data types—27 of them to be exact. All stored SQL Server data must be compatible with one of them. Let's briefly survey them.

■**Note** User-defined data types (UDTs), either *aliases* created from base data types or *Common Language Runtime (CLR) UDTs* based on .NET classes, are also supported. They are beyond the scope of this book.

Numeric Data Types

The eight T-SQL numeric data types map to C# simple types (see Table 3-7).

Table 3-7. *T-SQL Numeric Data Types*

SQL Data Type	C# Type	Description
bigint	long	64-bit signed integer
bit	bool	Unsigned number that can be 0, 1, or NULL
decimal (numeric)	decimal	128-bit signed number
float	double	64-bit floating-point number
int	int	32-bit signed integer
real	float	32-bit floating-point number
smallint	short	16-bit signed integer
tinyint	byte	8-bit unsigned integer

Money Data Types

Both T-SQL money data types (which are technically also numeric data types) map to a single C# type, decimal (see Table 3-8).

Table 3-8. *T-SQL Money Data Types*

SQL Data Type	C# Type	Description
money	decimal	Values from -922,337,203,605,477.5808 through 922,337,203,605,477.5807
smallmoney	decimal	Values from -214,748.3648 through 214,748.3647

Character String Data Types

All six T-SQL character string data types map to the C# string type (see Table 3-9).

Table 3-9. *T-SQL Character String Data Types*

SQL Data Type	C# Type	Description
char	string	Fixed-length string of 1 to 8,000 bytes
nchar	string	Fixed-length Unicode string of 1 to 4,000 bytes
text	string	Variable-length string of 1 to $2^{31}-1$ characters
ntext	string	Variable-length Unicode string of 1 to $2^{30}-1$ bytes
varchar	string	Variable-length string of 1 to $2^{31}-1$ bytes
nvarchar	string	Variable-length Unicode string of 1 to $2^{31}-1$ bytes

Date and Time Data Types

Both T-SQL date and time data types map to the .NET System.Data.SqlTypes.SqlDateTime type (see Table 3-10).

Table 3-10. *T-SQL Date/Time Data Types*

SQL Data Type	C# Type	Description
datetime	SqlDateTime	Date and time data from Jan. 1, 1753, through Dec. 31, 9999, accurate to 1/300th of a second. Equivalent to the standard SQL timestamp data type.
smalldatetime	SqlDateTime	Date and time data from Jan. 1, 1900, through June 6, 2079, accurate to the minute.

Binary Data Types

All three T-SQL binary data types map to C# byte arrays (see Table 3-11).

Table 3-11. *T-SQL Binary Data Types*

SQL Data Type	C# Type	Description
binary	byte[]	Fixed-length binary data of 1 to 8,000 bytes
image	byte[]	Variable-length binary data of 0 to 2^{31}-1 bytes
varbinary	byte[]	Variable-length binary data of 0 to 2^{31}-1 bytes

Other Data Types

Four of the other six T-SQL data types map to types compatible with C#. Two of the T-SQL data types, cursor and table, aren't accessible by C# (see Table 3-12).

Table 3-12. *Other T-SQL Data Types*

SQL Data Type	C# Type	Description
cursor		For internal SQL Server use only
sql_variant	object	Can hold int, binary, and char values
table		For internal SQL Server use only
timestamp	byte[]	8-byte database-unique integer, not to be confused with the datetime data type
uniqueidentifier	System.Guid	128-bit globally unique integer
xml	string	Can store XML documents up to 2GB in size

Data Type Precedence

When two expressions of different data types are operands in a larger expression, T-SQL attempts to implicitly convert the data type of lower precedence to the data type of higher precedence. If the conversion is not possible, an error is returned. When both operands are of the same data type, the result of the operation is that data type. Table 3-13 lists the T-SQL data types from highest to lowest precedence.

Table 3-13. *T-SQL Data Type Precedence*

Data Type
UDTs
sql_variant
xml
datetime
smalldatetime
float
real
decimal (numeric)
money
smallmoney
bigint
int

Continued

Table 3-13. *Continued*

Data Type
smallint
tinyint
bit
ntext
text
image
timestamp
uniqueidentifier
nvarchar
nchar
varchar
char
varbinary
binary

■**Note** Explicit conversions can be performed with the T-SQL CAST and CONVERT functions. We won't need them for our work in this book.

Summary

In this chapter, you saw how to use T-SQL to perform the four most common tasks against a database: SELECT, INSERT, UPDATE, and DELETE. You also saw how to use comparison and other operators to specify predicates that limit what rows are retrieved or manipulated. We surveyed the T-SQL data types and saw how they map to C# or .NET types. Understanding these T-SQL language elements is essential for retrieving and manipulating data with ADO.NET, the .NET facility for data (especially database) access, which we'll look at next.

Introducing ADO.NET

Now that you've seen essential T-SQL for retrieving and modifying data, let's look at ADO.NET, the interface between C# programs and databases. Understanding ADO.NET is the key to building powerful database applications.

In this chapter, we'll cover:

- Why ADO.NET was developed

- What the core ADO.NET architecture comprises

- How to use .NET Framework data providers

- That a .NET Framework data provider is an API

Why ADO.NET?

Before .NET, developers used data access technologies such as Open Database Connectivity (ODBC), OLE DB, and ActiveX Data Objects (ADO). With the introduction of .NET, Microsoft created a new way to work with data, called ADO.NET. Before we concentrate on ADO.NET in detail, we'll briefly look at older data access technologies, since OLE DB and ODBC still have a place in the ADO.NET environment.

From ADO to ADO.NET

ADO is a collection of ActiveX objects that are designed to work in a constantly *connected* environment. It was built on top of OLE DB (which we'll look at in the "OLE DB Data Provider" section). OLE DB provides access to non-SQL data as well as SQL databases, and ADO provides an interface designed to make it easier to work with OLE DB providers.

However, accessing data with ADO (and OLE DB under the hood) means you have to go through several layers of connectivity before you reach the data source. Just as OLE DB is there to connect to a large number of data sources, an older data access technology, ODBC, is still there to connect to even older data sources such as dBase and Paradox. To access ODBC data sources using ADO, you use an OLE DB provider for ODBC (since ADO only works directly with OLE DB), thus adding more layers to an already multilayered model.

With the multilayered data access model and the connected nature of ADO, you could easily end up sapping server resources and creating a performance bottleneck. ADO served well in its time, but ADO.NET has some great features that make it a far superior data access technology.

ADO.NET Isn't a New Version of ADO

ADO.NET is a completely new data access technology, with a new design that was built entirely from scratch. Let's first get this cleared up: ADO.NET *doesn't* stand for ActiveX Data Objects .NET. Why? For many reasons, but the following are the two most important ones:

- ADO.NET is an integral part of .NET, not an external entity.

- ADO.NET isn't a collection of ActiveX components.

The name ADO.NET is analogous to ADO because Microsoft wanted developers to feel at home using ADO.NET and didn't want them to think they'd need to "learn it all over again," so it purposely named and designed ADO.NET to offer similar features implemented in a different way.

During .NET design, Microsoft realized that ADO wasn't going to fit in. ADO was available as an external package based on Component Object Model (COM) objects, requiring .NET applications to explicitly include a reference to it. In contrast, .NET applications are designed to share a single model, where all libraries are integrated into a single framework, organized into logical namespaces, and declared public to any application that wants to use them. It was wisely decided that the .NET data access technology should comply with the .NET architectural model. So, ADO.NET was born.

ADO.NET is designed to accommodate both connected and disconnected access. Also, ADO.NET embraces the fundamentally important XML standard (more on this in Chapter 14), much more than ADO did, since the explosion in XML use came about after ADO was developed. With ADO.NET, you can not only use XML to transfer data between applications, but you can also export data from your application into an XML file, store it locally on your system, and retrieve it later when you need it.

Performance usually comes at a price, but in the case of ADO.NET, the price is definitely reasonable. Unlike ADO, ADO.NET doesn't transparently wrap OLE DB providers; instead, it uses *managed data providers* that are designed specifically for each type of data source, thus leveraging their true power and adding to overall application speed and performance.

ADO.NET also works in both connected and disconnected environments. You can connect to a database, remain connected while simply reading data, and then close your connection, which is a process similar to ADO. Where ADO.NET really begins to shine is in the disconnected world. If you need to edit database data, maintaining a continuous connection would be costly on the server. ADO.NET gets around this by providing a sophisticated disconnected model. Data is sent from the server and cached locally on the client. When you're ready to update the database, you can send the changed data back to the server, where updates and conflicts are managed for you.

In ADO.NET, when you retrieve data, you use an object known as a *data reader*. When you work with disconnected data, the data is cached locally in a relational data structure—either a *data table* or a *dataset*.

ADO.NET and the .NET Base Class Library

A dataset (a DataSet object) can hold large amounts of data in the form of tables (DataTable objects), their relationships (DataRelation objects), and constraints (Constraint objects) in an in-memory cache, which can then be exported to an external file or to another dataset. Since XML support is integrated into ADO.NET, you can produce XML schemas and transmit and share data using XML documents (much more on this in Chapter 14).

Table 4-1 describes the namespaces in which ADO.NET components are grouped.

Table 4-1. *ADO.NET Namespaces*

Namespace	Description
System.Data	Classes, interfaces, delegates, and enumerations that define and partially implement the ADO.NET architecture
System.Data.Common	Classes shared by .NET Framework data providers
System.Data.Design	Classes that can be used to generate a custom-typed dataset
System.Data.Odbc	The .NET Framework data provider for ODBC
System.Data.OleDb	The .NET Framework data provider for OLE DB
System.Data.Sql	Classes that support SQL Server-specific functionality
System.Data.OracleClient	The .NET Framework data provider for Oracle
System.Data.SqlClient	The .NET Framework data provider for SQL Server
System.Data.SqlServerCe	The .NET Compact Framework data provider for SQL Server Mobile
System.Data.SqlTypes	Classes for native SQL Server data types
Microsoft.SqlServer.Server	Components for integrating SQL Server and the CLR

Since XML support has been closely integrated into ADO.NET, some ADO.NET components in the `System.Data` namespace rely on components in the `System.Xml` namespace. So, you sometimes need to include both namespaces as references in Solution Explorer.

These namespaces are physically implemented as assemblies, and if you create a new application project in VCSE, references to the assemblies should be created automatically, along with the reference to the `System` assembly. However, if they're not present, simply perform the following steps to add the namespaces to your project:

1. Right-click the References item in Solution Explorer, and then click Add Reference... .

2. A dialog box with a list of available references displays. Select `System.Data`, `System.Xml`, and `System` (if not already present) one by one (hold down the Ctrl key for multiple selections), and then click the Select button.

3. Click OK, and the references will be added to the project.

■**Tip** Though we don't use it in this book, if you use the command-line C# compiler, you can use the following compiler options to include the assemblies: `/r:System.dll`, `/r:System.Data.dll`, `/r:System.Xml.dll`.

As you can see from the namespaces, ADO.NET can work with older technologies such as OLE DB and ODBC. However, the SQL Server data provider communicates directly with SQL Server without adding an OLE DB or ODBC layer, so it's the most efficient form of connection. Likewise, the Oracle data provider accesses Oracle directly.

■**Note** All major DBMS vendors support their own ADO.NET data providers. We'll stick to SQL Server in this book, but the same kind of C# code is written regardless of the provider.

Understanding ADO.NET Architecture

Figure 4-1 presents the most important architectural features of ADO.NET. We'll discuss them in far greater detail in later chapters.

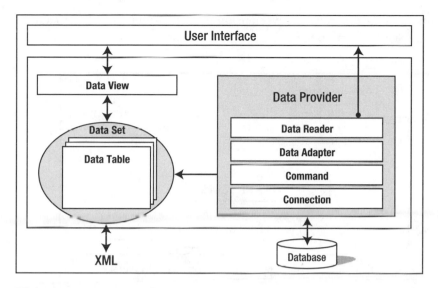

Figure 4-1. *ADO.NET architecture*

ADO.NET has two central components: data providers and datasets.

A *data provider* connects to a data source and supports data access and manipulation. You'll play with three different ones later in this chapter.

A *dataset* supports disconnected, independent caching of data in a relational fashion, updating the data source as required. A dataset contains one or more *data tables*. A data table is a row-and-column representation that provides much the same logical view as a SQL table. For example, you can store the data from the Northwind database's Employees table in a data table and manipulate the data as needed. You'll learn about datasets and data tables starting in Chapter 8.

In Figure 4-1, notice the DataView class (in the System.Data namespace). This isn't a data provider component. Data views are used primarily to bind data to Windows and Web forms. We'll cover data views in Chapter 9.

As you saw in Table 4-1, each data provider has its own namespace. In fact, each data provider is essentially an implementation of interfaces in the System.Data namespace, specialized for a specific type of data source. For example, if you use SQL Server, you should use the SQL Server data provider (System.Data.SqlClient) because it's the most efficient way to access SQL Server.

The OLE DB data provider supports access to older versions of SQL Server as well as to other databases, such as Access, DB2, MySQL, and Oracle. However, native data providers (such as System.Data.OracleClient) are preferable for performance, since the OLE DB data provider works through two other layers—the OLE DB service component and the OLE DB provider—before reaching the data source.

Figure 4-2 illustrates the difference between using the SQL Server and OLE DB data providers to access a SQL Server database.

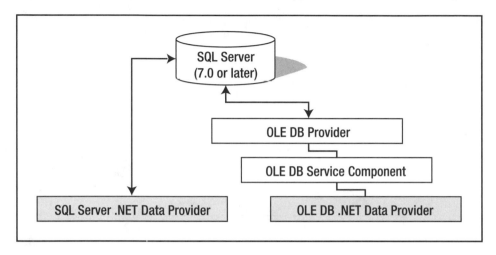

Figure 4-2. *SQL Server and OLE DB data provider differences*

If your application connects to an older version of SQL Server (6.5 or older) or to more than one kind of database server at the same time (for example, an Access and an Oracle database connected simultaneously), only then should you choose to use the OLE DB data provider.

No hard and fast rules exist; you can use both the OLE DB data provider for SQL Server and the Oracle data provider (System.Data.OracleClient) if you want, but it's important you choose the best provider for your purpose. Given the performance benefits of the server-specific data providers, if you use SQL Server 2005, 99% of the time you should be using the System.Data.SqlClient classes.

Before we look at what each kind of data provider does and how it's used, you need to be clear on their core functionality. Each .NET data provider is designed to do the following two things very well:

- Provide access to data with an active connection to the data source

- Provide data transmission to and from disconnected datasets and data tables

Database connections are established by using the data provider's connection class (for example, System.Data.SqlClient.SqlConnection). Other components such as data readers, commands, and data adapters support retrieving data, executing SQL statements, and reading or writing to datasets or data tables, respectively.

As you've seen, each data provider is prefixed with the type of data source it connects to. For instance, the SQL Server data provider is prefixed with Sql, so its connection class

is named SqlConnection. The OLE DB data provider's connection class is named
OleDbConnection.

Look now at the object model of these two providers in Figure 4-3. See how easy
it is to switch between data providers to populate a dataset. The OLE DB data provider
belongs to the System.Data.OleDb namespace; the SQL Server data provider belongs to
System.Data.SqlClient. Both data providers provide a similar architecture, though
they're actually very different internally.

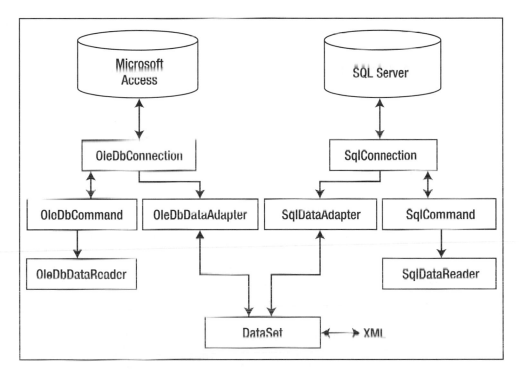

Figure 4-3. *ADO.NET concurrently accessing SQL Server and Access databases*

Let's see how to work with the three data providers that you can use with SQL Server.

Using the SQL Server Data Provider

The .NET data provider for SQL Server is in the System.Data.SqlClient namespace. This
data provider communicates directly with the server using its native network protocol
instead of through multiple layers.

Table 4-2 describes some important classes in the SqlClient namespace.

Table 4-2. *Commonly Used* SqlClient *Classes*

Class	Description
SqlCommand	Executes SQL queries, statements, or stored procedures
SqlConnection	Represents a connection to a SQL Server database
SqlDataAdapter	Represents a bridge between a dataset and a data source
SqlDataReader	Provides a forward-only, read-only data stream of the results
SqlError	Holds information on SQL Server errors and warnings
SqlException	The exception thrown on a SQL Server error or warning
SqlParameter	Represents a command parameter
SqlTransaction	Represents a SQL Server transaction

Another namespace, System.Data.SqlTypes, maps SQL Server data types to .NET types, both enhancing performance and making developers' lives a lot easier.

Let's look at an example that uses the SQL Server data provider. It won't cover connections and data retrieval in detail, but will familiarize you with what you'll encounter in upcoming chapters.

Try It Out: Creating a Simple Console Application Using the SQL Server Data Provider

You'll build a simple console application that opens a connection and runs a query, using the SqlClient namespace against the SSE Northwind database. You'll display the retrieved data in a console window. Follow these steps:

1. Open VCSE and create a new Console Application project named Chapter04. In Solution Explorer, save the solution with Ctrl+S.

2. Right-click the Chapter04 project and rename it to SqlServerProvider.

3. Right-click the Program.cs file and rename it to SqlServerProvider.cs. When prompted to rename all references to Program, you can click either Yes or No.

4. Since you'll be creating this example from scratch, open SqlServerProvider.cs in Code Editor and replace it with the code in Listing 4-1 (available in the code download, in bcs2005db\code\Chapter04\Listing4_1.txt).

Listing 4-1. SqlServerProvider.cs

```csharp
using System;
using System.Data;
using System.Data.SqlClient;

namespace Chapter04
{
    class SqlServerProvider
    {
        static void Main(string[] args)
        {
            // Set up connection string
            string connString = @"
                server = .\sqlexpress;
                integrated security = true;
                database = northwind
            ";

            // Set up query string
            string sql = @"
                select
                    *
                from
                    employees
            ";

            // Declare connection and data reader variables
            SqlConnection conn = null;
            SqlDataReader reader = null;

            try
            {
                // Open connection
                conn = new SqlConnection(connString);
                conn.Open();

                // Execute the query
                SqlCommand cmd = new SqlCommand(sql, conn);
                reader = cmd.ExecuteReader();
```

```csharp
                // Display output header
                Console.WriteLine(
                   "This program demonstrates the use of "
                 + "the SQL Server Data Provider."
                );
                Console.WriteLine(
                   "Querying database {0} with query {1}\n"
                 , conn.Database
                 , cmd.CommandText
                );
                Console.WriteLine("First Name\tLast Name\n");

                // Process the result set
                while(reader.Read()) {
                   Console.WriteLine(
                      "{0} | {1}"
                    , reader["FirstName"].ToString().PadLeft(10)
                    , reader[1].ToString().PadLeft(10)
                   );
                }
            }
            catch (Exception e)
            {
                Console.WriteLine("Error: " + e);
            }
            finally
            {
                // Close connection
                reader.Close();
                conn.Close();
            }
        }
    }
}
```

5. Save the project, and press Ctrl+F5 to run it. The results should appear as in Figure 4-4.

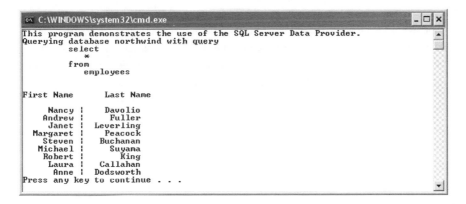

Figure 4-4. *Accessing Northwind via the SQL Server data provider*

How It Works

Let's take a look at how the code works, starting with the using directives:

```
using System;
using System.Data;
using System.Data.SqlClient;
```

The reference to System.Data is actually not needed in this small program, since you don't explicitly use any of its members, but it's a good habit to always include it. The reference to System.Data.SqlClient is necessary, since you want to use the simple names of its members.

You specify the connection string with *parameters* (key-value pairs) suitable for an SSE session:

```
// Set up connection string
string connString = @"
   server = .\sqlexpress;
   integrated security - true;
   database = northwind
";
```

The connection string contains the parameter

```
integrated security=true;
```

which specifies Windows Authentication, so any user logged onto Windows can access the SQLEXPRESS instance.

■**Note** We use Windows Authentication throughout this book. SQL Server Authentication is also available, but it requires users to be defined to the SQLEXPRESS instance. For information on how SQL Server
handles user authentication and authorization, see Robin Dewson's *Beginning SQL Server 2005 Express
for Developers: From Novice to Professional* (Berkeley, CA: Apress, 2007).

You then code the SQL query:

```
// Set up query string
string sql = @"
   select
      *
   from
      employees
";
```

■**Tip** We use verbatim strings for both connection strings and SQL, because it allows us to indent the
source code conveniently. The connection string is actually parsed before it's assigned to the connection's `ConnectionString` property, so the new lines and extra spaces are inconsequential. SQL can
contain extraneous new lines and spaces, so you can format it flexibly to make it more readable and
maintainable.

You next declare variables for the connection and data reader, so they're available to
the rest of your code:

```
// Declare connection and data reader variables
SqlConnection conn = null;
SqlDataReader reader = null;
```

You then create the connection and open it:

```
try
{
   // Open connection
   conn = new SqlConnection(connString);
   conn.Open();
```

You do this (and the rest of your database work) in a `try` block to handle exceptions,
in particular exceptions thrown by ADO.NET in response to database errors, though in
this simple example you're not interested in distinguishing them from other exceptions.

Here, ADO.NET will throw an exception if the connection string parameters aren't syntactically correct, so you may as well be prepared. If you wait until you enter the try block to declare the connection (and data reader) variable, you won't have it available in the finally block to close the connection. Note that creating a connection doesn't actually connect to the database. You need to call the Open method on the connection.

To execute the query, you first create a command object, passing its constructor the SQL to run and the connection on which to run it. Next, you create a data reader by calling ExecuteReader() on the command object. This not only executes the query but also sets up the data reader. Note that unlike most objects, you have no way to create a data reader with a new expression:

```
// Execute the query
SqlCommand cmd = new SqlCommand(sql, conn);
reader = cmd.ExecuteReader();
```

You then produce a header for your output, using connection and command properties (Database and CommandText, respectively) to get the database name and query text:

```
// Display output header
Console.WriteLine(
    "This program demonstrates the use of "
  + "the SQL Server Data Provider."
);
Console.WriteLine(
    "Querying database {0} with query {1}\n"
  , conn.Database
  , cmd.CommandText
);
Console.WriteLine("First Name\tLast Name\n");
```

You retrieve all the rows in the result set by calling the data reader's Read method, which returns true if there are more rows and false otherwise. Note that the data reader is positioned immediately *before* the first row prior to the first call to Read:

```
// Process the result set
while(reader.Read()) {
    Console.WriteLine(
        "{0} | {1}"
      , reader["FirstName"].ToString().PadLeft(10)
      , reader[1].ToString().PadLeft(10)
    );
}
}
```

You access each row's columns with the data reader's *indexer* (here, the `SqlDataReader.Item` property), which is overloaded to accept either a column name or a zero-based integer index. You use both to demonstrate the indexer's use, but using column numbers is more efficient than using column names.

Next, you handle any exceptions, quite simplistically, but at least you're developing a good habit (we'll cover exception handling much more thoroughly in Chapter 15):

```
catch (Exception e)
{
   Console.WriteLine("Error: " + e);
}
```

Finally, in a `finally` block, close the data reader and the connection by calling their `Close` methods. As a general rule, you should close things in a `finally` block to be sure they get closed no matter what happens within the `try` block:

```
finally
{
   // Close connection
   reader.Close();
   conn.Close();
}
```

Technically, closing the connection also closes the data reader, but closing both (in the previous order) is another good habit. A connection with an open data reader can't be used for any other purpose until the data reader has been closed.

Using the OLE DB Data Provider

Outside .NET, OLE DB is still Microsoft's high-performance data access technology. You can use it to access data stored in any format, so even in ADO.NET it plays an important role in accessing data sources that don't have their own ADO.NET data providers.

The .NET Framework data provider for OLE DB is in the namespace `System.Data.OleDb`. Table 4-3 describes some important classes in the `OleDb` namespace.

Table 4-3. *Commonly Used* OleDb *Classes*

Class	Description
OleDbCommand	Executes SQL queries, statements, or stored procedures
OleDbConnection	Represents a connection to an OLE DB data source
OleDbDataAdapter	Represents a bridge between a dataset and a data source
OleDbDataReader	Provides a forward-only, read-only data stream of rows from a data source
OleDbError	Holds information on errors and warnings returned by the data source
OleDbParameter	Represents a command parameter
OleDbTransaction	Represents a SQL transaction

Notice the similarity between the two data providers, SqlClient and OleDb. The differences in their implementations are transparent, and the user interface is fundamentally the same.

The ADO.NET OLE DB data provider requires that an OLE DB provider be specified in the connection string. Table 4-4 describes some OLE DB providers.

Table 4-4. *Some OLE DB Providers*

Provider	Description
DB2OLEDB	Microsoft OLE DB provider for DB2
SQLOLEDB	Microsoft OLE DB provider for SQL Server
Microsoft.Jet.OLEDB.4.0	Microsoft OLE DB provider for Access (which uses the Jet engine)
MSDAORA	Microsoft OLE DB provider for Oracle
MSDASQL	Microsoft OLE DB provider for ODBC

Let's use the OLE DB data provider (SQLOLEDB) to access the Northwind database, making a few straightforward changes to the code in Listing 4-1. (Of course, you'd use the SQL Server data provider for real work since it's more efficient.)

Try It Out: Creating a Simple Console Application Using the OLE DB Data Provider

Let's access Northwind with OLE DB:

1. In Solution Explorer, add a new C# console application project named
   OleDbProvider to the Chapter04 solution. Rename the Program.cs file to
   OleDbProvider.cs. In Code Editor, replace the generated code with the code
   in Listing 4-2, which shows the changes to Listing 4-1 in bold.

Listing 4-2. `OleDbProvider.cs`

```csharp
using System;
using System.Data;
using System.Data.OleDb;

namespace Chapter04
{
    class OleDbProvider
    {
        static void Main(string[] args)
        {
            // Set up connection string
            string connString = @"
                provider = sqloledb;
                data source = .\sqlexpress;
                integrated security = sspi;
                initial catalog = northwind
            ";

            // Set up query string
            string sql = @"
                select
                    *
                from
                    employees
            ";

            // Declare connection and data reader variables
            OleDbConnection conn = null;
            OleDbDataReader reader = null;

            try
            {
                // Open connection
                conn = new OleDbConnection(connString);
                conn.Open();

                // Execute the query
                OleDbCommand cmd = new OleDbCommand(sql, conn);
                reader = cmd.ExecuteReader();
```

```
        // Display output header
        Console.WriteLine(
            "This program demonstrates the use of "
          + "the OLE DB Data Provider."
        );
        Console.WriteLine(
            "Querying database {0} with query {1}\n"
          , conn.Database
          , cmd.CommandText
        );
        Console.WriteLine("First Name\tLast Name\n");

        // Process the result set
        while(reader.Read()) {
            Console.WriteLine(
                "{0} | {1}"
              , reader["FirstName"].ToString().PadLeft(10)
              , reader[1].ToString().PadLeft(10)
            );
        }
    }
    catch (Exception e)
    {
        Console.WriteLine("Error: " + e);
    }
    finally
    {
        // Close connection
        reader.Close();
        conn.Close();
    }
    }
  }
}
```

2. Since you now have two projects in your solution, you need to make this project the startup project so it runs when you click Ctrl+F5. Right-click the project name in Solution Explorer, and then click Set As StartUp Project (see Figure 4-5).

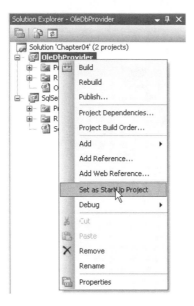

Figure 4-5. *Setting the Startup Project*

3. Run the application with Ctrl+F5. The results should appear as in Figure 4-6.

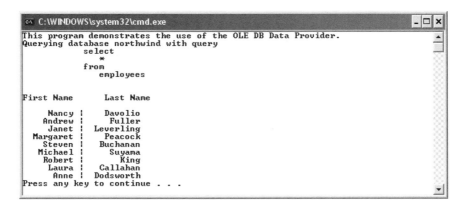

Figure 4-6. *Accessing Northwind via OLE DB*

How It Works

This program does the same thing as the first example, so we'll discuss only the things that changed. First, you replace SqlClient with OleDb in the third using directive:

```
using System;
using System.Data;
using System.Data.OleDb;
```

The connection string requires the most change, since the OLE DB data provider doesn't accept the same parameters as the SQL Server data provider. In addition, it requires a `provider` parameter:

```
// Set up connection string
string connString = @"
    provider = sqloledb;
    data source = .\sqlexpress;
    integrated security = sspi;
    initial catalog = northwind
";
```

Only four other lines have to change to use the OLE DB data provider classes for the connection, command, and data reader:

```
// Declare connection and data reader variables
OleDbConnection conn = null;
OleDbDataReader reader = null;

try
{
    // Open connection
    conn = new OleDbConnection(connString);
    conn.Open();

    // Execute the query
    OleDbCommand cmd = new OleDbCommand(sql, conn);
    reader = cmd.ExecuteReader();
```

The final change is a semantic one and isn't required by ADO.NET:

```
// Display output header
Console.WriteLine(
    "This program demonstrates the use of "
+ "the OLE DB Data Provider."
);
```

Using the ODBC Data Provider

ODBC was Microsoft's original general-purpose data access technology. It's still widely used for data sources that don't have OLE DB providers or .NET Framework data providers. ADO.NET includes an ODBC data provider in the namespace `System.Data.Odbc`.

The ODBC architecture is essentially a three-tier process. An application uses ODBC functions to submit database requests. ODBC converts the function calls to the protocol (*call-level interface*) of a *driver* specific to a given data source. The driver communicates with the data source, passing any results or errors back up to ODBC. Obviously, this is less efficient than a database-specific data provider's direct communication with a database, so for performance, it's preferable to avoid the ODBC data provider, since it merely offers a simpler interface to ODBC but still involves all the ODBC overhead. Table 4-5 describes some important classes in the Odbc namespace.

Table 4-5. *Commonly Used* Odbc *Classes*

Class	Description
OdbcCommand	Executes SQL queries, statements, or stored procedures
OdbcConnection	Represents a connection to an ODBC data source
OdbcDataAdapter	Represents a bridge between a dataset and a data source
OdbcDataReader	Provides a forward-only, read-only data stream of rows from a data source
OdbcError	Holds information on errors and warnings returned by the data source
OdbcParameter	Represents a command parameter
OdbcTransaction	Represents a SQL transaction

Let's use the ODBC data provider to access the Northwind database, making the same kind of straightforward changes (highlighted in Listing 4-3) to the code in Listing 4-1 as you did in using the OLE DB data provider.

Before you do, though, you need to create an ODBC data source—actually, you configure a data source name (DSN) for use with a data source accessible by ODBC—for the Northwind database, since, unlike the SQL Server and OLE DB data providers, the ODBC data provider doesn't let you specify the server or database in the connection string. (The following works on Windows XP, and the process is similar for other versions of Windows.)

Creating an ODBC Data Source

To create an ODBC data source, follow these steps:

1. In the Control Panel, double-click Administrative Tools (see Figure 4-7).

2. In Administrative Tools, double-click Data Sources (ODBC) (see Figure 4-8).

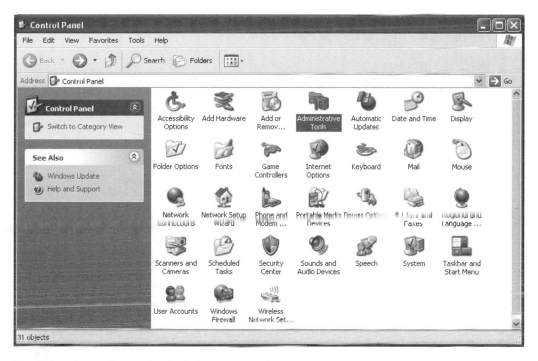

Figure 4-7. *Control Panel: Administrative Tools*

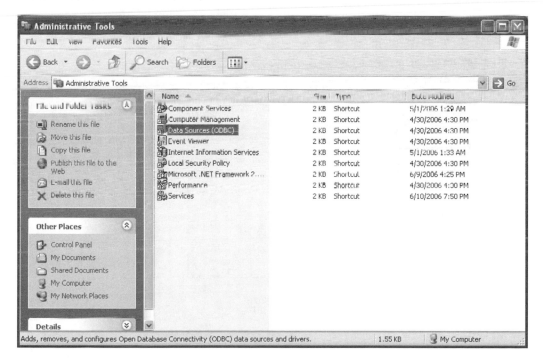

Figure 4-8. *Administrative Tools: Data Sources (ODBC)*

3. When the ODBC Data Source Administrator window opens, click the User DSN tab and then click Add... (see Figure 4-9).

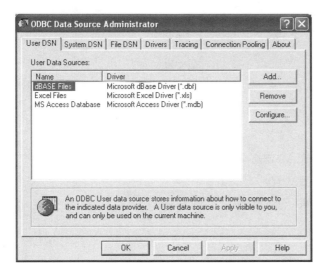

Figure 4-9. *ODBC Data Source Administrator*

4. The Create New Data Source wizard starts. Follow its instructions carefully! First, select the SQL Server driver; second, click Finish (see Figure 4-10).

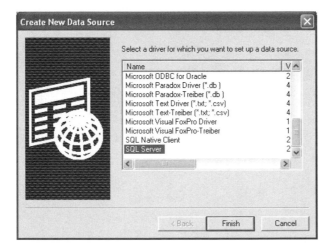

Figure 4-10. *Create New Data Source wizard*

5. The next window prompts for the data source name and server. Fill the entries as in Figure 4-11, and then click Next.

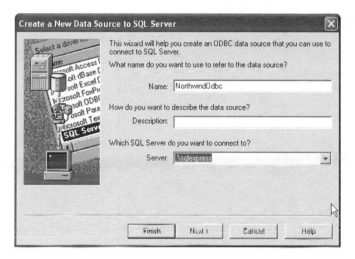

Figure 4-11. *Specify data source name and SQL Server to connect to*

6. Accept the defaults in the authentication window by clicking Next (see Figure 4-12).

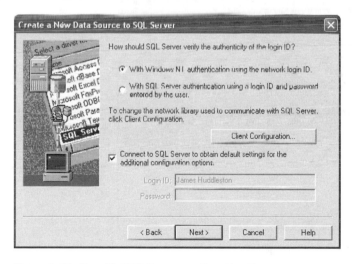

Figure 4-12. *Specify SQL Server authentication*

7. In the next window, check the "Change the default database to:" option, specify
the Northwind database, and click Next (see Figure 4-13).

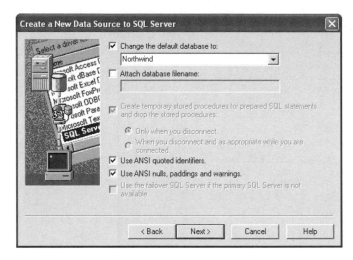

Figure 4-13. *Specify default database*

8. In the next window, simply click Finish (see Figure 4-14).

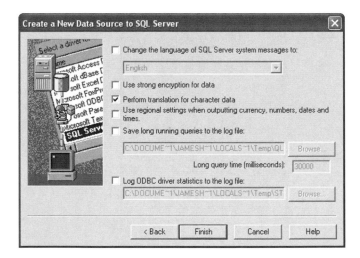

Figure 4-14. *Finish DSN creation*

9. A confirmation window appears, describing the new data source. Click Test Data Source... (see Figure 4-15).

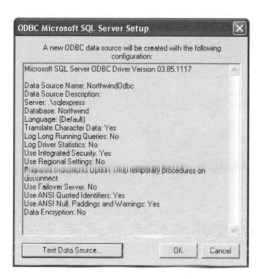

Figure 4-15. *Testing the Northwind data source connection*

10. A window reporting a successful test should appear (see Figure 4-16). (If it doesn't, cancel your work and *carefully* try again.) Click OK.

Figure 4-16. *Connection to Northwind is successful*

11. When the confirmation window reappears, click OK. When the ODBC Data
Source Administrator window reappears, the new data source will be on the list
(see Figure 4-17). Click OK.

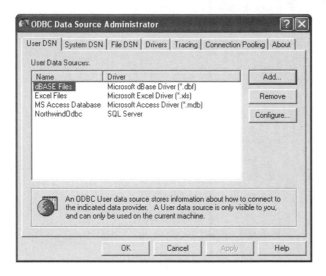

Figure 4-17. *New data source appears in data source list*

Gee, that was simple, wasn't it? Now that you have an ODBC data source, you can get
back to programming!

Try It Out: Creating a Simple Console Application Using the ODBC Data Provider

Let's access Northwind with ODBC:

1. In Solution Explorer, add a new C# console application project named
OdbcProvider to the Chapter04 solution. Rename the Program.cs file to
OdbcProvider.cs. In Code Editor, replace the generated code with the code in
Listing 4-3, which shows the changes to Listing 4-1 in bold.

Listing 4-3. OdbcProvider.cs

```
using System;
using System.Data;
using System.Data.Odbc;
```

```csharp
namespace Chapter04
{
    class OdbcProvider
    {
        static void Main(string[] args)
        {
            // Set up connection string
            string connString = @"dsn=northwindodbc";

            // Set up query string
            string sql = @"
                select
                    *
                from
                    employees
            ";

            // Declare connection and data reader variables
            OdbcConnection conn = null;
            OdbcDataReader reader = null;

            try
            {
                // Open connection
                conn = new OdbcConnection(connString);
                conn.Open();

                // Execute the query
                OdbcCommand cmd = new OdbcCommand(sql, conn);
                reader = cmd.ExecuteReader();

                // Display output header
                Console.WriteLine(
                    "This program demonstrates the use of "
                  + "the ODBC Data Provider."
                );
                Console.WriteLine(
                    "Querying database {0} with query {1}\n"
                  , conn.Database
                  , cmd.CommandText
                );
                Console.WriteLine("First Name\tLast Name\n");
```

```csharp
            // Process the result set
            while(reader.Read()) {
                Console.WriteLine(
                    "{0} | {1}"
                    , reader["FirstName"].ToString().PadLeft(10)
                    , reader[1].ToString().PadLeft(10)
                );
            }
        }
        catch (Exception e)
        {
            Console.WriteLine("Error: " + e);
        }
        finally
        {
            // Close connection
            reader.Close();
            conn.Close();
        }
    }
}
}
```

2. Make this project the startup project by right-clicking the project name in Solution Explorer and then clicking Set As StartUp Project.

3. Run the application with Ctrl+F5. The results should appear as in Figure 4-18.

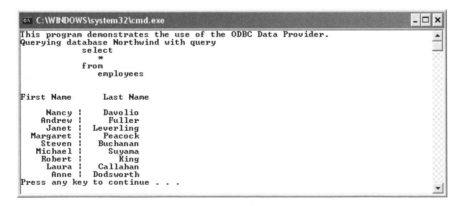

Figure 4-18. *Accessing Northwind via ODBC*

How It Works

Once you create a DSN, the rest is easy. You simply change `Sql` to `Odbc` in the class names (and, of course, the output header), just as you did to modify the program to work with OLE DB. The biggest change, and the only one that really deserves attention, is to the connection string:

```
// Set up connection string
string connString = @"dsn=northwindodbc";
```

The ODBC connection string isn't limited only to the DSN, but it doesn't allow blanks or newlines anywhere in the string.

Tip Each data provider has its own rules regarding both the parameters and syntax of its connection string. Consult the documentation for the provider you're using when coding connection strings. Connection strings can be very complicated. We don't cover the details here, but documentation for connection strings is included with the description of the `ConnectionString` property for the connection class for each data provider.

Now that you've played with all the data providers that access SQL Server (the SQL Server CE data provider is beyond the scope of this book), let's make sure you clearly understand what a data provider is.

Data Providers Are APIs

The .NET Framework data providers, sophisticated as they are (and you'll learn plenty about exploiting their sophistication later), are simply APIs for accessing data sources, most often relational databases. (ADO.NET is essentially one big API of which data providers are a major part.)

Newcomers to ADO.NET are often understandably confused by the Microsoft documentation. They read about `Connection`, `Command`, `DataReader`, and other ADO.NET objects, but they see no classes named `Connection`, `Command`, or `DataReader` in any of the ADO.NET namespaces. The reason is that data provider classes implement *interfaces* in the `System.Data` namespace. These interfaces define the data provider methods of the ADO.NET API.

The key concept is simple. A data provider, such as `System.Data.SqlClient`, consists of classes whose methods provide a uniform way of accessing a specific kind of data source. In this chapter, you used three different data providers (SQL Server, OLE DB, and ODBC) to access the same SSE database. The only real difference in the code was the connection string. Except for choosing the appropriate data provider, the rest of the programming was effectively the same. This is true of all ADO.NET facilities, whatever kind of data source you need to access.

The SQL Server data provider is optimized to access SQL Server and can't be used for any other DBMS. The OLE DB data provider can access any OLE DB data source—and you can use it without knowing anything about OLE DB (a major study in itself). The ODBC data provider lets you use an even older data access technology, again without knowing anything about it. Working at such an abstract level enables you to do a lot more, a lot more quickly, than you could have otherwise.

ADO.NET isn't just an efficient data access technology, but it's also an elegant one. Data providers are only one aspect of it. The art of ADO.NET programming is founded more on conceptualizing than on coding. First, get a clear idea of what ADO.NET offers, and then look for the right method in the right class to make the idea a reality.

Since conceptual clarity is so important, you can view (and refer to) connections, commands, data readers, and other ADO.NET components primarily as abstractions rather than merely objects used in database programs. If you concentrate on concepts, learning when and how to use relevant objects and methods will be easy.

Summary

In this chapter, you saw why ADO.NET was developed and how it supersedes other data access technologies in .NET. We gave an overview of its architecture and then focused on one of its core components, the data provider. You built three simple examples to practice basic data provider use and experienced the uniform way data access code is written, regardless of the data provider. Finally, we offered the opinion that conceptual clarity is the key to understanding and using both data providers and the rest of the ADO.NET API.

Next, we'll study the details of ADO.NET, starting with connections.

CHAPTER 5

■ ■ ■

Introducing Connections

Before you can do anything useful with a database, you need to establish a *session* with the database server. You do this with an object called a *connection*, which is an instance of a class that implements the System.Data.IDbConnection interface for a specific data provider. In this chapter, you'll use various data providers to establish connections, and you'll look at problems that may arise and learn how to solve them.

In this chapter, we'll cover:

- How to create and use connections

- How to solve common connection problems

Introducing the Data Provider Connection Classes

As you saw in Chapter 4, each data provider has its own namespace. Each has a connection class that implements the System.Data.IDbConnection interface. Table 5-1 summarizes the data providers supplied by Microsoft.

Table 5-1. *Data Provider Namespaces and Connection Classes*

Data Provider	Namespace	Connection Class
ODBC	System.Data.Odbc	OdbcConnection
OLE DB	System.Data.OleDb	OleDbConnection
Oracle	System.Data.OracleClient	OracleConnection
SQL Server	System.Data.SqlClient	SqlConnection
SQL Server CE	System.Data.SqlServerCe	SqlCeConnection

As you can see, the names follow a convention, using Connection prefixed by an identifier for the data provider. Since all connection classes implement System.Data. IDbConnection, the use of each one is similar. Each has additional members that provide methods specific to a particular database. You used connections in Chapter 4. Let's take a closer look at one of them, SqlConnection, in the namespace System.Data.SqlClient.

Connecting to SSE with SqlConnection

In this example, you'll again connect to the SSE Northwind database.

Try It Out: Using SqlConnection

We'll write a simple program that opens and checks a connection:

1. In VCSE, create a new Windows Console application project named Chapter05. When Solution Explorer opens, save the solution.

2. Rename the Chapter05 project ConnectionSql. Rename the Program.cs file to ConnectionSql.cs, and replace the generated code with the code in Listing 5-1.

Listing 5-1. ConnectionSql.cs

```
using System;
using System.Data;
using System.Data.SqlClient;

namespace Chapter05
{
    class ConnectionSql
    {
        static void Main(string[] args)
        {
            // Connection string
            string connString = @"
                server = .\sqlexpress;
                integrated security = true;
            ";

            // Create connection
            SqlConnection conn = new SqlConnection(connString);
```

```
    try {
        // Open connection
        conn.Open();
        Console.WriteLine("Connection opened.");
    }
    catch (SqlException e) {
        // Display error
        Console.WriteLine("Error: " + e);
    }
    finally {
        // Close connection
        conn.Close();
        Console.WriteLine("Connection closed.");
    }
    }
  }
}
```

3. Run it with Ctrl+F5. If the connection is successful, you'll see the output shown in Figure 5-1.

Figure 5-1. *Connecting and disconnecting*

If the connection failed, you'll see an error message as in Figure 5-2. (You can get this by shutting down SSE first, with net stop mssql$netsdk entered at a command prompt. If you try this, remember to restart it with net start mssql$sqlexpress.)

Don't worry about the specifics of this message right now. Connections often fail for reasons that have nothing to do with your code. It may be because a server isn't started, as in this case, because a password is wrong, or because some other configuration problem exists. You'll soon look at common problems in establishing database connections.

Figure 5-2. *Error on connecting and disconnecting*

How It Works

Let's examine the code in Listing 5-1 to understand the steps in the connection process. First, you specify the ADO.NET and the SQL Server data provider name-spaces, so you can use the simple names of their members:

```
using System;
using System.Data;
using System.Data.SqlClient;
```

Then you create a connection string. A connection string consists of parameters—in other words, key=value pairs separated by semicolons—that specify connection information. Although some parameters are valid for all data providers, each data provider has specific parameters it will accept, so it's important to know which parameters are valid in a connection string for the data provider you're using:

```
// Connection string
string connString = @"
    server = .\sqlexpress;
    integrated security = true;
";
```

Let's briefly examine each of the connection string parameters in this example. The server parameter specifies the SQL Server instance to which you want to connect:

```
server = .\sqlexpress;
```

The next clause indicates that you should use Windows Authentication (i.e., any valid logged-on Windows user can log onto SSE):

```
integrated security = true;
```

Alternatively, you could use sspi instead of true, as they both have the same effect. Other parameters are available. You'll use one later to specify the database to which you want to connect.

Next, create a connection (a SqlConnection object), passing it the connection string. This doesn't create a database session. It simply creates the object you'll use later to open a session:

```
// Create connection
SqlConnection conn = new SqlConnection(connString);
```

Now you have a connection, but you still need to establish a session with the database by calling the Open method on the connection. If the attempt to open a session fails, an exception will be thrown, so you use a try statement to enable exception handling. You display a message after calling Open, but this line will be executed only if the connection is opened successfully:

```
try {
    // Open connection
    conn.Open();
    Console.WriteLine("Connection opened.");
}
```

At this stage in the code, you'd normally issue a query or perform some other database operation over the open connection. However, we'll save that for later chapters and concentrate here on just connecting.

Next comes an exception handler in case the Open() fails:

```
catch (SqlException e) {
    // Display error
    Console.WriteLine("Error: " + e);
}
```

Each data provider has a specific exception class for its error handling; SqlException is the class for the SQL Server data provider. Specific information about database errors is available from the exception, but here you're just displaying its raw contents.

When you're finished with the database, you call Close() to terminate the session and then print a message to show that Close() was called:

```
finally {
    // Close connection
    conn.Close();
    Console.WriteLine("Connection closed.");
}
```

You call Close() within the finally block to ensure it *always* gets called.

Note Establishing connections (database sessions) is relatively expensive. They use resources on both the client and the server. Although connections may eventually get closed, through garbage collection or by timing out, leaving one open when it's no longer needed is a bad practice. Too many open connections can slow a server down or prevent new connections from being made.

Note that you can call Close() on a closed connection, and no exception will be thrown. So, your message would have been displayed if the connection had been closed earlier or even if it had never been opened. See Figure 5-2, where the connection failed but the close message was still displayed.

In one typical case, multiple calls to both Open() and Close() make sense. ADO.NET supports disconnected processing of data, even when the connection to the data provider has been closed. The pattern looks like this:

```
try
{
    conn.Open(); // Open connection
    //
    // Online processing (e.g., queries) here
    //
    conn.Close(); // Close connection

    //
    // Offline processing here
    //
```

```
    conn.Open(); // Reopen connection
    //
    // Online processing(e.g., INSERT/UPDATE/DELETE) here
    //
    conn.Close(); // Reclose connection
}
finally {
    //Close connection
    conn.Close();
}
```

The `finally` block still calls `Close()`, calling it unnecessarily if no exceptions are encountered, but this isn't a problem or expensive, and it ensures the connection will be closed. Although many programmers hold connections open until program termination, this is usually wasteful in terms of server resources. With *connection pooling*, opening and closing a connection as needed is actually more efficient than opening it once and for all.

That's it! You're finished with the first connection example. Since, however, you saw a possible error, let's look at typical causes of connection errors.

Debugging Connections to SQL Server

Writing the C# code to use a connection is usually the easy part of getting a connection to work. Problems often lie not in the code, but rather in a mismatch in the connection parameters between the client (your C# program) and the database server. All appropriate connection parameters must be used and must have correct values. Even experienced database professionals often have problems getting a connection to work the first time.

More parameters are available than the ones shown here, but you get the idea. A corollary of Murphy's Law applies to connections: If several things can go wrong, surely one of them will. Your goal is to check both sides of the connection to make sure all of your assumptions are correct and that everything the client program specifies is matched correctly on the server.

Often the solution is on the server side. If the SQL Server instance isn't running, then the client will be trying to connect to a server that doesn't exist. If Windows Authentication isn't used and the user name and password on the client don't match the name and password of a user authorized to access the SQL Server instance, then the connection will be rejected. If the database requested in the connection doesn't exist, an error will occur. If the client's network information doesn't match the server's, then the server may not receive the client's connection request, or the server response may not reach the client.

For connection problems, using the debugger to locate the line of code where the error occurs usually doesn't help—the problem almost always occurs on the call to the Open method. The question is, why? You need to look at the error message.

A typical error is as follows

```
Unhandled Exception: System.ArgumentException: Keyword not supported . . .
```

The cause for this is either using an invalid parameter or value or misspelling a parameter or value in your connection string. Make sure you've entered what you really mean to enter.

Figure 5-2 shows probably the most common message when trying to connect to SQL Server. In this case, most likely SQL Server simply isn't running. Restart the SSE service with net start mssql$sqlexpress.

Other possible causes of this message are as follows:

- *The SQL Server instance name is incorrect*: For example, you used .\sqlexpress, but SSE was installed with a different name. It's also possible that SSE was installed as the default instance (with no instance name) or is on another machine (see the next section); correct the instance name if this is the case.

- *SSE program hasn't been installed*: Go back to Chapter 1 and follow the instructions there for installing SSE.

- *A security problem*: Your Windows login and password aren't valid on the server. This is unlikely to be the problem when connecting to a local SSE instance, but it might happen in trying to connect to a SQL Server instance on another server.

- *A hardware problem*: Again, this is unlikely if you're trying to connect to a server on the same machine.

Security and Passwords in SqlConnection

There are two kinds of user authentication in SSE. The preferred way is to use Windows Authentication (integrated security), as we do in this book. SQL Server uses your Windows login to access the instance. Your Windows login must exist on the machine where SQL Server is running, and your login must be authorized to access the SQL Server instance or be a member of a user group that has access.

If you don't include the Integrated Security = true (or Integrated Security = sspi) parameter in the connection string, the connection defaults to SQL Server security, which uses a separate login and password within SQL Server.

How to Use SQL Server Security

If you really do intend to use SQL Server security because that's how your company or department has set up access to your SQL Server (perhaps because some clients are non-Microsoft), then you need to specify a user name and password in the connection string, as shown here:

```
thisConnection.ConnectionString = @"
    server = .\sqlexpress;
    user id = sa;
    password = x1y2z3
";
```

The sa user name is the default system administrator account for SQL Server. If a specific user has been set up, such as george or payroll, then specify that name. The password for sa is set when SQL Server is installed. If the user name you use has no password, you can omit the password clause entirely or specify an empty password, as follows:

```
password =;
```

However, a blank password is bad practice and should be avoided, even in a test environment.

Connection String Parameters for SqlConnection

Table 5-2 summarizes the basic parameters for the SQL Server data provider connection string.

Table 5-2. *SQL Server Data Provider Connection String Parameters*

Name	Alias	Default Value	Allowed Values	Description
Application Name		.Net SqlClient Data Provider	Any string	Name of application
AttachDBFileName	extended properties, Initial File Name	None	Any path	Full path of an attachable database file
Connect Timeout	Connection Timeout	15	0–32767	Seconds to wait to connect
Data Source	Server, Address, Addr, Network Address	None	Server name or network address	Name of the target SQL Server instance

Continued

Table 5-2. *Continued*

Name	Alias	Default Value	Allowed Values	Description
Encrypt		false	true, false, yes, no	Specifies whether to use SSL encryption
Initial Catalog	Database	None	Any database that exists on server	Database name
Integrated Security	Trusted_Connection	false	true, false, yes, no, sspi	Specifies the authentication mode
Network Library	Net	dbmssocn	dbnmpntw, dbmsrpcn, dbmsadsn, dbmsgnet, dbmslpcn, dbmsspxn, dbmssocn	Network .dll
Packet Size		8192	Multiple of 512	Network packet size in bytes
Password	PWD	None	Any string	Password if not using Windows Authentication
Persist Security Info		false	true, false, yes, no	Specifies whether sensitive information should be passed back after connecting
User ID	UID		None	User name if not using Windows Authentication
Workstation ID		Local computer name	Any string	Workstation connecting to SQL Server

The Alias column in Table 5-2 gives alternate parameter names. For example, you can specify the server using any of the following:

```
data source = .\sqlexpress
server = .\sqlexpress
address = .\sqlexpress
addr = .\sqlexpress
network address = .\sqlexpress
```

> **■Tip** (local) is an alternative to the dot (.) to specify the local machine, so you can replace
> .\sqlexpress with (local)\sqlexpress.

Connection Pooling

One low-level detail that's worth noting—even though you shouldn't change it—is *connection pooling*. Recall that creating connections is expensive in terms of memory and time. With pooling, a closed connection isn't immediately destroyed but is kept in memory in a pool of unused connections. If a new connection request comes in that matches the properties of one of the unused connections in the pool, then the unused connection is used for the new database session.

Creating a totally new connection over the network can take seconds, whereas reusing a pooled connection can happen in milliseconds; it's much faster to use pooled connections. The connection string has parameters that can change the size of the connection pool or even turn off connection pooling. The default values (for example, connection pooling is on by default) are appropriate for the vast majority of applications. See the BOL for details.

Improving Your Use of Connection Objects

The code in the first sample program was trivial, so you could concentrate on how connections work. Let's enhance it a bit.

Using the Connection String in the Connection Constructor

In ConnectionSql, you created the connection and specified the connection string in separate steps. Since you always have to specify a connection string, you can use an overloaded version of the constructor that takes the connection string as an argument:

```
// Create connection
SqlConnection conn = new SqlConnection(@"
    server = (local)\netsdk;
    integrated security = sspi;
");
```

This constructor sets the ConnectionString property when creating the SqlConnection object. We will try it in the next examples and use it in later chapters.

Displaying Connection Information

Connections have several properties that provide information about the connection. Most of these properties are read-only, since their purpose is to display rather than set information. (You set connection values in the connection string.) These properties are often useful when debugging, to verify that the connection properties are what you expect them to be.

Here, we'll describe the connection properties common to most data providers. The complete list of properties and methods is available in the BOL. Later, you'll see some of the properties specific to other data providers.

Try It Out: Displaying Connection Information

Let's write a program to display connection information:

1. Add a C# Console Application project named ConnectionDisplay to the Chapter05 solution.

2. Rename Program.cs to ConnectionDisplay.cs. Replace the code with that in Listing 5-2.

Listing 5-2. ConnectionDisplay.cs

```
using System;
using System.Data;
using System.Data.SqlClient;

namespace Display
{
   class Display
   {
      static void Main()
      {
         // Connection string
         string connString = @"
            server = (local)\netsdk;
            integrated security = sspi;
         ";

         // Create connection
         SqlConnection conn = new SqlConnection(connString);
```

```
            try {
                // Open connection
                conn.Open();
                Console.WriteLine("Connection opened.");

                // Display connection properties
                Console.WriteLine("Connection Properties:");
                Console.WriteLine(
                    "\tConnection String: {0}",
                    conn.ConnectionString);
                Console.WriteLine(
                    "\tDatabase: {0}",
                    conn.Database);
                Console.WriteLine(
                    "\tDataSource: {0}",
                    conn.DataSource);
                Console.WriteLine(
                    "\tServerVersion: {0}",
                    conn.ServerVersion);
                Console.WriteLine(
                    "\tState: {0}",
                    conn.State);
                Console.WriteLine(
                    "\tWorkstationId: {0}",
                    conn.WorkstationId);
            }
            catch (SqlException e) {
                // Display error
                Console.WriteLine("Error: " + e);
            }
            finally {
                // Close connection
                conn.Close();
                Console.WriteLine("Connection closed.");
            }
        }
    }
}
```

3. Make it the startup project, and run it with Ctrl+F5. If the connection is successful, you'll see output like that shown in Figure 5-3.

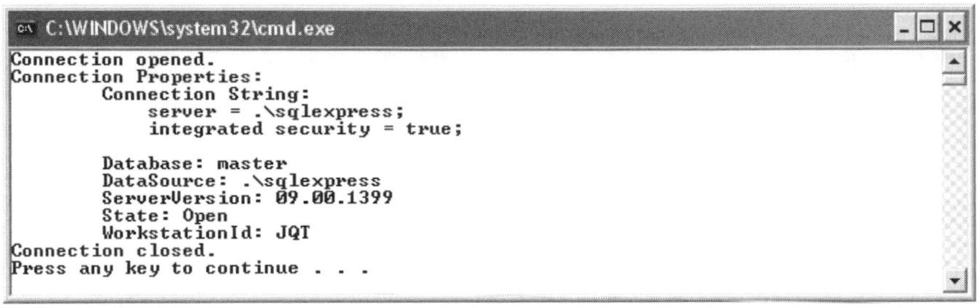

Figure 5-3. *Displaying connection information*

How It Works

The ConnectionString property can be both read and written. Here you just display it:

```
Console.WriteLine(
    "\tConnection String: {0}",
    conn.ConnectionString);
```

You'll see the value you assigned to it, including the whitespace, in the verbatim string.

What's the point? Well, it's handy when debugging connections to verify that the connection string really contains the values you thought you assigned. For example, if you're trying out different connection options, you may have different connection string parameters in the program. You may have commented out one intending to use it later but forgot about it. Displaying the ConnectionString property helps you to see that a parameter is missing.

The next statement displays the Database property. Since each SQL Server instance has several databases, this property shows which one you're initially using when you connect:

```
Console.WriteLine(
    "\tDatabase: {0}",
    conn.Database);
```

In this program, it displays:

```
Database: master
```

Since you didn't specify a database in the connection string, you were connected to the default database, which for this SSE instance is master. If you want to connect to the Northwind database, then you'll need to specify the Database parameter, for example:

```
// Connection string
string connString = @"
    server = (local)\netsdk;
    integrated security = sspi;
    database = northwind
";
```

Again, this is a handy property to display for debugging purposes. If you get an error saying that a particular table doesn't exist, often the problem isn't that the table doesn't exist but that it isn't in the database to which you're connected. Displaying the Database property helps you to find that kind of error quickly.

Tip If you specify a database in the connection string that doesn't exist on the server, you may see this error: System.Data.SqlClient.SqlException: Cannot open database "*database*" requested by the login. The login failed.

You can change the database currently used on a connection with the ChangeDatabase method.

The next statement displays the DataSource property, which gives the server instance name for SQL Server database connections:

```
Console.WriteLine(
    "\tDataSource: {0}",
    conn.DataSource);
```

In this program, this statement displays the same SQL Server instance name you've used in all the examples so far.

```
DataSource: .\sqlexpress
```

The utility of this, again, is mainly for debugging purposes.

The ServerVersion property displays the server version information:

```
Console.WriteLine(
    "\tServerVersion: {0}",
    conn.ServerVersion);
```

It shows the version of SSE you installed in Chapter 1. (Your version may differ.)

```
ServerVersion: 09.00.1399
```

The version number is useful for debugging. This information actually comes from the server, so it indicates the connection is working.

■Note SQL Server 2005 (and SSE) is version 9. SQL Server 2000 is version 8.

The State property indicates whether the connection is open or closed:

```
Console.WriteLine(
    "\tState: {0}",
    conn.State);
```

Since you display this property after the Open() call, it shows that the connection is open:

```
State: Open
```

You've been displaying your own message that the connection is open, but this property contains the current state. If the connection is closed, then the State property would be Closed.

You then display the workstation ID, a string identifying the client computer. The WorkstationId property is specific to SQL Server and can be handy for debugging:

```
Console.WriteLine(
    "\tWorkstationId: {0}",
    conn.WorkstationId);
```

It defaults to the computer name. Our computer is named JQT, but yours, of course, will be different:

```
WorkstationId: JQT
```

What makes this useful for debugging is that the SQL Server tools on the server can display which workstation ID issued a particular command. If you don't know which machine is causing a problem, you can modify your programs to display the WorkstationId property and compare it to the workstation IDs displayed on the server.

You can also set this property with the `Workstation ID` connection string parameter as follows, so if you want all the workstations in, say, Building B to show that information on the server, you can indicate that in the program:

```
// Connection string
string connString = @"
    server = .\sqlexpress;
    workstation id = Building B;
    integrated security = true;
";
```

That completes the discussion of the fundamentals of connecting to SQL Server with `SqlClient`. Now let's look at connecting with another data provider.

Connecting to SSE with OleDbConnection

As you saw in Chapter 4, you can use the OLE DB data provider to work with any OLE DB-compatible data store. Microsoft provides OLE DB data providers for SQL Server, Microsoft Access (Jet), Oracle, and a variety of other database and data file formats.

If a native data provider is available for a particular database or file format (such as the `SqlClient` data provider for SQL Server), then it's generally better to use it rather than the generic OLE DB data provider. This is because OLE DB introduces an extra layer of indirection between the C# program and the data source. One common database format for which no native data provider exists is the Microsoft Access database (`.mdb` file) format, also known as the Jet database engine format, so in this case you need to use the OLE DB (or the ODBC) data provider.

We don't assume you have an Access database to connect to, so we'll use OLE DB with SSE, as we did in Chapter 4.

Try It Out: Connecting to SSE with the OLE DB Data Provider

Follow these steps:

1. Add a C# Console Application project, named `ConnectionOleDb`, and rename `Program.cs` to `ConnectionOleDb.cs`.

2. Replace the code in `ConnectionOleDb.cs` with that in Listing 5-3. This is basically the same code as `Connection.cs`, with the changed code in bold.

Listing 5-3. ConnectionOleDb.cs

```csharp
using System;
using System.Data;
using System.Data.OleDb;

namespace Chapter05
{
    class ConnectionOleDb
    {
        static void Main()
        {
            // Create connection
            OleDbConnection conn = new OleDbConnection(@"
                provider = sqloledb;
                data source = .\sqlexpress;
                integrated security = sspi;
            ");

            try
            {
                // Open connection
                conn.Open();
                Console.WriteLine("Connection opened.");

                // Display connection properties
                Console.WriteLine("Connection Properties:");
                Console.WriteLine(
                    "\tConnection String: {0}",
                    conn.ConnectionString);
                Console.WriteLine(
                    "\tDatabase: {0}",
                    conn.Database);
                Console.WriteLine(
                    "\tDataSource: {0}",
                    conn.DataSource);
                Console.WriteLine(
                    "\tServerVersion: {0}",
                    conn.ServerVersion);
                Console.WriteLine(
                    "\tState: {0}",
                    conn.State);
```

```
        }
        catch (OleDbException e)
        {
            // Display error
            Console.WriteLine("Error: " + e);
        }
        finally
        {
            // Close connection
            conn.Close();
            Console.WriteLine("Connection closed.");
        }
    }
  }
}
```

3. Make it the startup project, and run it with Ctrl+F5. If the connection is successful, you'll see output like that shown in Figure 5-4.

Figure 5-4. *Displaying OLE DB connection information*

How It Works

We'll discuss only the differences between this example and the previous one.

The first step is to reference the OLE DB data provider namespace, System.Data.OleDb:

```
using System.Data.OleDb;
```

Next, you create an OleDbConnection object instead of a SqlConnection object. Note the changes to the connection string. Instead of the server parameter, you use Provider and Data Source. Notice the value of the Integrated Security parameter must be sspi, not true:

```
// Create connection
OleDbConnection conn = new OleDbConnection(@"
    provider = sqloledb;
    data source = .\sqlexpress;
    integrated security = sspi;
");
```

Finally, note that you omit the WorkstationId property in your display. The OLE DB data provider doesn't support it.

This is the pattern for accessing any data source with any .NET data provider. Specify the connection string with parameters specific to the data provider. Use the appropriate objects from the data provider namespace. Use only the properties and methods provided by that data provider.

Summary

In this chapter, you created, opened, and closed connections, using two data providers and their appropriate connection string parameters and values. You displayed information about connections after creating them, using connection properties. You also saw how to handle various exceptions associated with connections.

In the next chapter, you'll look at ADO.NET *commands* and see how to use them to access data.

Introducing Commands

Once you've established a connection to the database, you want to start interacting with it and getting it to do something useful for you. You may need to add, update, or delete some data, or perhaps modify the database in some other way. Whatever the task, it will inevitably involve a *command*.

In this chapter, we'll explain commands, which are objects that encapsulate the SQL for the action you want to perform and that provide methods for submitting it to the database. Each data provider has a command class that implements the System.Data.IDbCommand interface.

In this chapter, we'll cover:

- Creating commands

- Associating commands with connections

- Using connection methods that apply to commands

- Using command properties and methods

- Setting command text

- Executing commands

- Processing command results

- Using command parameters and the Prepare method

We'll use the SQL Server data provider (System.Data.SqlClient) in our examples. Its command is named SqlCommand. The commands for the other data providers work the same way.

Creating a Command

You can create a command either using the `SqlCommand` constructor or using methods that create the object for you. Let's look at the first of these alternatives.

Try It Out: Creating a Command with a Constructor

In this example, you'll create a `SqlCommand` object but not yet do anything with it:

1. Create a new Console Application project named `Chapter06`. When Solution Explorer opens, save the solution.

2. Rename the `Chapter06` project `CommandSql`. Rename the `Program.cs` file to `CommandSql.cs`, and replace the generated code with the code in Listing 6-1.

Listing 6-1. `CommandSql.cs`

```
using System;
using System.Data;
using System.Data.SqlClient;

namespace Chapter06
{
    class CommandSql
    {
        static void Main()
        {
            // create connection
            SqlConnection conn = new SqlConnection(@"
                server = .\sqlexpress;
                integrated security = true;
                database = northwind
            ");

            // create command
            SqlCommand cmd = new SqlCommand();
            Console.WriteLine("Command created.");
```

```
        try
        {
            // open connection
            conn.Open();
        }
        catch (SqlException ex)
        {
            Console.WriteLine(ex.ToString());
        }
        finally
        {
            conn.Close();
            Console.WriteLine("Connection Closed.");
        }
    }
  }
}
```

3. Run the program with Ctrl+F5. You should see the output as shown in Figure 6-1.

Figure 6-1. *Connecting after creating a command*

How It Works

You create a SqlCommand object using the default constructor, and you print a message indicating you've created it:

```
// create SqlCommand
SqlCommand cmd = new SqlCommand();
Console.WriteLine("Command created.");
```

In this example, the command is empty. It isn't associated with a connection, and it doesn't have its text (in other words, the SQL) set. You can't do much with it here, so let's move on and see how you can associate a command with a connection.

Associating a Command with a Connection

For your commands to be executed against a database, each command must be associated with a connection to the database. You do this by setting the Connection property of the command, and in order to save resources, multiple commands can use the same connection. You have a couple of ways to set up this association, so let's modify our example to try them.

Try It Out: Setting the Connection Property

To set the Connection property:

1. Add the following bold code to the try block of Listing 6-1:

```
try
{
    // open connection
    conn.Open();

    // connect command to connection
    cmd.Connection = conn;
    Console.WriteLine("Connnected command to this connection.");
}
```

2. Run it with Ctrl+F5. You should see the result shown in Figure 6-2.

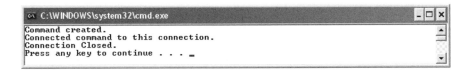

Figure 6-2. *Connecting a command to a connection*

How It Works

As you saw in the previous example, you start the code by creating the connection and command:

```
// create connection
SqlConnection conn = new SqlConnection(@"
   server = .\sqlexpress;
   integrated security = true;
   database = northwind
");

// create command
SqlCommand cmd = new SqlCommand();
Console.WriteLine("Command created.");
```

At this point, both the connection and command exist, but they aren't associated with each other in any way. It's only when you assign the connection to the command's Connection property that they become associated:

```
// connect command to connection
cmd.Connection = conn;
Console.WriteLine("Connected command to this connection.");
```

The actual assignment occurs after the call to conn.Open in this particular example, but you could have done it before calling Open(); the connection doesn't have to be open for the Connection property of the command to be set.

As mentioned earlier, you have a second option for associating a connection with a command: calling the connection's CreateCommand method will return a new command with the Connection property set to that connection:

```
SqlCommand cmd = conn.CreateCommand();
```

This is equivalent to:

```
SqlCommand cmd = new SqlCommand();
cmd.Connection = conn;
```

In both cases, you end up with a command associated with a connection.

You still need one more thing in order to use the command, and that's the text of the command. Let's see how to set that next.

Assigning Text to a Command

Every command has a property, CommandText, that holds the SQL to execute. You can assign to this property directly or specify it when constructing the command. Let's look at these alternatives.

Try It Out: Setting the CommandText Property

To set the CommandText property:

1. Modify the try block with the following bold code:

```
try
{
    // open connection
    conn.Open();

    // connect command to connection
    cmd.Connection = conn;
    Console.WriteLine("Connnected command to this connection.");

    // associate SQL with command
    cmd.CommandText = @"
        select
            count(*)
        from
            employees
    ";
    Console.WriteLine(
        "Ready to execute SQL: {0}"
        , cmd.CommandText
    );
}
```

2. Run it with Ctrl+F5. You should see the result shown in Figure 6-3.

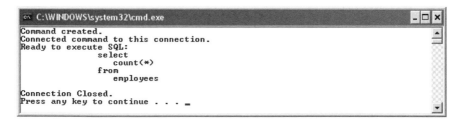

Figure 6-3. *Setting command text*

How It Works

CommandText is just a string, so you can print it with Console.WriteLine() just like any other string. The SQL will return the number of employees in the Northwind Employees table when you eventually execute it.

■Note You must set both the Connection and the CommandText properties of a command before the command can be executed.

You can set the Connection and the CommandText properties when you create the command with yet another variation of its constructor, as shown here:

```
// create command (with both text and connection)
string sql = @"
    select
        count(*)
    from
        employees
";
SqlCommand cmd =
    new SqlCommand(sql, thisConnection);
```

This is equivalent to the previous code that assigns each property explicitly. This is the most commonly used variation of the SqlCommand constructor, and you'll use this one for the rest of the chapter.

Executing Commands

Commands aren't much use unless you can execute them, so let's look at that now. Commands have several different methods for executing SQL. The differences between these methods depend on the results you expect from the SQL. Queries return rows of data (*result sets*), but statements don't. You determine which method to use by considering what you expect to be returned (see Table 6-1).

Table 6-1. *Command Execution Methods*

If the Command Is Going to Return ...	You Should Use ...
Nothing (because it isn't a query)	ExecuteNonQuery
A single value	ExecuteScalar
Zero or more rows	ExecuteReader
XML (which you'll learn more about in Chapter 17)	ExecuteXmlReader

The SQL you just used in the example should return one value, the number of employees. Looking at Table 6-1, you can see that you should use the ExecuteScalar method of SqlCommand to return this one result. Let's try it.

Try It Out: Using the ExecuteScalar Method

To use the ExecuteScalar method:

1. Add a new C# Console Application project named CommandScalar to your Chapter06 solution. Rename Program.cs to CommandScalar.cs.

2. Replace the code in CommandScalar.cs with the code in Listing 6-2.

Listing 6-2. CommandScalar.cs

```
using System;
using System.Data;
using System.Data.SqlClient;

namespace Chapter06
{
    class CommandScalar
    {
        static void Main()
        {
            // create connection
            SqlConnection conn = new SqlConnection(@"
                server = .\sqlexpress;
                integrated security = true;
                database = northwind
            ");
```

```
      // create command (with both text and connection)
      string sql = @"
         select
            count(*)
         from
            employees
      ";

      SqlCommand cmd = new SqlCommand(sql, conn);
      Console.WriteLine("Command created and connected.");

      try
      {
         // open connection
         conn.Open();

         // execute query
         Console.WriteLine(
            "Number of Employees is {0}"
          , cmd.ExecuteScalar()
         );
      }
      catch (SqlException ex)
      {
         Console.WriteLine(ex.ToString());
      }
      finally
      {
         conn.Close();
         Console.WriteLine("Connection Closed.");
      }
   }
  }
}
```

3. Make it the startup project, and then run it with Ctrl+F5. You should see the result shown in Figure 6-4.

Figure 6-4. *Executing a scalar command*

How It Works

All you did was add a call to ExecuteScalar() within a call to WriteLine():

```
// execute query
Console.WriteLine(
    "Number of Employees is {0}"
  , cmd.ExecuteScalar()
);
```

ExecuteScalar() takes the CommandText property and sends it to the database using the command's Connection property. It returns the result, 9, as a single object, which you display with Console.WriteLine().

This is pretty simple to follow, but it's worth noting this really is simpler than usual because Console.WriteLine() takes any kind of object as its input. In fact, ExecuteScalar()'s return type is object, the base class of all types in the .NET Framework, which makes perfect sense when you remember that a database can hold any type of data. So, if you want to assign the returned object to a variable of a specific type (int, for example), you must cast the object to the specific type. If the types aren't compatible, the system will generate a runtime error that indicates an invalid cast.

The following is an example that demonstrates this idea. In it, you store the result from ExecuteScalar() in the variable count, casting it to the specific type int:

```
int count = (int) cmd.ExecuteScalar();
Console.WriteLine("Number of Employees is: {0}", count);
```

If you're sure the type of the result will always be an int (a safe bet with COUNT(*)), then the previous code is safe. However, if you left the cast to int in place and changed the CommandText of the command to

```
select
    firstname
from
    employees
where
    lastname = 'Davolio'
```

then ExecuteScalar() would return the string "Nancy" instead of an integer, and you'd get this exception

```
Unhandled Exception: System.InvalidCastException: Specified cast is not valid.
```

because you can't cast a string to an int.

Another problem may occur if a query actually returns multiple rows where you thought it would return only one; for example, what if there were multiple employees with the last name Davolio? In this case, ExecuteScalar() just returns the first row of the result and ignores the rest. If you use ExecuteScalar(), make sure you not only expect but actually get a single value returned.

Executing Commands with Multiple Results

For queries where you're expecting multiple rows and columns to be returned, use the command's ExecuteReader() method.

ExecuteReader() returns a data reader, an instance of the SqlDataReader class that you'll study in the next chapter. Data readers have methods that allow you to read successive rows in result sets and retrieve individual column values.

We'll leave the details of data readers for the next chapter, but for comparison's sake, we'll give a brief example here of using the ExecuteReader() method to create a SqlDataReader from a command to display query results.

Try It Out: Using the ExecuteReader Method

To use the ExecuteReader method, follow these steps:

1. Add a new C# Console Application project named CommandReader to your Chapter06 solution. Rename Program.cs to CommandReader.cs.

2. Replace the code in CommandReader.cs with the code in Listing 6-3.

Listing 6-3. CommandReader.cs

```
using System;
using System.Data;
using System.Data.SqlClient;

namespace Chapter06
{
    class CommandReader
    {
        static void Main()
```

```csharp
{
    // create connection
    SqlConnection conn = new SqlConnection(@"
        server = .\sqlexpress;
        integrated security = true;
        database = northwind
    ");

    // create command (with both text and connection)
    string sql = @"
        select
            firstname,
            lastname
        from
            employees
    ";

    SqlCommand cmd = new SqlCommand(sql, conn);
    Console.WriteLine("Command created and connected.");

    try
    {
        // open connection
        conn.Open();

        // execute query
        SqlDataReader rdr = cmd.ExecuteReader();

        while (rdr.Read())
        {
            Console.WriteLine("Employee name: {0} {1}",
                rdr.GetValue(0),
                rdr.GetValue(1)
            );
        }
    }
    catch (SqlException ex)
    {
        Console.WriteLine(ex.ToString());
    }
```

```
        finally
        {
            conn.Close();
            Console.WriteLine("Connection Closed.");
        }
    }
  }
}
```

3. Make it the startup project, and then run it with Ctrl+F5. You should see the result shown in Figure 6-5, displaying the first and last names of all nine employees.

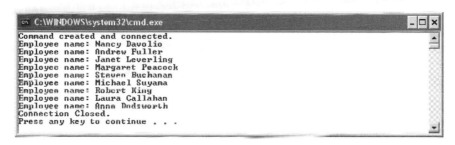

Figure 6-5. *Using a data reader*

How It Works

In this example, you use the ExecuteReader method to retrieve and then output the first and last names of all the employees in the Employees table. As with ExecuteScalar(), ExecuteReader() takes the CommandText property and sends it to the database using the connection from the Connection property.

When you use the ExecuteScalar method, you produce only a single scalar value. In contrast, using ExecuteReader() returns a SqlDataReader object:

```
// execute query
SqlDataReader rdr = cmd.ExecuteReader();

while (rdr.Read())
{
    Console.WriteLine("Employee name: {0} {1}",
        rdr.GetValue(0),
        rdr.GetValue(1)
    );
}
```

The `SqlDataReader` object has a `Read` method that gets each row in turn and a `GetValue` method that gets the value of a column in the row. The particular column whose value it retrieves is given by the integer parameter indicating the index of the column. Note that `GetValue()` uses a zero-based index, so the first column is column zero, the second column is column one, and so on. Since the query asks for two columns, `FirstName` and `LastName`, these are the columns numbered 0 and 1 in this query result.

Executing Statements

The `ExecuteNonQuery` method of the command executes SQL statements instead of queries. Let's try it.

Try It Out: Using the ExecuteNonQuery Method

To use the `ExecuteNonQuery` method, follow these steps:

1. Add a new C# Console Application project named `CommandNonQuery` to your `Chapter06` solution. Rename `Program.cs` to `CommandNonQuery.cs`.

2. Replace the code in `CommandNonQuery.cs` with the code in Listing 6-4.

Listing 6-4. `CommandNonQuery.cs`

```
using System;
using System.Data;
using System.Data.SqlClient;

namespace Chapter06
{
    class CommandNonQuery
    {
        static void Main()
        {
            // create connection
            SqlConnection conn = new SqlConnection(@"
                server = .\sqlexpress;
                integrated security = true;
                database = northwind
            ");
```

```csharp
// define scalar query
string sqlqry = @"
   select
      count(*)
   from
      employees
";

// define insert statement
string sqlins = @"
   insert into employees
      (
      firstname,
      lastname
      )
   values('Zachariah', 'Zinn')
";

// define delete statement
string sqldel = @"
   delete from employees
   where
      firstname = 'Zachariah'
      and
      lastname = 'Zinn'
";

// create commands
SqlCommand cmdqry = new SqlCommand(sqlqry, conn);
SqlCommand cmdnon = new SqlCommand(sqlins, conn);

try
{
   // open connection
   conn.Open();

   // execute query to get number of employees
   Console.WriteLine(
      "Before INSERT: Number of employees {0}\n"
      , cmdqry.ExecuteScalar()
   );
```

```
            // execute nonquery to insert an employee
            Console.WriteLine(
               "Executing statement {0}"
              , cmdnon.CommandText
            );
            cmdnon.ExecuteNonQuery();
            Console.WriteLine(
               "After INSERT: Number of employees {0}\n"
              , cmdqry.ExecuteScalar()
            );

            // execute nonquery to delete an employee
            cmdnon.CommandText = sqldel;
            Console.WriteLine(
               "Executing statement {0}"
              , cmdnon.CommandText
            );
            cmdnon.ExecuteNonQuery();
            Console.WriteLine(
               "After DELETE: Number of employees {0}\n"
              , cmdqry.ExecuteScalar()
            );
         }
         catch (SqlException ex)
         {
            Console.WriteLine(ex.ToString());
         }
         finally
         {
            conn.Close();
            Console.WriteLine("Connection Closed.");
         }
      }
   }
}
```

3. Make it the startup project, and then run it with Ctrl+F5. You should see the result shown in Figure 6-6.

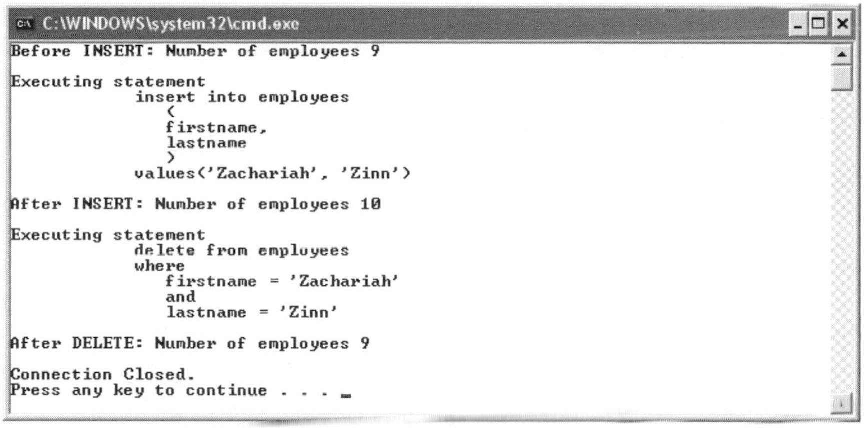

```
Before INSERT: Number of employees 9

Executing statement
            insert into employees
                (
                firstname,
                lastname
                )
            values('Zachariah', 'Zinn')
After INSERT: Number of employees 10

Executing statement
            delete from employees
            where
                firstname = 'Zachariah'
                and
                lastname = 'Zinn'

After DELETE: Number of employees 9

Connection Closed.
Press any key to continue . . . _
```

Figure 6-6. *Executing statements*

How It Works

In this program, you use a scalar query and two statements, storing the SQL in three string variables:

```csharp
// define scalar query
string sqlqry = @"
   select
       count(*)
   from
       employees
";

// define insert statement
string sqlins = @"
   insert into employees
       (
       firstname,
       lastname
       )
   values('Zachariah', 'Zinn')
";

// define delete statement
```

```
string sqldel = @"
    delete from employees
    where
        firstname = 'Zachariah'
        and
        lastname = 'Zinn'
";
```

Then you create two commands. The first is cmdqry, which encapsulates the scalar query to count the rows in the Employees table. You use this command several times to monitor the number of rows as you insert and delete employees. The second is cmdnon, which you use twice, first to insert a row, then to delete the same row. You initially set its CommandText to the INSERT statement SQL

```
SqlCommand cmdnon = new SqlCommand(sqlins, conn);
```

and later reset it to the DELETE statement SQL

```
cmdnon.CommandText = sqldel;
```

executing the SQL statements with two calls to

```
cmdnon.ExecuteNonQuery();
```

ExecuteNonQuery() returns an int indicating how many rows are affected by the command. Since you want to display the number of affected rows, you put the call to ExecuteNonQuery() within a call to Console.WriteLine(). You use ExecuteScalar() to display the number of rows, before and after the INSERT and DELETE operations:

```
Console.WriteLine("After INSERT: Number of Employees is: {0}",
    selectCommand.ExecuteScalar() );
```

Note that both cmdqry and cmdnon are SqlCommand objects. The difference between submitting queries and statements is the method you use to submit them.

■**Note** With ExecuteNonQuery(), you can submit virtually any SQL statement, including Data Definition Language (DDL) statements to create and drop database objects such as tables and indexes. We'll create tables in Chapter 11, using SSMSE, because that's how they're typically created, but the SQL you learn there can be submitted from a C# program with ExecuteNonQuery().

Command Parameters

When you insert the new row into Employees, you hard-code the values. Although this is perfectly valid SQL, it's something you almost never want (or need) to do. You need to be able to store whatever values are appropriate at any given time. There are two approaches to doing this. Both are reasonable, but one is far more efficient than the other.

The less efficient alternative is to dynamically build a SQL statement, producing a string that contains all the necessary information in the CommandText property. For example, you could do something like this:

```
string fname = "Zachariah";
string lname = "Zinn";
string vals = "('" + fname + "'," + "'" + lname +"')" ;
string sqlins = @"
   insert into employees
   (
      firstname,
      lastname
   )
   values"
 + vals
;
```

You'd then assign sqlins to some command's CommandText before executing the statement.

Note Of course, we're using fname and lname simply as rudimentary sources of data. Data most likely comes from some dynamic input source and involves many rows over time, but the technique is nonetheless the same: building a SQL string from a combination of hard-coded SQL keywords and values contained in variables.

A much better way to handle this is with *command parameters*. A command parameter is a placeholder in the command text where a value will be substituted. In SQL Server, *named parameters* are used. They begin with @ followed by the parameter name with no intervening space. So, in the following INSERT statement, @MyName and @MyNumber are both parameters:

```
INSERT INTO MyTable VALUES (@MyName, @MyNumber)
```

■**Note** Some data providers use the standard SQL *parameter marker*, a question mark (?), instead of named parameters.

Command parameters have several advantages:

- The mapping between the variables and where they're used in SQL is clearer.

- Parameters let you use the type definitions that are specific to a particular ADO.NET data provider to ensure that your variables are mapped to the correct SQL data types.

- Parameters let you use the Prepare method, which can make your code run faster because SQL Server parses the SQL in a "prepared" command only the first time it's executed. Subsequent executions run the same SQL, changing only parameter values.

- Parameters are used extensively in other programming techniques, such as stored procedures (see Chapter 13) and working with irregular data (see Chapter 18).

Try It Out: Using Command Parameters

Follow these steps:

1. Add a new C# Console Application project named CommandParameters to your Chapter06 solution. Rename Program.cs to CommandParameters.cs.

2. Replace the code in CommandParameters.cs with the code in Listing 6-5. This is a variation of Listing 6-4, with salient changes highlighted.

Listing 6-5. CommandParameters.cs

```
using System;
using System.Data;
using System.Data.SqlClient;

namespace Chapter06
{
    class CommandParameters
    {
        static void Main()
```

```
{
    // set up rudimentary data
    string fname = "Zachariah";
    string lname = "Zinn";

    // create connection
    SqlConnection conn = new SqlConnection(@"
        server = .\sqlexpress;
        integrated security = true;
        database = northwind
    ");

    // define scalar query
    string sqlqry = @"
        select
            count(*)
        from
            employees
    ";

    // define insert statement
    string sqlins = @"
        insert into employees
        (
            firstname,
            lastname
        )
        values(@fname, @lname)
    ";

    // define delete statement
    string sqldel = @"
        delete from employees
        where
            firstname = @fname
            and
            lastname = @lname
    ";
```

```
// create commands
SqlCommand cmdqry = new SqlCommand(sqlqry, conn);
SqlCommand cmdnon = new SqlCommand(sqlins, conn);

// add parameters to the command for statements
cmdnon.Parameters.Add("@fname", SqlDbType.NVarChar, 10);
cmdnon.Parameters.Add("@fname", SqlDbType.NVarChar, 20);

try
{
   // open connection
   conn.Open();

   // execute query to get number of employees
   Console.WriteLine(
      "Before INSERT: Number of employees {0}\n"
     , cmdqry.ExecuteScalar()
   );

   // execute nonquery to insert an employee
   cmdnon.Parameters["@fname"].Value = fname;
   cmdnon.Parameters["@lname"].Value = lname;
   Console.WriteLine(
      "Executing statement {0}"
     , cmdnon.CommandText
   );
   cmdnon.ExecuteNonQuery();
   Console.WriteLine(
      "After INSERT: Number of employees {0}\n"
     , cmdqry.ExecuteScalar()
   );

   // execute nonquery to delete an employee
   cmdnon.CommandText = sqldel;
   Console.WriteLine(
      "Executing statement {0}"
     , cmdnon.CommandText
   );
```

```
            cmdnon.ExecuteNonQuery();
            Console.WriteLine(
                "After DELETE: Number of employees {0}\n"
                , cmdqry.ExecuteScalar()
            );
        }
        catch (SqlException ex)
        {
            Console.WriteLine(ex.ToString());
        }
        finally
        {
            conn.Close();
            Console.WriteLine("Connection Closed.");
        }
    }
}
}
```

3. Make it the startup project, and then run it with Ctrl+F5. You should see the result shown in Figure 6-7.

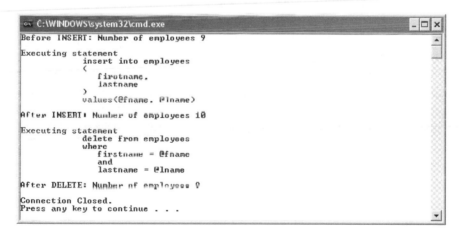

Figure 6-7. *Using command parameters*

How It Works

First, you set up the sample data:

```
// set up rudimentary data
```

```
string fname = "Zachariah";
string lname = "Zinn";
```

Then you add two parameters, @fname and @lname, to the Parameters collection property of the command you want to parameterize:

```
// create commands
SqlCommand cmdqry = new SqlCommand(sqlqry, conn);
SqlCommand cmdnon = new SqlCommand(sqlins, conn);

// add parameters to the command for statements
cmdnon.Parameters.Add("@fname", SqlDbType.NVarChar, 10);
cmdnon.Parameters.Add("@fname", SqlDbType.NVarChar, 20);
```

Note that you provide the parameter names as strings, then specify the data types of the columns you expect to use them with. The SqlDbType enumeration contains a member for every SQL Server data type except cursor and table, which C# programs can't directly use. The Add method is overloaded. Since nvarchar requires you to specify its maximum length, you include that as the third argument.

Finally, you set the parameter values before executing the command:

```
// execute nonquery to insert an employee
cmdnon.Parameters["@fname"].Value = fname;
cmdnon.Parameters["@lname"].Value = lname;
```

■**Note** The same command, cmdnon, is used to execute both the INSERT and DELETE statements. The parameter values don't change, even though the SQL in CommandText does. The Parameters collection is the source of parameter values for whatever SQL is in CommandText. The SQL doesn't have to use all or even any of the parameters, but it cannot use any parameters not in the command's Parameters collection.

Notice in Figure 6-7 that when you display the SQL in CommandText, you see the parameter names rather than their values. Values are substituted for parameters when the SQL is submitted to the database server, not when the values are assigned to the members of the Parameters collection.

The Prepare Method

When you expect to execute a parameterized command multiple times, you should prepare it with the Prepare method. The syntax is simple:

```
command.Prepare();
```

You can execute it any time after the parameters have been added to the command and before the command is executed.

Prepare() avoids SQL parsing overhead. The query or statement associated with the command is parsed only on first execution. After that, the cached SQL is executed, changing only parameter values. You never have to prepare any commands, but it's always the best practice to do this if you expect to execute a command multiple times.

Note If you change its CommandText after you prepare a command, you must prepare the command again to gain the advantage of prepared SQL. For a command to stay prepared, only parameter values can change between command executions.

You can use Prepare() even if you only execute a command once, but it's a waste of your time and the computer's. For example, you could change CommandParameters.cs by adding the following line in bold:

```
// execute nonquery to insert an employee
cmdnon.Parameters["@fname"].Value = fname;
cmdnon.Parameters["@lname"].Value = lname;
Console.WriteLine(
    "Executing statement {0}"
  , cmdnon.CommandText
);
cmdnon.Prepare();
cmdnon.ExecuteNonQuery();
Console.WriteLine(
    "After INSERT: Number of employees {0}\n"
  , cmdqry.ExecuteScalar()
);
```

It would still run as expected, but now you've added an unnecessary call to Prepare(). Further, the prepared command is discarded when you change the CommandText before performing the DELETE

```
cmdnon.CommandText = sqldel;
```

because the new SQL statement is different (though it still uses the same parameters and they stay in effect).

■**Tip** If you prepare commands, use them for only one SQL query or statement. Create as many command objects as you need to prepare.

Summary

In this chapter, we covered quite a few things:

- What an ADO.NET command is and does

- How to create a command

- How to associate a command with a connection

- How to set command text

- How to use ExecuteScalar() for queries that return single values

- How to use ExecuteReader() to process result sets

- How to use ExecuteNonQuery() for statements

- What command parameters are and how to use them

- How to use the Prepare method

In the next chapter, we'll look at data readers.

CHAPTER 7

■■■

Introducing Data Readers

In Chapter 4, you used data readers to retrieve data from a multirow result set. In this chapter, we'll look at data readers in more detail. You'll see how they're used and their importance in ADO.NET programming.

In particular, you'll see how to use data readers to do the following:

- Retrieve query results

- Get information with ordinal and column name indexers

- Get result set information

- Get schema information

- Process multiple result sets

Understanding Data Readers in General

The third component of a data provider, in addition to connections and commands, is the *data reader*. Once you've connected to a database and queried it, you need some way to access the result set. This is where the data reader comes in.

Note If you're from an ADO background, an ADO.NET data reader is like an ADO forward-only/read-only client-side recordset, but it's not a COM object.

Data readers are objects that implement the System.Data.IDataReader interface. A data reader is a fast, unbuffered, forward-only, read-only *connected* stream that retrieves data on a per-row basis. It reads one row at a time as it loops through a result set.

You can't instantiate a data reader directly; instead, you create one with the ExecuteReader method of a command. For example, assuming cmd is a SqlClient command object for a query, here's how to create a SqlClient data reader:

```
SqlDataReader rdr = cmd.ExecuteReader();
```

You can now use this data reader to access the query's result set.

■**Tip** One point that we'll discuss further in the next chapter is choosing a data reader vs. a dataset. The general rule is to always use a data reader for simply retrieving data. If all you need to do is display data, all you need to use in most cases is a data reader.

We'll demonstrate basic data reader usage with a few examples. The first example is the most basic; it simply uses a data reader to loop through a result set.

Let's say you've successfully established a connection with the database, a query has been executed, and everything seems to be going fine—what now? The next sensible thing to do would be to retrieve the rows and process them.

Try It Out: Looping Through a Result Set

The following steps show how to use a SqlDataReader to loop through a result set and retrieve rows:

1. Create a new Console Application project named Chapter07. When Solution Explorer opens, save the solution.

2. Rename the Chapter07 project to DataLooper. Rename the Program.cs file to DataLooper.cs, and replace the generated code with the code in Listing 7-1.

Listing 7-1. DataLooper.cs

```
using System;
using System.Data;
using System.Data.SqlClient;
```

```
namespace Chapter07
{
    class DataLooper
    {
        static void Main(string[] args)
        {
            // connection string
            string connString = @"
                server = .\sqlexpress;
                integrated security = true;
                database = northwind
            ";

            // query
            string sql = @"
                select
                    contactname
                from
                    customers
            ";

            // create connection
            SqlConnection conn = new SqlConnection(connString);

            try
            {
                // open connection
                conn.Open();

                // create command
                SqlCommand cmd = new SqlCommand(sql, conn);

                // create data reader
                SqlDataReader rdr = cmd.ExecuteReader();

                // loop through result set
                while (rdr.Read())
                {
                    // print one row at a time
                    Console.WriteLine("{0}", rdr[0]);
                }
```

```
            // close data reader
            rdr.Close();
        }
        catch(Exception e)
        {
            Console.WriteLine("Error Occurred: " + e);
        }
        finally
        {
            //close connection
            conn.Close();
        }
    }
  }
}
```

3. Run it with Ctrl+F5. You should see the result shown in Figure 7-1. (Only the last 20 rows are displayed in the figure.)

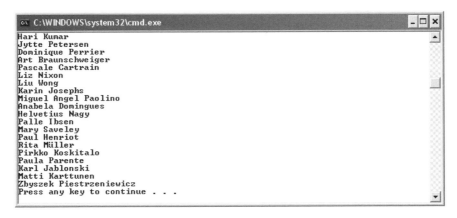

Figure 7-1. *Looping through a result set*

How It Works

SqlDataReader is an abstract class that you can't instantiate explicitly. For this reason, you obtain an instance of a SqlDataReader by executing the ExecuteReader method of SqlCommand:

```
            // create data reader
            SqlDataReader rdr = cmd.ExecuteReader();
```

ExecuteReader() doesn't just create a data reader, it sends the SQL to the connection for execution. When it returns, you can loop through each row of the result set and retrieve values column by column. To do this, you call the Read method of SqlDataReader, which returns true if a row is available and advances the *cursor* (the internal pointer to the next row in the result set) or returns false if another row isn't available. Since Read() advances the cursor to the next available row, you have to call it for all the rows in the result set, so you call it as the condition in a while loop:

```
// loop through result set
while (rdr.Read())
{
    // print one row at a time
    Console.WriteLine("{0}", rdr[0]);
}
```

Once you call the Read method, the next row is returned as a collection and stored in the SqlDataReader object itself. To access data from a specific column, you can use a number of methods (we'll cover these in the next section), but for this application, you use the ordinal indexer lookup method, giving the column number to the reader to retrieve values (just as you'd specify an index for an array). Since in this case you choose a single column from the Customers table while querying the database, only the "zero[th]" indexer is accessible, so you hard-code the index as rdr[0].

To use the *connection* for another purpose or to run another query on the database, it's important to call the Close method of SqlDataReader to close the reader explicitly. Once a reader is attached to an active connection, the connection remains busy fetching data for the reader and remains unavailable for other use until the reader has been detached from it. That's why you close the reader in the try block rather than in the finally block (even though this simple program doesn't need to use the connection for another purpose):

```
// close data reader
rdr.Close();
```

Using Ordinal Indexers

You use an ordinal indexer to retrieve column data from the result set. Let's learn more about ordinal indexers. The code

```
rdr[0]
```

is a reference to the data reader's Item property, and returns the value in the column specified for the current row. The value is returned as an object.

Try It Out: Using Ordinal Indexers

Let's build a console application that uses an ordinal indexer:

1. Add a new C# Console Application project named OrdinalIndexer to your Chapter07 solution. Rename Program.cs to OrdinalIndexer.cs.

2. Replace the code in OrdinalIndexer.cs with the code in Listing 7-2.

Listing 7-2. OrdinalIndexer.cs

```csharp
using System;
using System.Data;
using System.Data.SqlClient;

namespace Chapter07
{
    class OrdinalIndexer
    {
        static void Main(string[] args)
        {
            // connection string
            string connString = @"
                server = .\sqlexpress;
                integrated security = true;
                database = northwind
            ";

            // query
            string sql = @"
                select
                    companyname,
                    contactname
                from
                    customers
                where
                    contactname like 'M%'
            ";

            // create connection
            SqlConnection conn = new SqlConnection(connString);
```

```csharp
      try
      {
          // Open connection
          conn.Open();

          // create command
          SqlCommand cmd = new SqlCommand(sql, conn);

          // create data reader
          SqlDataReader rdr = cmd.ExecuteReader();

          // print headings
          Console.WriteLine("\t{0}   {1}",
              "Company Name".PadRight(25),
              "Contact Name".PadRight(20));

          Console.WriteLine("\t{0}   {1}",
              "============".PadRight(25),
              "============".PadRight(20));

          // loop through result set
          while (rdr.Read())
          {
              Console.WriteLine(" {0} | {1}",
                  rdr[0].ToString().PadLeft(25),
                  rdr[1].ToString().PadLeft(20));
          }

          // close reader
          rdr.Close();
      }
      catch(Exception e)
      {
          Console.WriteLine("Error Occurred: " + e);
      }
      finally
      {
          // close connection
          conn.Close();
      }
   }
  }
}
```

3. Make this the startup project, and run it with Ctrl+F5. You should see the result shown in Figure 7-2.

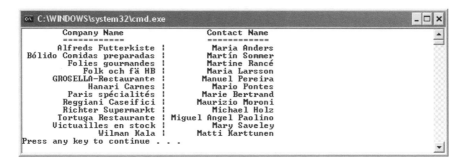

Figure 7-2. *Displaying multiple columns*

How It Works

You query the Customers table for the columns CompanyName and ContactName, where contact names begin with the letter *M*:

```
// query
string sql = @"
    select
        companyname,
        contactname
    from
        customers
    where
        contactname like 'M%'
";
```

Since your query selects two columns, the returned data also comprises a collection of rows from only these two columns, thus allowing access to only two possible ordinal indexers, 0 and 1.

You read each row in a while loop, fetching values of the two columns with their indexers. Since the returned value is an object, you need to explicitly convert the value to a string so that you can use the PadLeft method to format the output:

```
// loop through result set
while (rdr.Read())
{
    Console.WriteLine(" {0} | {1}",
        rdr[0].ToString().PadLeft(25),
        rdr[1].ToString().PadLeft(20));
}
```

After processing all rows in the result set, you explicitly close the reader to free the connection:

```
// close reader
rdr.Close();
```

Using Column Name Indexers

Most of the time we don't really keep track of column numbers and instead prefer retrieving values by their respective column names, simply because it's much easier to remember them by their names, which also makes the code more self-documenting.

You use column name indexing by specifying column names instead of ordinal index numbers. This has its advantages. For example, a table may be changed by the addition or deletion of one or more columns, upsetting column ordering and raising exceptions in older code that uses ordinal indexers. Using column name indexers avoids this issue, but ordinal indexers are faster, since they directly reference columns rather than look them up by name.

The following code snippet retrieves the same columns (CompanyName and ContactName) that the last example did, using column name indexers:

```
// loop through result set
while (rdr.Read())
{
    Console.WriteLine(" {0} | {1}",
        rdr["companyname"].ToString().PadLeft(25),
        rdr["contactname"].ToString().PadLeft(20));
}
```

Replace the ordinal indexers in OrdinalIndexer.cs with column name indexers, rerun the project, and you'll get the same results as shown in Figure 7-2.

The next section discusses a better approach for most cases.

Using Typed Accessor Methods

When a data reader returns a value from a data source, the resulting value is retrieved and stored locally in a .NET type rather than in the original data source type. This in-place type-conversion feature is a trade-off between consistency and speed, so to give some control over the data being retrieved, the data reader exposes typed accessor methods that you can use if you know the specific type of the value being returned.

Typed accessor methods all begin with Get, take an ordinal index for data retrieval, and are type safe; C# won't allow you to get away with unsafe casts. These methods turn out to be faster than both the ordinal and the column name indexer methods. Being faster than column name indexing seems only logical, as the typed accessor methods take ordinals for referencing; however, we need to explain how it's faster than ordinal indexing. This is because even though both techniques take in a column number, the conventional ordinal indexing method needs to look up the data source data type of the result and then go through a type conversion. This overhead of looking up the schema is avoided with typed accessors. .NET types and typed accessor methods are available for almost all data types supported by SQL Server and OLE DB databases.

Table 7-1 should give you a brief idea of when to use typed accessors and with what data type. It lists SQL Server data types, their corresponding .NET types, .NET typed accessors, and special SQL Server–specific typed accessors designed particularly for returning objects of type System.Data.SqlTypes.

Table 7-1. *SQL Server Typed Accessors*

SQL Server Data Type	.NET Type	.NET Typed Accessor
bigint	Int64	GetInt64
binary	Byte[]	GetBytes
bit	Boolean	GetBoolean
char	String or Char[]	GetString or GetChars
datetime	DateTime	GetDateTime
decimal	Decimal	GetDecimal
float	Double	GetDouble
image or long varbinary	Byte[]	GetBytes
int	Int32	GetInt32
money	Decimal	GetDecimal
nchar	String or Char[]	GetString or GetChars
ntext	String or Char[]	GetString or GetChars
numeric	Decimal	GetDecimal
nvarchar	String or Char[]	GetString or GetChars

SQL Server Data Type	.NET Type	.NET Typed Accessor
real	Single	GetFloat
smalldatetime	DateTime	GetDateTime
smallint	Int16	GetInt16
smallmoney	Decimal	GetDecimal
sql_variant	Object	GetValue
long varchar	String or Char[]	GetString or GetChars
timestamp	Byte[]	GetBytes
tinyint	Byte	GetByte
uniqueidentifier	Guid	GetGuid
varbinary	Byte[]	GetBytes
varchar	String or Char[]	GetString or GetChars

Table 7-2 shows some available OLE DB data types, their corresponding .NET types, and their .NET typed accessors.

Table 7-2. *OLE DB Typed Accessors*

OLE DB Type	.NET Type	.NET Typed Accessor
DBTYPE_I8	Int64	GetInt64
DBTYPE_BYTES	Byte[]	GetBytes
DBTYPE_BOOL	Boolean	GetBoolean
DBTYPE_BSTR	String	GetString
DBTYPE_STR	String	GetString
DBTYPE_CY	Decimal	GetDecimal
DBTYPE_DATE	DateTime	GetDateTime
DBTYPE_DBDATE	DateTime	GetDateTime
DBTYPE_DBTIME	DateTime	GetDateTime
DBTYPE_DBTIMESTAMP	DateTime	GetDateTime
DBTYPE_DECIMAL	Decimal	GetDecimal
DBTYPE_R8	Double	GetDouble
DBTYPE_ERROR	ExternalException	GetValue
DBTYPE_FILETIME	DateTime	GetDateTime
DBTYPE_GUID	Guid	GetGuid

Continued

Table 7-2. *Continued*

OLE DB Type	.NET Type	.NET Typed Accessor
DBTYPE_I4	Int32	GetInt32
DBTYPE_LONGVARCHAR	String	GetString
DBTYPE_NUMERIC	Decimal	GetDecimal
DBTYPE_R4	Single	GetFloat
DBTYPE_I2	Int16	GetInt16
DBTYPE_I1	Byte	GetByte
DBTYPE_UI8	UInt64	GetValue
DBTYPE_UI4	UInt32	GetValue
DBTYPE_UI2	UInt16	GetValue
DBTYPE_VARCHAR	String	GetString
DBTYPE_VARIANT	Object	GetValue
DBTYPE_WVARCHAR	String	GetString
DBTYPE_WSRT	String	GetString

To see typed accessors in action, let's build a console application that uses them. For this example, you'll use the Products table from the Northwind database.

Table 7-3 shows the data design of the table. Note that you can look up the data types given in the table for their corresponding typed accessor methods in Table 7-1, so you can use them correctly in your application.

Table 7-3. *Northwind* Products *Table Data Types*

Column Name	Data Type	Length	Allow Nulls?
ProductID (unique)	int	4	No
ProductName	nvarchar	40	No
SupplierID	int	4	Yes
CategoryID	int	4	Yes
QuantityPerUnit	nvarchar	20	Yes
UnitPrice	money	8	Yes
UnitsInStock	smallint	2	Yes
UnitsOnOrder	smallint	2	Yes
ReorderLevel	smallint	2	Yes
Discontinued	bit	1	No

Try It Out: Using Typed Accessor Methods

Let's build a console application that uses typed accessors:

1. Add a new C# Console Application project named TypedAccessors to your Chapter07 solution. Rename Program.cs to TypedAccessors.cs.

2. Replace the code in TypedAccessors.cs with the code in Listing 7-3.

Listing 7-3. TypedAccessors.cs

```csharp
using System;
using System.Data;
using System.Data.SqlClient;

namespace Chapter07
{
    class TypedAccessors
    {
        static void Main(string[] args)
        {
            // connection string
            string connString = @"
                server = .\sqlexpress;
                integrated security = true;
                database = northwind
            ";

            // query
            string sql = @"
                select
                    productname,
                    unitprice,
                    unitsinstock,
                    discontinued
                from
                    products
            ";

            // create connection
            SqlConnection conn = new SqlConnection(connString);
```

```
try
{
    // open connection
    conn.Open();

    // create command
    SqlCommand cmd = new SqlCommand(sql, conn);

    // create data reader
    SqlDataReader rdr = cmd.ExecuteReader();

    // fetch data
    while (rdr.Read())
    {
        Console.WriteLine(
            "{0}\t {1}\t\t {2}\t {3}",
            // nvarchar
            rdr.GetString(0).PadRight(30),
            // money
            rdr.GetDecimal(1),
            // smallint
            rdr.GetInt16(2),
            // bit
            rdr.GetBoolean(3));
    }

    // close data reader
    rdr.Close();
}
catch(Exception e)
{
    Console.WriteLine("Error Occurred: " + e);
}
finally
{
    // close connection
    conn.Close();
}
        }
    }
}
```

3. Make this the startup project, and run it with Ctrl+F5. You should see the result shown in Figure 7-3. (Only the first 20 rows are displayed in the figure.)

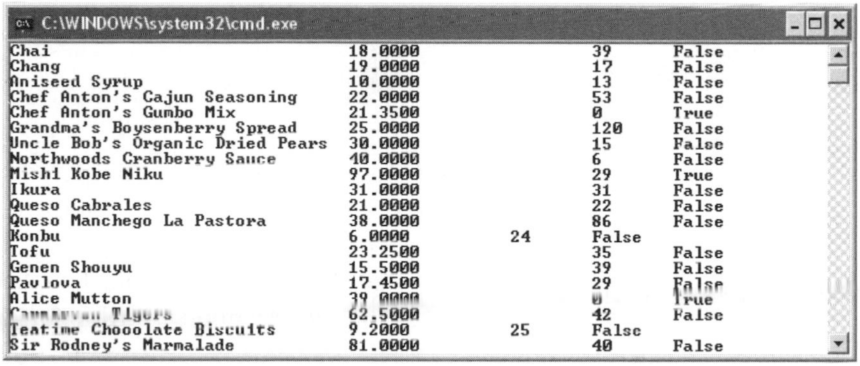

Figure 7-3. *Using typed accessors*

How It Works

You query the Products table for ProductName, UnitPrice, UnitsInStock, and Discontinued:

```
// query
string sql = @"
    select
        productname,
        unitprice,
        unitsinstock,
        discontinued
    from
        products
";
```

We chose these columns to deal with different kinds of data types and to show how to use relevant typed accessors to obtain the correct results:

```
// fetch data
while (rdr.Read())
{
    Console.WriteLine(
        "{0}\t {1}\t\t {2}\t {3}",
        // nvarchar
        rdr.GetString(0).PadRight(30),
```

```
        // money
        rdr.GetDecimal(1),
        // smallint
        rdr.GetInt16(2),
        // bit
        rdr.GetBoolean(3));
}
```

Looking at Table 7-1, you can see that you can access the nvarchar, money, smallint, and bit data types in SQL Server with the GetString, GetDecimal, GetInt16, and GetBoolean accessor methods, respectively.

This technique is fast and completely type safe. By this, we mean that if implicit conversions from native data types to .NET types fail, an exception is thrown for invalid casts. For instance, if you try using the GetString method on a bit data type instead of using the GetBoolean method, a "Specified cast is not valid" exception will be thrown.

Getting Data About Data

So far, all you've done is retrieve data from a data source. Once you have a populated data reader in your hands, you can do a lot more. Here are a number of useful methods for retrieving schema information or retrieving information directly related to a result set. Table 7-4 describes some of the metadata methods and properties of a data reader.

Table 7-4. *Data Reader Metadata Properties and Methods*

Method or Property Name	Description
Depth	A property that gets the depth of nesting for the current row
FieldCount	A property that holds the number of columns in the current row
GetDataTypeName	A method that accepts an index and returns a string containing the name of the column data type
GetFieldType	A method that accepts an index and returns the .NET Framework type of the object
GetName	A method that accepts an index and returns the name of the specified column
GetOrdinal	A method that accepts a column name and returns the column index
GetSchemaTable	A method that returns column metadata
HasRows	A property that indicates if the data reader has any rows
RecordsAffected	A property that gets the number of rows changed, inserted, or deleted

Try It Out: Getting Information About a Result Set with a Data Reader

Let's use some of these methods and properties:

1. Add a new C# Console Application project named `ResultSetInfo` to your `Chapter07` solution. Rename `Program.cs` to `ResultSetInfo.cs`.

2. Replace the code in `ResultSetInfo.cs` with the code in Listing 7-4.

Listing 7-4. `ResultSetInfo.cs`

```
using System;
using System.Data;
using System.Data.SqlClient;

namespace Chapter07
{
   class ResultSetInfo
   {
      static void Main(string[] args)
      {
         // connection string
         string connString = @"
            server = .\sqlexpress;
            integrated security = true;
            database = northwind
         ";

         // query
         string sql = @"
            select
               contactname,
               contacttitle
            from
               customers
            where
               contactname like 'M%'
         ";
```

```
// create connection
SqlConnection conn = new SqlConnection(connString);

try
{
    conn.Open();

    SqlCommand cmd = new SqlCommand(sql, conn);

    SqlDataReader rdr = cmd.ExecuteReader();

    // get column names
    Console.WriteLine(
        "Column Name:\t{0} {1}",
        rdr.GetName(0).PadRight(25),
        rdr.GetName(1));

    // get column data types
    Console.WriteLine(
        "Data Type:\t{0} {1}",
        rdr.GetDataTypeName(0).PadRight(25),
        rdr.GetDataTypeName(1));

    Console.WriteLine();

    while (rdr.Read())
    {
        // get column values for all rows
        Console.WriteLine(
            "\t\t{0} {1}",
            rdr.GetString(0).ToString().PadRight(25),
            rdr.GetString(1));
    }

    // get number of columns
    Console.WriteLine();
    Console.WriteLine(
        "Number of columns in a row: {0}",
        rdr.FieldCount);

    // get info about each column
    Console.WriteLine(
        "'{0}' is at index {1} " +
        "and its type is: {2}",
```

```
            rdr.GetName(0),
            rdr.GetOrdinal("contactname"),
            rdr.GetFieldType(0));

        Console.WriteLine(
            "'{0}' is at index {1} " +
            "and its type is: {2}",
            rdr.GetName(1),
            rdr.GetOrdinal("contacttitle"),
            rdr.GetFieldType(1));

        rdr.Close();
    }
    catch(Exception e)
    {
        Console.WriteLine("Error Occurred: " + e);
    }
    finally
    {
        conn.Close();
    }
    }
  }
}
```

3. Make this the startup project, and run it with Ctrl+F5. You should see the result shown in Figure 7-4.

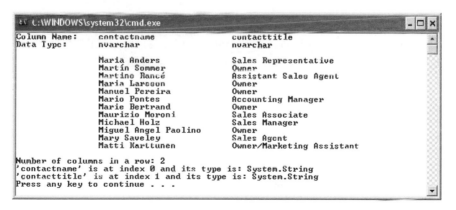

Figure 7-4. *Displaying result set metadata*

How It Works

The GetName method gets a column name by its index. This method returns information *about* the result set, so you can call it before the first call to Read():

```
// get column names
Console.WriteLine(
    "Column Name:\t{0} {1}",
    rdr.GetName(0).PadRight(25),
    rdr.GetName(1));
```

The GetDataTypeName method returns the database data type of a column. You can call it as well before the first call to Read():

```
// get column data types
Console.WriteLine(
    "Data Type:\t{0} {1}",
    rdr.GetDataTypeName(0).PadRight(25),
    rdr.GetDataTypeName(1));
```

The FieldCount property of the data reader contains the number of columns in the result set. This is useful for looping through columns without knowing their names or other attributes:

```
// get number of columns
Console.WriteLine();
Console.WriteLine(
    "Number of columns in a row: {0}",
    rdr.FieldCount);
```

Finally, we demonstrate how the GetOrdinal and GetFieldType methods are used. The former returns a column index based on its name; the latter returns the C# type. These are the converses of GetName() and GetDataTypeName(), respectively:

```
// get info about each column
Console.WriteLine(
    "'{0}' is at index {1} " +
    "and its type is: {2}",
    rdr.GetName(0),
    rdr.GetOrdinal("contactname"),
    rdr.GetFieldType(0));
```

So much for obtaining information about result sets. You'll now learn how to get information about schemas.

Getting Data About Tables

The term *schema* has several meanings in relational databases. Here, we use it to refer to the design of a data structure, particularly a database table. A table consists of rows and columns, and each column can have a different data type. The columns and their attributes (data type, length, and so on) make up the table's schema.

To retrieve schema information easily, you can call the GetSchemaTable method on a data reader. As the name suggests, this method returns a System.Data.DataTable object, which is a representation (schema) of the table queried and contains a collection of rows and columns in the form of DataRow and DataColumn objects. These rows and columns are returned as collection objects by the properties Rows and Columns of the DataTable class.

However, here's where a slight confusion usually occurs. Data column objects aren't column values but rather are column definitions that represent and control the behavior of individual columns. They can be looped through by using a column name indexer and can tell you a lot about the dataset.

Try It Out: Getting Schema Information

Let's see a practical demonstration of the GetSchemaTable method:

1. Add a new C# Console Application project named SchemaTable to your Chapter07 solution. Rename Program.cs to SchemaTable.cs.

2. Replace the code in SchemaTable.cs with the code in Listing 7-5.

Listing 7-5. SchemaTable.cs

```
using System;
using System.Data;
using System.Data.SqlClient;

namespace Chapter07
{
    class SchemaTable
    {
        static void Main(string[] args)
        {
            // connection string
            string connString = @"
```

```csharp
        server = .\sqlexpress;
        integrated security = true;
        database = northwind
";

// query
string sql = @"
    select
        *
    from
        employees
";

// create connection
SqlConnection conn = new SqlConnection(connString);

try
{
    conn.Open();

    SqlCommand cmd = new SqlCommand(sql, conn);
    SqlDataReader rdr = cmd.ExecuteReader();

    // store Employees schema in a data table
    DataTable schema = rdr.GetSchemaTable();

    // display info from each row in the data table.
    // each row describes a column in the database table.
    foreach (DataRow row in schema.Rows)
    {
        foreach (DataColumn col in schema.Columns)
            Console.WriteLine(col.ColumnName + " = " + row[col]);
        Console.WriteLine("----------------");
    }

    rdr.Close();
}
catch(Exception e)
{
    Console.WriteLine("Error Occurred: " + e);
}
```

```
      finally
      {
         conn.Close();
      }
   }
 }
}
```

3. Make this the startup project, and run it with Ctrl+F5. You should see the result shown in Figure 7-5. (Only the information for the table and the first column are displayed in the figure.)

Figure 7-5. *Displaying schema metadata*

How It Works

This code is a bit different from what you've written earlier. When the call to the GetSchemaTable method is made, a populated instance of a data table is returned:

```
// store Employees schema in a data table
DataTable schema = rdr.GetSchemaTable();
```

You can use a data table to represent a complete table in a database, either in the form of a table that represents its schema or in the form of a table that holds all its original data for offline use.

In this example, once you grab hold of a schema table, you retrieve a collection of rows through the Rows property of DataTable and a collection of columns through the Columns property of DataTable. (You can use the Rows property to add a new row into the table altogether or remove one, and you can use the Columns property for adding or deleting an existing column—we'll cover this in Chapter 8.) Each row returned by the table describes one column in the original table, so for each of these rows, you traverse through the column's schema information one by one, using a nested foreach loop:

```
// display info from each row in the data table.
// each row describes a column in the database table.
foreach (DataRow row in schema.Rows)
{
    foreach (DataColumn col in schema.Columns)
        Console.WriteLine(col.ColumnName + " = " + row[col]);
    Console.WriteLine("----------------");
}
```

Notice how you use the ColumnName property of the DataColumn object to retrieve the current schema column name in the loop, and then you retrieve the value related to that column's definition by using the familiar indexer-style method that uses a DataRow object. DataRow has a number of overloaded indexers, and this is only one of several ways of doing it.

Using Multiple Result Sets with a Data Reader

Sometimes you may really want to get a job done quickly and also want to query the database with two or more queries at the same time. And, you wouldn't want the overall application performance to suffer in any way by instantiating more than one command or data reader or by exhaustively using the same objects over and over again, adding to the code as you go.

So, is there a way you can get a single data reader to loop through multiple result sets? Yes, data readers have a method, NextResult(), that advances the reader to the next result set.

Try It Out: Handling Multiple Result Sets

Let's use NextResult() to process multiple result sets:

1. Add a new C# Console Application project named MultipleResults to your Chapter07 solution. Rename Program.cs to MultipleResults.cs.

2. Replace the code in MultipleResults.cs with the code in Listing 7-6.

Listing 7-6. MultipleResults.cs

```
using System;
using System.Data;
using System.Data.SqlClient;

namespace Chapter07
{
    class MultipleResults
    {
        static void Main(string[] args)
        {
            // connection string
            string connString = @"
                server = .\sqlexpress;
                integrated security = true;
                database = northwind
            ";

            // query 1
            string sql1 = @"
                select
                    companyname,
                    contactname
                from
                    customers
                where
                    companyname like 'A%'
            ";
```

```csharp
// query 2
string sql2 = @"
    select
        firstname,
        lastname
    from
        employees
";

// combine queries
string sql = sql1 + sql2;

// create connection
SqlConnection conn = new SqlConnection(connString);

try
{
    // open connection
    conn.Open();

    // create command
    SqlCommand cmd = new SqlCommand(sql, conn);

    // create data reader
    SqlDataReader rdr = cmd.ExecuteReader();

    // loop through result sets
    do
    {
        while (rdr.Read())
        {
            // Print one row at a time
            Console.WriteLine("{0} : {1}", rdr[0], rdr[1]);
        }
        Console.WriteLine("".PadLeft(60, '='));
    }
    while (rdr.NextResult());
```

```
      // close data reader
      rdr.Close();
   }
   catch(Exception e)
   {
      Console.WriteLine("Error Occurred: " + e);
   }
   finally
   {
      // Close connection
      conn.Close();
   }
}
}
}
```

3. Make this the startup project, and run it with Ctrl+F5. You should see the result shown in Figure 7-6.

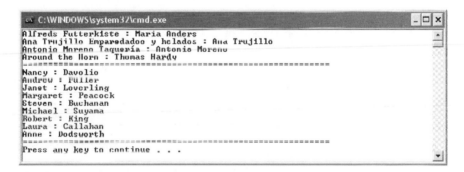

Figure 7-6. *Handling multiple result sets*

How It Works

This program is essentially the same as the first, DataLooper.cs (Listing 7-1). Here, you define two separate queries and then combine them:

```
// query 1
string sql1 = @"
   select
      companyname,
      contactname
```

```
        from
            customers
        where
            companyname like 'A%'
    ";

    // query 2
    string sql2 = @"
        select
            firstname,
            lastname
        from
            employees
    ";

    // combine queries
    string sql = sql1 + sql2;
```

■**Caution** Some DBMSs require an explicit character as a separator between multiple queries, but SQL Server requires only whitespace before subsequent SELECT keywords, which you have because of the verbatim strings.

The only other change is that you loop through result sets. You nest the loop that retrieves rows inside one that loops through result sets:

```
    // loop through result sets
    do
    {
        while (rdr.Read())
        {
            // Print one row at a time
            Console.WriteLine("{0} : {1}", rdr[0], rdr[1]);
        }
        Console.WriteLine("".PadLeft(60, '='));
    }
    while (rdr.NextResult());
```

We chose only two character-string columns per query to simplify things. Extending this to handle result tables with different numbers of columns and column data types is straightforward.

Summary

In this chapter, you used data readers to perform a variety of common tasks, from simply looping through single result sets to handling multiple result sets. You learned how to retrieve values for columns by column name and index, and you learned about methods available for handling values of different data types. You also learned how to get information about result sets and get schema information.

In the next chapter, we'll cover the really interesting aspects of ADO.NET, handling database data while disconnected from the database.

CHAPTER 8

■ ■ ■

Introducing Datasets and Data Adapters

In Chapter 7, you saw how to use data readers to access database data in a connected, forward-only, read-only fashion. Often, this is all you want to do, and a data reader suits your purposes perfectly.

In this chapter, you'll look at a new object for accessing data—the *dataset*. Unlike data readers, which are objects of data provider-specific classes that implement the System.Data.IDataReader interface, datasets are objects of the class System.Data.DataSet, a distinct ADO.NET component used by all data providers. Datasets are completely independent of and can be used either connected to or disconnected from data sources. Their fundamental purpose is to provide a relational view of data stored in an in-memory cache.

Note In yet another somewhat confusing bit of terminology, the class is named DataSet, but the generic term is spelled *dataset* (when one expects *data set*). Why Microsoft does this is unclear, especially since *data set* is the more common usage outside ADO.NET. Nonetheless, we'll follow the .NET convention and call DataSet objects *datasets*.

So, if a dataset doesn't have to be connected to a database, then how do you populate it with data and save its data back to the database? This is where *data adapters* come in. Think of data adapters as bridges between datasets and data sources. Without a data adapter, a dataset can't access any kind of data source. The data adapter takes care of all connection details for the dataset, populates it with data, and updates the data source.

In this chapter, we'll cover the following:

- Datasets and data adapters

- How data is stored in a dataset with data tables, data rows, and data columns

- How to get different views of the data in a dataset

- How to manipulate data in a dataset

- How to persist changes in the dataset back to the original data source

- Working with datasets and XML

- Using data tables without datasets

- Typed and untyped datasets

Understanding the Object Model

We'll start this chapter with a quick presentation of all the new objects you'll need to understand in order to work with datasets and data adapters. You'll start by looking at the difference between datasets and data readers and then move on to look in more detail at how data is structured within a dataset and how a dataset works in collaboration with a data adapter.

Datasets vs. Data Readers

If you simply want to read and display data, then you need to use only a data reader, as you saw in the previous chapter, particularly if you're working with large quantities of data. In situations where you need to loop through thousands or millions of rows, you want a fast sequential reader (reading rows from the result set one at a time), and the data reader does this job in an efficient way.

If you need to manipulate the data in any way and then update the database, then you need to use a dataset. A data adapter fills a dataset by using a data reader; additional resources are needed to save data for disconnected use. You need to think about whether you really need a dataset; otherwise, you'll just be wasting resources. Unless you need to update the data source or use other dataset features such as reading and writing to XML files, exporting database schemas, and creating XML views of a database, you should use a data reader.

A Brief Introduction to Datasets

The notion of a dataset in ADO.NET is a big step in the world of multi-tiered database application development. When retrieving or modifying large amounts of data, maintaining an open connection to a data source while waiting for users to make requests is an enormous waste of precious resources.

Datasets help tremendously here, because they enable you to store and modify large amounts of data in a local cache, view the data as tables, and process the data in an *offline* mode (in other words, disconnected from the database).

Let's look at an example. Imagine you're trying to connect to a remote database server over the Internet for detailed information about some business transactions. You search on a particular date for all available transactions, and the results are displayed. Behind the scenes, your application creates a connection with the data source, joins a couple of tables, and retrieves the results. Suppose you now want to edit this information and add or remove details. Whatever the reason, your application goes through the same cycle over and over again: creating a new connection, joining tables, and retrieving data. Not only is there overhead in creating a new connection each time, but you may be doing a lot of other redundant work, especially if you're dealing with the same data. Wouldn't it be better if you could connect to the data source once, store the data locally in a structure that resembles a relational database, close the connection, modify the local data, and then propagate the changes to the data source when the time is right?

This is exactly what the dataset is designed to do. A dataset stores relational data as collections of *data tables*. You met data tables briefly in the previous chapter when you used a System.Data.DataTable object to hold schema information. In that instance, however, the data table contained only schema information. In a dataset, the data tables contain both metadata describing the structure of the data and the data itself.

Figure 8-1 shows the dataset architecture.

The architecture mirrors the logical design of a relational database. You'll see how to use data tables, data rows, and data columns in this chapter, but we won't cover constraints and will leave relationships until Chapter 11.

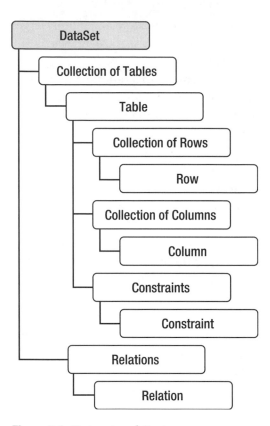

Figure 8-1. *Dataset architecture*

A Brief Introduction to Data Adapters

When you first instantiate a dataset, it contains no data. You obtain a populated dataset by passing it to a data adapter, which takes care of connection details and is a component of a data provider. A dataset isn't part of a data provider. It's like a bucket, ready to be filled with water, but it needs an external pipe to let the water in. In other words, the dataset needs a data adapter to populate it with data and to support access to the data source.

Each data provider has its own data adapter in the same way that it has its own connection, command, and data reader. Figure 8-2 depicts the interactions between the dataset, data adapter, and data source.

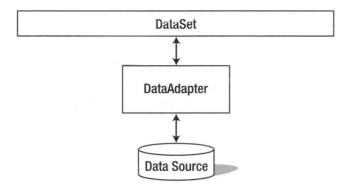

Figure 8-2. *Dataset, data adapter, and data source interaction*

The data adapter constructor is overloaded. You can use any of the following to get a new data adapter. We're using the SQL Server data provider, but the constructors for the other data providers are analogous:

```
SqlDataAdapter da = new SqlDataAdapter();
SqlDataAdapter da = new SqlDataAdapter(cmd);
SqlDataAdapter da = new SqlDataAdapter(sql, conn);
SqlDataAdapter da = new SqlDataAdapter(sql, connString);
```

So, you can create a data adapter in four ways:

- You can use its parameterless constructor (assigning SQL and the connection later).

- You can pass its constructor a command (here, cmd is a SqlCommand object).

- You can pass a SQL string and a connection.

- You can pass a SQL string and a connection string.

You'll see all this working in action shortly. For now, we'll move on and show how to use data tables, data columns, and data rows. You'll use these in upcoming sections.

A Brief Introduction to Data Tables, Data Columns, and Data Rows

A data table is an instance of the class System.Data.DataTable. It's conceptually analogous to a relational table. As shown in Figure 8-1, a data table has collections of data rows and data columns. You can access these nested collections via the Rows and Columns properties of the data table.

A data table can represent a stand-alone independent table, either inside a dataset—
as you'll see in this chapter—or as an object created by another method, as you saw in
the previous chapter, when a data table was returned by calling the method
GetSchemaTable on a data reader.

A data column represents the schema of a column within a data table and can be
used to set or get column properties. For example, you could use it to set the default
value of a column by assigning a value to the DefaultValue property of the data column.

You obtain the collection of data columns using the data table's Columns property,
whose indexer accepts either a column name or a zero-based index; for example
(where dt is a data table):

```
DataColumn col = dt.Columns["ContactName"];
DataColumn col = dt.Columns[2];
```

A data row represents the data in a row. You can programmatically add, update, or
delete rows in a data table. To access rows in a data table, you use its Rows property, whose
indexer accepts a zero-based index; for example (where dt is a data table):

```
DataRow row = dt.Rows[2];
```

That's enough theory for now. It's time to do some coding and see how these objects
work together in practice!

Working with Datasets and Data Adapters

The dataset constructor is overloaded:

```
DataSet ds = new DataSet();
DataSet ds = new DataSet("MyDataSet");
```

If you use the parameterless constructor, the dataset name defaults to NewDataSet.
If you need more than one dataset, it's good practice to use the other constructor and
name it explicitly. However, you can always change the dataset name by setting its
DataSetName property.

You can populate a dataset in several ways, including

- Using a data adapter

- Reading from an XML document

In this chapter, we'll use data adapters. However, in the "Using Datasets and XML"
section, you'll take a quick peek at the converse of the second method, and you'll write
from a dataset to an XML document.

Try It Out: Populating a Dataset with a Data Adapter

In this example, you'll create a dataset, populate it with a data adapter, and then display its contents:

1. Create a new Console Application project named Chapter08. When Solution Explorer opens, save the solution.

2. Rename the Chapter07 project to PopDataset. Rename the Program.cs file to PopDataset.cs, and replace the generated code with the code in Listing 8-1.

Listing 8-1. PopDataSet.cs

```
using System;
using System.Data;
using System.Data.SqlClient;

namespace Chapter08
{
    class PopDataSet
    {
        static void Main(string[] args)
        {
            // connection string
            string connString = @"
                server = .\sqlexpress;
                integrated security = true;
                database = northwind
            ";

            // query
            string sql = @"
                select
                    productname,
                    unitprice
                from
                    products
                where
                    unitprice < 20
            ";
```

```csharp
        // create connection
        SqlConnection conn = new SqlConnection(connString);

        try
        {
            // open connection
            conn.Open();

            // create data adapter
            SqlDataAdapter da = new SqlDataAdapter(sql, conn);

            // create dataset
            DataSet ds = new DataSet();

            // fill dataset
            da.Fill(ds, "products");

            // get data table
            DataTable dt = ds.Tables["products"];

            // display data
            foreach (DataRow row in dt.Rows)
            {
                foreach (DataColumn col in dt.Columns)
                    Console.WriteLine(row[col]);
                Console.WriteLine("".PadLeft(20, '='));
            }
        }
        catch(Exception e)
        {
            Console.WriteLine("Error: " + e);
        }
        finally
        {
            // close connection
            conn.Close();
        }
    }
  }
}
```

3. Run it with Ctrl+F5. You should see the result in Figure 8-3. (Only the last ten rows are displayed.)

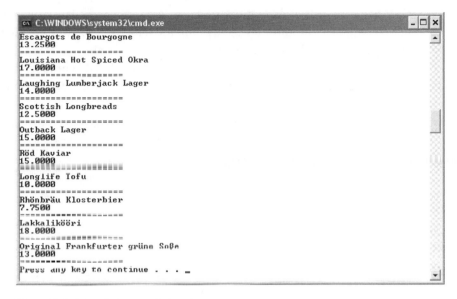

Figure 8-3. *Populating a dataset*

How It Works

After defining a query and opening a connection, you create and initialize a data adapter:

```
// create data adapter
SqlDataAdapter da = new SqlDataAdapter(sql, conn);
```

You then create a dataset:

```
// create dataset
DataSet ds = new DataSet();
```

At this stage, all you have is an empty dataset. The key line is where you use the Fill method on the data adapter to execute the query, retrieve the data, and populate the dataset:

```
// fill dataset
da.Fill(ds, "products");
```

The Fill method uses a data reader internally to access the table schema and data and then use them to populate the dataset. Note that this method isn't just used for filling datasets. It has a number of overloads and can also be used for filling an individual data table without a dataset, if needed.

If you don't provide a name for the table to the Fill method, it will automatically be named TableN, where N starts as an empty string (the first table name is simply Table) and increments every time a new table is inserted into the dataset. It's better practice to name data tables explicitly, but here it doesn't really matter.

If the same query is run more than once on the dataset that already contains data, then Fill() updates the data, skipping the process of redefining the table based on the schema.

It's worth mentioning here that the following code would have produced the same result. Instead of passing the SQL and connection to the data adapter's constructor, you could have set its SelectCommand property with a command that you create with the appropriate SQL and connection:

```
// Create data adapter
SqlDataAdapter da = new SqlDataAdapter();
da.SelectCommand = new SqlCommand(sql, conn);
```

With a populated dataset at your disposal, you can now access the data in individual data tables (this dataset contains only one data table):

```
// get data table
DataTable dt = ds.Tables["products"];
```

Finally, you use nested foreach loops to access the columns in each row and output their data values to the screen:

```
// display data
foreach (DataRow row in dt.Rows)
{
    foreach (DataColumn col in dt.Columns)
        Console.WriteLine(row[col]);
    Console.WriteLine("".PadLeft(20, '='));
}
```

Filtering and Sorting in a Dataset

In the previous example, you saw how to extract data from a dataset. However, if you're working with datasets, then chances are that you're going to want to do more with the data than merely display it. Often, you'll want to dynamically filter or sort the data. In the following example, you'll see how you can use data rows to do this.

Try It Out: Dynamically Filtering and Sorting Data in a Dataset

We'll get all the rows and columns from the Customers table, filter the result for only German customers, and sort it by company. We'll use a separate query to find products, and we'll fill two data tables in the same dataset:

1. Add a new C# Console Application project named FilterSort to your Chapter07 solution. Rename Program.cs to FilterSort.cs.

2. Replace the code in FilterSort.cs with the code in Listing 8-2.

Listing 8-2. FilterSort.cs

```
using System;
using System.Data;
using System.Data.SqlClient;

namespace Chapter08
{
    class FilterSort
    {
        static void Main(string[] args)
        {
            // connection string
            string connString = @"
                server = .\sqlexpress;
                integrated security = true;
                database = northwind
            ";

            // query 1
            string sql1 = @"
                select
                    *
                from
                    customers
            ";
```

```
// query 2
string sql2 = @"
   select
      *
   from
      products
   where
      unitprice < 10
";

// combine queries
string sql = sql1 + sql2;

// create connection
SqlConnection conn = new SqlConnection(connString);

try
{
   // create data adapter
   SqlDataAdapter da = new SqlDataAdapter();
   da.SelectCommand = new SqlCommand(sql, conn);

   // create and fill dataset
   DataSet ds = new DataSet();
   da.Fill(ds, "customers");

   // get the data tables collection
   DataTableCollection dtc = ds.Tables;

   // display data from first data table
   //
   // display output header
   Console.WriteLine("Results from Customers table:");
   Console.WriteLine(
      "CompanyName".PadRight(20) +
      "ContactName".PadLeft(23) + "\n");

   // set display filter
   string fl = "country = 'Germany'";
```

```csharp
        // set sort
        string srt = "companyname asc";

        // display filtered and sorted data
        foreach (DataRow row in dtc["customers"].Select(fl, srt))
        {
          Console.WriteLine(
              "{0}\t{1}",
              row["CompanyName"].ToString().PadRight(25),
              row["ContactName"]);
        }

        // display data from second data table
        //
        // display output header
        Console.WriteLine("\n-----                    -----------");
        Console.WriteLine("Results from Products table:");
        Console.WriteLine(
            "ProductName".PadRight(20) +
            "UnitPrice".PadLeft(21) + "\n");

        // display data
        foreach (DataRow row in dtc[1].Rows)
        {
            Console.WriteLine("{0}\t{1}",
                row["productname"].ToString().PadRight(25),
                row["unitprice"]);
        }
      }
      catch(Exception e)
      {
        Console.WriteLine("Error: " + e);
      }
      finally
      {
        // close connection
        conn.Close();
      }
    }
  }
}
```

3. Make this the startup project, and run it with Ctrl+F5. You should see the result shown in Figure 8-4.

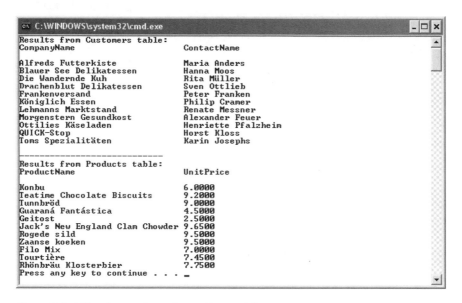

Figure 8-4. *Filtering and sorting a data table*

How It Works

You code and combine two queries for execution on the same connection:

```
// query 1
string sql1 = @"
   select
      *
   from
      customers
";

// query 2
string sql2 = @"
   select
      *
   from
      products
   where
      unitprice < 10
";
```

```
// combine queries
string sql = sql1 + sql2;

// create connection
SqlConnection conn = new SqlConnection(connString);
```

You create a data adapter, assigning to its SelectCommand property a command that encapsulates the query and connection (for internal use by the data adapter's Fill method):

```
// create data adapter
SqlDataAdapter da = new SqlDataAdapter();
da.SelectCommand = new SqlCommand(sql, conn);
```

You then create and fill a dataset:

```
// create and fill dataset
DataSet ds = new DataSet();
da.Fill(ds, "customers");
```

Each query returns a separate result set, and each result set is stored in a separate data table (in the order in which the queries were specified). The first table is explicitly named customers; the second is given the default name customers1.

You get the data table collection from the dataset Tables property for ease of reference later:

```
// get the data tables collection
DataTableCollection dtc = ds.Tables;
```

As part of displaying the first data table, you declare two strings:

```
// set display filter
string fl = "country - 'Germany'";

// set sort
string srt = "companyname asc";
```

The first string is a *filter expression* that specifies row-selection criteria. It's syntactically the same as a SQL WHERE clause predicate. You want only rows where the Country column equals 'Germany'. The second string specifies your sort criteria and is syntactically the same as a SQL ORDER BY clause, giving a data column name and sort sequence.

You use a foreach loop to display the rows selected from the data table, passing the filter and sort strings to the Select method of the data table. This particular data table is the one named customers in the data table collection:

```
// display filtered and sorted data
foreach (DataRow row in dtc["customers"].Select(fl, srt))
{
  Console.WriteLine(
    "{0}\t{1}",
    row["CompanyName"].ToString().PadRight(25),
    row["ContactName"]);
}
```

You obtain a reference to a single data table from the data table collection (the dtc object) using the table name that you specified when creating the dataset. The overloaded Select method does an internal search on the data table, filters out rows not satisfying the selection criterion, sorts the result as prescribed, and finally returns an array of data rows. You access each column in the row, using the column name in the indexer.

It's important to note that you could have achieved the same result—much more efficiently—had you simply used a different query for the Customer data:

```
select
    *
from
    customers
where
    country = 'Germany'
order by
    companyname
```

This would be ideal in terms of performance, but it'd be feasible only if the data you need were limited to these specific rows in this particular sequence. However, if you were building a more elaborate system, it might be better to pull all the data once from the database (as you do here) and then filter and sort it in different ways. ADO.NET's rich suite of methods for manipulating datasets and their components gives you a broad range of techniques for meeting specific needs in an optimal way.

■**Tip** In general, try to exploit SQL, rather than code C# procedures, to get the data you need from the database. Database servers are optimized to perform selections and sorts, as well as other things. Queries can be far more sophisticated and powerful than the ones you've been playing with in this book. By carefully (and creatively) coding queries to return *exactly* what you need, you not only minimize resource demands (on memory, network bandwidth, and so on), but you also reduce the code you must write to manipulate and format result set data.

The loop through the second data table is interesting mainly for its first line

```
foreach (DataRow row in dtc[1].Rows)
```

which uses an ordinal index. Since you don't rename the second data table (you could have done so with its TableName property), it's better to use the index rather than the name (customers1), since a change to the name in the Fill() call would require you to change it here, an unlikely thing to remember to do, if the case ever arose.

Comparing FilterSort to PopDataSet

In the first example, PopDataSet (Listing 8-1), you saw how simple it is to get data into a dataset. The second example, FilterSort (Listing 8-2), was just a variation, demonstrating how multiple result sets are handled and how to filter and sort data tables. However, the two programs have one major difference. Did you notice it?

FilterSort doesn't explicitly open a connection! In fact, it's the first (but won't be the last) program you've written that doesn't. Why doesn't it?

The answer is simple but *very* important. The Fill method *automatically* opens a connection if it's not open when Fill() is called. It then closes the connection after filling the dataset. However, if a connection is open when Fill() is called, it uses that connection and *doesn't* close it afterward.

So, although datasets are completely independent of databases (and connections), just because you're using a dataset doesn't mean you're running disconnected from a database. If you want to run disconnected, use datasets, but don't open connections before filling them (or, if a connection is open, close it first). Datasets in themselves don't imply either connected or disconnected operations.

You left the standard conn.Close(); in the finally block. Since you can call Close() without error on a closed connection, it presents no problems if called unnecessarily, but it definitely guarantees that the connection will be closed, whatever may happen in the try block.

Note If you want to prove this for yourself, simply open the connection in FilterSort before calling Fill() and then display the value of the connection's State property. It will be Open. Comment out the Open() call, and run it again. State will be closed.

Using Data Views

In the previous example, you saw how to dynamically filter and sort data in a data table using the Select method. However, ADO.NET has another approach for doing much the same thing and more: *data views*. A data view (an instance of class `System.Data.DataView`) enables you to create dynamic views of the data stored in an underlying data table, reflecting all the changes made to its content and its ordering. This differs from the `Select` method, which returns an array of data rows whose contents reflect the changes to data values but not the data ordering.

■**Note** A *data view* is a dynamic representation of the contents of a data table. Like a SQL view, it doesn't actually hold data.

Try It Out: Refining Data with a Data View

We won't cover all aspects of data views here, as they're beyond the scope of this book. However, to show how you can use them, we'll present a short example that uses a data view to dynamically sort and filter an underlying data table:

1. Add a new C# Console Application project named `DataViews` to your `Chapter08` solution. Rename `Program.cs` to `DataViews.cs`.

2. Replace the code in `DataViews.cs` with the code in Listing 8-3.

Listing 8-3. `DataViews.cs`

```
using System;
using System.Data;
using System.Data.SqlClient;

namespace Chapter08
{
    class DataViews
    {
        static void Main(string[] args)
        {
            // connection string
            string connString = @"
                server = .\sqlexpress;
                integrated security = true;
                database = northwind
            ";
```

```csharp
// query
string sql = @"
    select
        contactname,
        country
    from
        customers
";

// create connection
SqlConnection conn = new SqlConnection(connString);

try
{
    // Create data adapter
    SqlDataAdapter da = new SqlDataAdapter();
    da.SelectCommand = new SqlCommand(sql, conn);

    // create and fill dataset
    DataSet ds = new DataSet();
    da.Fill(ds, "customers");

    // get data table reference
    DataTable dt = ds.Tables["customers"];

    // create data view
    DataView dv = new DataView(
        dt,
        "country = 'Germany'",
        "country",
        DataViewRowState.CurrentRows
    );

    // display data from data view
    foreach (DataRowView drv in dv)
    {
        for (int i = 0; i < dv.Table.Columns.Count; i++)
            Console.Write(drv[i] + "\t");
            Console.WriteLine();
    }
}
```

```
        catch(Exception e)
        {
           Console.WriteLine("Error: " + e);
        }
        finally
        {
           // close connection
           conn.Close();
        }
      }
   }
}
```

3. Make this the startup project, and run it with Ctrl+F5. You should see the result shown in Figure 8-5.

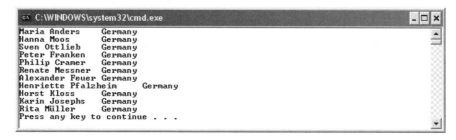

Figure 8-5. *Using a data view*

How It Works

This program is basically the same as the other examples, so we'll focus on its use of a data view. You create a new data view and initialize it by passing four parameters to its constructor:

```
// create data view
DataView dv = new DataView(
    dt,
    "country = 'Germany'",
    "country",
    DataViewRowState.CurrentRows
);
```

The first parameter is a data table, the second is a filter for the contents of the data table, the third is the sort column, and the fourth specifies the types of rows to include in the data view.

System.Data.DataViewRowState is an enumeration of states that rows can have in a data view's underlying data table. Table 8-1 summarizes the states.

Table 8-1. *Data View Row States*

DataViewRowState Member	Description
Added	A new row
CurrentRows	Current rows, including unchanged, new, and modified ones
Deleted	A deleted row
ModifiedCurrent	The current version of a modified row
ModifiedOriginal	The original version of a modified row
None	None of the rows
OriginalRows	Original rows, including unchanged and deleted
Unchanged	A row that hasn't been modified

Every time you add, modify, or delete a row, its row state changes to the appropriate one in Table 8-1. This is useful if you're interested in retrieving, sorting, or filtering specific rows based on their state (for example, all new rows in the data table or all rows that have been modified).

You then loop through the rows in the data view:

```
// display data from data view
foreach (DataRowView drv in dv)
{
    for (int i = 0; i < dv.Table.Columns.Count; i++)
        Console.Write(drv[i] + "\t");
        Console.WriteLine();
}
```

Just as a data row represents a single row in a data table, a *data row view* (perhaps it would have been better to call it a *data view row*) represents a single row in a data view. You retrieve the filtered and the sorted column data for each data row view and output it to the console.

As this simple example suggests, data views offer a powerful and flexible means of dynamically changing what data one works with in a data table.

Modifying Data in a Dataset

In the following sections, you'll work through a practical example showing a number of ways to update data in data tables programmatically. Note that here you'll just modify the data in the dataset but not update the data in the database. You'll see in the "Propagating Changes to a Data Source" section how to persist in the original data source changes made to a dataset.

■**Note** Changes you make to a dataset aren't automatically propagated to a database. To save the changes in a database, you need to connect to the database again and explicitly perform the necessary updates.

Try It Out: Modifying a Data Table in a Dataset

Let's update a row and add a row in a data table:

1. Add a new C# Console Application project named ModifyDataTable to your Chapter08 solution. Rename Program.cs to ModifyDataTable.cs.

2. Replace the code in ModifyDataTable.cs with the code in Listing 8-4.

Listing 8-4. ModifyDataTable.cs

```
using System;
using System.Data;
using System.Data.SqlClient;

namespace Chapter08
{
    class ModifyDataTable
    {
        static void Main(string[] args)
        {
            // connection string
            string connString = @"
                server = .\sqlexpress;
                integrated security = true;
                database = northwind
            ";
```

```csharp
// query
string sql = @"
   select
      *
   from
      employees
   where
      country = 'UK'
";

// create connection
SqlConnection conn = new SqlConnection(connString);

try
{
   // create data adapter
   SqlDataAdapter da = new SqlDataAdapter();
   da.SelectCommand = new SqlCommand(sql, conn);

   // create and fill dataset
   DataSet ds = new DataSet();
   da.Fill(ds, "employees");

   // get data table reference
   DataTable dt = ds.Tables["employees"];

   // FirstName column should be nullable
   dt.Columns["firstname"].AllowDBNull = true;

   // modify City in first row
   dt.Rows[0]["city"] = "Wilmington";

   // add a row
   DataRow newRow = dt.NewRow();
   newRow["firstname"] = "Roy";
   newRow["lastname"] = "Beatty";
   newRow["titleofcourtesy"] = "Sir";
   newRow["city"] = "Birmingham";
   newRow["country"] = "UK";
   dt.Rows.Add(newRow);
```

```
    // display Rows
    foreach (DataRow row in dt.Rows)
    {
        Console.WriteLine(
            "{0} {1} {2}",
            row["firstname"].ToString().PadRight(15),
            row["lastname"].ToString().PadLeft(25),
            row["city"]);
    }

    //
    // code for updating the database would come here
    //
}
catch(Exception e)
{
    Console.WriteLine("Error: " + e);
}
finally
{
    // close connection
    conn.Close();
}
        }
    }
}
```

3. Make this the startup project, and run it with Ctrl+F5. You should see the result
   shown in Figure 8-6.

Figure 8-6. *Modifying a data table*

How It Works

As before, you use a single data table in a dataset:

```
// get data table reference
DataTable dt = ds.Tables["employees"];
```

Next, you can see an example of how you can change the schema information. You select the FirstName column, whose AllowNull property is set to false in the database, and you change it—just for the purposes of demonstration—to true:

```
// FirstName column should be nullable
dt.Columns["firstname"].AllowDBNull = true;
```

Note that you could have used an ordinal index (for example, dt.Columns[1]) if you knew what the index for the column was, but using * to select all columns makes this less reliable, since the position of a column may change if the database table schema changes.

You can modify a row using the same technique. You simply select the appropriate row and set its columns to whatever values you want, consistent with the column data types, of course. The following line shows the City column of the first row of the dataset being changed to Wilmington:

```
// modify City in first row
dt.Rows[0]["city"] = "Wilmington";
```

Next you add a new row to the data table:

```
// add a row
DataRow newRow = dt.NewRow();
newRow["firstname"] = "Roy";
newRow["lastname"] = "Beatty";
newRow["titleofcourtesy"] = "Sir";
newRow["city"] = "Birmingham";
newRow["country"] = "UK";
dt.Rows.Add(newRow);
```

The NewRow method creates a data row (a System.Data.DataRow instance). You use the data row's indexer to assign values to its columns. Finally, you add the new row to the data table, calling the Add method on the data table's Rows property, which references the rows collection.

Note that you don't provide a value for `EmployeeID`, since it's an `IDENTITY` column. If you persist the changes to the database, then SQL Server will automatically provide a value for it.

Updating data sources requires learning more about data adapter methods and properties. Let's take a look at these now.

Propagating Changes to a Data Source

You've seen how a data adapter populates a dataset's data tables. What you haven't looked at yet is how a data adapter updates and synchronizes a data source with data from a dataset. It has three properties that support this (analogous to its `SelectCommand` property that supports queries):

- `UpdateCommand`

- `InsertCommand`

- `DeleteCommand`

We'll describe each of these properties briefly and then put them to work.

UpdateCommand Property

The `UpdateCommand` property of the data adapter holds the command used to update the data source when the data adapter's `Update` method is called.

For example, to update the `City` column in the `Employees` table with the data from a data table, one approach is to write code such as the following (where `da` is the data adapter, `dt` is the data table, `conn` is the connection, and `ds` is the dataset):

```
// Create command to update Employees City column
da.UpdateCommand = new SqlCommand(
    "update employees "
  + "set "
  + "   city = "
  +          "'" + dt.Rows[0]["city"] + "' "
  + "where employeeid = "
  +          "'" + dt.Rows[0]["employeeid"] + "' "
  , conn);

// Update Employees table
da.Update(ds, "employees");
```

This isn't very pretty—or useful. Basically, you code an UPDATE statement and embed two data column values for the first row in a data table in it. It's valid SQL, but that's its only virtue, and it's not much of one, since it updates only one database row—the row in Employees corresponding to the first data row in the employees data table.

Another approach works for any number of rows. Recall from the CommandParameters program in Chapter 6 how you used command parameters for INSERT statements. You can use them in any query or data-manipulation statement. Let's recode the previous code with command parameters.

Try It Out: Propagating Dataset Changes to a Data Source

Let's change the city in the first row of the Employees table and persist the change in the database:

1. Add a new C# Console Application project named PersistChanges to your Chapter08 solution. Rename Program.cs to PersistChanges.cs.

2. Replace the code in PersistChanges.cs with the code in Listing 8-5. (This is a variation on ModifyDataTable.cs in Listing 8-4, with the nullability and insertion logic removed, since they're irrelevant here.)

Listing 8-5. PersistChanges.cs

```
using System;
using System.Data;
using System.Data.SqlClient;

namespace Chapter08
{
    class PersistChanges
    {
        static void Main(string[] args)
        {
            // connection string
            string connString = @"
                server = .\sqlexpress;
                integrated security = true;
                database = northwind
            ";
```

```csharp
// query
string qry = @"
   select
      *
   from
      employees
   where
      country = 'UK'
";

// SQL to update employees
string upd = @"
   update employees
   set
      city = @city
   where
      employeeid = @employeeid
";

// create connection
SqlConnection conn = new SqlConnection(connString);

try
{
   // create data adapter
   SqlDataAdapter da = new SqlDataAdapter();
   da.SelectCommand = new SqlCommand(qry, conn);

   // create and fill dataset
   DataSet ds = new DataSet();
   da.Fill(ds, "employees");

   // get data table reference
   DataTable dt = ds.Tables["employees"];

   // modify city in first row
   dt.Rows[0]["city"] = "Wilmington";
```

```
        // display rows
        foreach (DataRow row in dt.Rows)
        {
            Console.WriteLine(
                "{0} {1} {2}",
                row["firstname"].ToString().PadRight(15),
                row["lastname"].ToString().PadLeft(25),
                row["city"]);
        }

        // update Employees
        //
        // create command
        SqlCommand cmd = new SqlCommand(upd, conn);
        //
        // map parameters
        //
        // City
        cmd.Parameters.Add(
            "@city",
            SqlDbType.NVarChar,
            15,
            "city");
        //
        // EmployeeID
        SqlParameter parm =
            cmd.Parameters.Add(
                "@employeeid",
                SqlDbType.Int,
                4,
                "employeeid");
        parm.SourceVersion = DataRowVersion.Original;
        //
        // Update database
        da.UpdateCommand = cmd;
        da.Update(ds, "employees");
    }
    catch(Exception e)
    {
        Console.WriteLine("Error: " + e);
    }
```

```
        finally
        {
            // close connection
            conn.Close();
        }
    }
  }
}
```

3. Make this the startup project, and run it with Ctrl+F5. You should see the result shown in Figure 8-7.

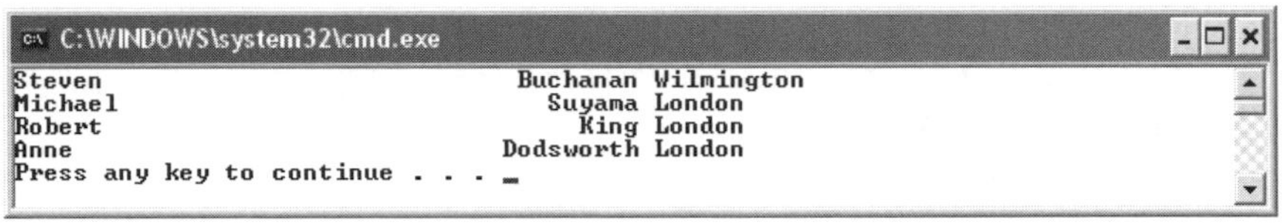

Figure 8-7. *Modifying a row*

How It Works

You add an UPDATE statement and change the name of the original query string variable from sql to upd in order to clearly distinguish it from this statement:

```
// SQL to update employees
string upd = @"
    update employees
    set
        city = @city
    where
        employeeid = @employeeid
";
```

You replace the update comment in the try block with quite a bit of code. Let's look at it piece by piece. Creating a command is nothing new, but notice that you use the update SQL variable (upd), not the query one (sql):

```
// update Employees
//
// create command
SqlCommand cmd = new SqlCommand(upd, conn);
```

Then you configure the command parameters. The @city parameter is mapped to a data column named city. Note that you don't specify the data table, but you must be sure the type and length are compatible with this column in whatever data table you eventually use:

```
// City
cmd.Parameters.Add(
    "@city",
    SqlDbType.NVarChar,
    15,
    "city");
```

Next, you configure the @employeeid parameter, mapping it to a data column named employeeid. Unlike @city, which by default takes values from the current version of the data table, you want to make sure that @employeeid gets values from the version *before* any changes. Although it doesn't really matter here, since you didn't change any employee IDs, it's a good habit to specify the original version for primary keys, so if they do change, the correct rows are accessed in the database table. Note also that you save the reference returned by the Add method so you can set its SourceVersion property. Since you don't need to do anything else with @city, you don't have to save a reference to it:

```
// EmployeeID
SqlParameter parm =
    cmd.Parameters.Add(
        "@employeeid",
        SqlDbType.Int,
        4,
        "employeeid");
parm.SourceVersion = DataRowVersion.Original;
```

Finally, you set the data adapter's UpdateCommand property with the command to update the Employees table, so it will be the SQL the data adapter executes when you call its Update method. You then call Update on the data adapter to propagate the change to the database. Here you have only one change, but since the SQL is parameterized, the data adapter looks for all changed rows in the employees data table and submits updates for all of them to the database:

```
// Update database
da.UpdateCommand = cmd;
da.Update(ds, "employees");
```

Figure 8-7 shows the change to the city, and if you check with Database Explorer or the SSMSE, you'll see the update has been propagated to the database. The city for employee Steven Buchanan is now Wilmington, not London.

InsertCommand Property

The data adapter uses the `InsertCommand` property for inserting rows into a table. Upon calling the `Update` method, all rows added to the data table will be searched for and propagated to the database.

Try It Out: Propagating New Dataset Rows to a Data Source

Let's propagate a new row to the database, in another variation on `ModifyDataTable.cs` in Listing 8-4:

1. Add a new C# Console Application project named `PersistAdds` to your `Chapter08` solution. Rename `Program.cs` to `PersistAdds.cs`.

2. Replace the code in `PersistAdds.cs` with the code in Listing 8-6.

Listing 8-6. `PersistAdds`

```
using System;
using System.Data;
using System.Data.SqlClient;

namespace Chapter08
{
    class PersistAdds
    {
        static void Main(string[] args)
        {
            // connection string
            string connString = @"
                server = .\sqlexpress;
                integrated security = true;
                database = northwind
            ";
```

```csharp
// query
string qry = @"
   select
      *
   from
      employees
   where
      country = 'UK'
";

// SQL to insert employees
string ins = @"
   insert into employees
   (
      firstname,
      lastname,
      titleofcourtesy,
      city,
      country
   )
   values
   (
      @firstname,
      @lastname,
      @titleofcourtesy,
      @city,
      @country
   )
";

// Create connection
SqlConnection conn = new SqlConnection(connString);

try
{
   // create data adapter
   SqlDataAdapter da = new SqlDataAdapter();
   da.SelectCommand = new SqlCommand(qry, conn);
```

```
// create and fill dataset
DataSet ds = new DataSet();
da.Fill(ds, "employees");

// get data table reference
DataTable dt = ds.Tables["employees"];

// add a row
DataRow newRow = dt.NewRow();
newRow["firstname"] = "Roy";
newRow["lastname"] = "Beatty";
newRow["titleofcourtesy"] = "Sir";
newRow["city"] = "Birmingham";
newRow["country"] = "UK";
dt.Rows.Add(newRow);

// display rows
foreach (DataRow row in dt.Rows)
{
   Console.WriteLine(
      "{0} {1} {2}",
      row["firstname"].ToString().PadRight(15),
      row["lastname"].ToString().PadLeft(25),
      row["city"]);
}

// insert employees
//
// create command
SqlCommand cmd = new SqlCommand(ins, conn);
//
// map parameters
cmd.Parameters.Add(
   "@firstname",
   SqlDbType.NVarChar,
   10,
   "firstname");
cmd.Parameters.Add(
   "@lastname",
   SqlDbType.NVarChar,
   20,
   "lastname");
```

```
        cmd.Parameters.Add(
            "@titleofcourtesy",
            SqlDbType.NVarChar,
            25,
            "titleofcourtesy");
        cmd.Parameters.Add(
            "@city",
            SqlDbType.NVarChar,
            15,
            "city");
        cmd.Parameters.Add(
            "@country",
            SqlDbType.NVarChar,
            15,
            "country");
        //
        // insert employees
        da.InsertCommand = cmd;
        da.Update(ds, "employees");
    }
    catch(Exception e)
    {
        Console.WriteLine("Error: " + e);
    }
    finally
    {
        // close connection
        conn.Close();
    }
  }
 }
}
```

3. Make this the startup project, and run it with Ctrl+F5. You should see the result
   shown in Figure 8-8.

Figure 8-8. *Adding a row*

How It Works

You add an INSERT statement and change the name of the original query string variable
from sql to ins in order to clearly distinguish it from this statement:

```
// SQL to insert employees
string ins = @"
   insert into employees
   (
       firstname,
       lastname,
       titleofcourtesy,
       city,
       country
   )
   values
   (
       @firstname,
       @lastname,
       @titleofcourtesy,
       @city,
       @country
   )
";
```

You replace the update comment in the try block with quite a bit of code. Let's look at
it piece by piece. Creating a command is nothing new, but notice that you use the insert
SQL variable (ins), not the query one (sql):

```
// insert employees
//
// create command
SqlCommand cmd = new SqlCommand(ins, conn);
```

Then you configure the command parameters. The five columns for which you'll
provide values are each mapped to a named command parameter. You don't supply the
primary key value, since SQL Server generates it, and the other columns are nullable, so
you don't have to provide values for them. Note that all the values are current values,
so you don't have to specify the SourceVersion property:

```
// map parameters
cmd.Parameters.Add(
    "@firstname",
    SqlDbType.NVarChar,
    10,
    "firstname");
cmd.Parameters.Add(
    "@lastname",
    SqlDbType.NVarChar,
    20,
    "lastname");
cmd.Parameters.Add(
    "@titleofcourtesy",
    SqlDbType.NVarChar,
    25,
    "titleofcourtesy");
cmd.Parameters.Add(
    "@city",
    SqlDbType.NVarChar,
    15,
    "city");
cmd.Parameters.Add(
    "@country",
    SqlDbType.NVarChar,
    15,
    "country");
```

Finally, you set the data adapter's InsertCommand property with the command to insert into the Employees table so it will be the SQL the data adapter executes when you call its Update method. You then call Update on the data adapter to propagate the change to the database. Here you add only one row, but since the SQL is parameterized, the data adapter looks for all new rows in the employees data table and submits inserts for all of them to the database:

```
// insert employees
da.InsertCommand = cmd;
da.Update(ds, "employees");
```

Figure 8-8 shows the new row, and if you check with Database Explorer or the SSMSE, you'll see the row has been propagated to the database. Roy Beatty is now in the Employees table.

DeleteCommand Property

You use the `DeleteCommand` property to execute SQL `DELETE` statements.

Try It Out: Propagating New Dataset Rows to a Data Source

Let's again modify `ModifyDataTable.cs` (Listing 8-4) to delete a row from the database:

1. Add a new C# Console Application project named `PersistDeletes` to your `Chapter08` solution. Rename `Program.cs` to `PersistDeletes.cs`.

2. Replace the code in `PersistDeletes.cs` with the code in Listing 8-7.

Listing 8-7. `PersistDeletes.cs`

```
using System;
using System.Data;
using System.Data.SqlClient;

namespace Chapter08
{
    class PersistDeletes
    {
        static void Main(string[] args)
        {
            // connection string
            string connString = @"
                server = .\sqlexpress;
                integrated security = true;
                database = northwind
            ";

            // query
            string qry = @"
                select
                    *
                from
                    employees
                where
                    country = 'UK'
            ";
```

```
// SQL to delete employees
string del = @"
   delete from employees
   where
      employeeid = @employeeid
";

// create connection
SqlConnection conn = new SqlConnection(connString);

try
{
   // create data adapter
   SqlDataAdapter da = new SqlDataAdapter();
   da.SelectCommand = new SqlCommand(qry, conn);

   // create and fill dataset
   DataSet ds = new DataSet();
   da.Fill(ds, "employees");

   // get data table reference
   DataTable dt = ds.Tables["employees"];

   // delete employees
   //
   // create command
   SqlCommand cmd = new SqlCommand(del, conn);
   //
   // map parameters
   cmd.Parameters.Add(
      "@employeeid",
      SqlDbType.Int,
      4,
      "employeeid");
   //
   // select employees
   string filt = @"
         firstname = 'Roy'
         and
         lastname = 'Beatty'
   ";
   //
```

```
            // delete employees
            foreach (DataRow row in dt.Select(filt))
            {
                row.Delete();
            }
            da.DeleteCommand = cmd;
            da.Update(ds, "employees");

            // display rows
            foreach (DataRow row in dt.Rows)
            {
                Console.WriteLine(
                    "{0} {1} {2}",
                    row["firstname"].ToString().PadRight(15),
                    row["lastname"].ToString().PadLeft(25),
                    row["city"]);
            }
        }
        catch(Exception e)
        {
            Console.WriteLine("Error: " + e);
        }
        finally
        {
            // close connection
            conn.Close();
        }
    }
  }
}
```

3. Make this the startup project, and run it with Ctrl+F5. You should see the output shown in Figure 8-9.

Figure 8-9. *Deleting a row*

How It Works

You add a DELETE statement (and change the name of the original query string variable from sql to del in order to clearly distinguish it from this statement):

```
// SQL to delete employees
string del = @"
   delete from employees
   where
      employeeid = @employeeid
";
```

You insert the delete code ahead of the display, after creating a command and mapping a parameter:

```
// delete employees
//
// create command
SqlCommand cmd = new SqlCommand(del, conn);
//
// map parameters
cmd.Parameters.Add(
    "@employeeid",
    SqlDbType.Int,
    4,
    "employeeid");
```

You select the row to delete and delete it. Actually, you select all rows for employees named Roy Beatty, since you don't know (or care about) their employee IDs. Although you expect only one row to be selected, you use a loop to delete all the rows (If you ran the PropagateInserts program multiple times, you'd have more than one row that matches this selection criteria):

```
// select employees
string filt = @"
      firstname = 'Roy'
      and
      lastname = 'Beatty'
";
//
```

```
// delete employees
foreach (DataRow row in dt.Select(filt))
{
    row.Delete();
}
```

Finally, you set the data adapter's `DeleteCommand` property with the command to delete from the `Employees` table so it will be the SQL the data adapter executes when you call its `Update` method. You then call `Update()` on the data adapter to propagate the changes to the database:

```
da.DeleteCommand = cmd;
da.Update(ds, "employees");
```

Whether you delete one row or several, your SQL is parameterized, and the data adapter will look for all deleted rows in the `employees` data table and submit deletes for all of them to the `Employees` database table.

If you check with Database Explorer or the SSMSE, you'll see the row has been removed from the database. Sir Roy Beatty is no longer in the `Employees` table.

Command Builders

Although it's straightforward, it's a bit of a hassle to code SQL statements for the `UpdateCommand`, `InsertCommand`, and `DeleteCommand` properties, so each data provider has its own *command builder*. If a data table corresponds to a single database table, then you can use a command builder to automatically generate the appropriate `UpdateCommand`, `InsertCommand`, and `DeleteCommand` properties for a data adapter. This is all done transparently when you make a call to the data adapter's `Update` method.

To be able to dynamically generate `INSERT`, `DELETE`, and `UPDATE` statements, the command builder uses the data adapter's `SelectCommand` property to extract metadata for the database table. If you make any changes to the `SelectCommand` property after invoking the `Update` method, you should call the `RefreshSchema` method on the command builder to refresh the metadata accordingly.

To create a command builder, you create an instance of the data provider's command builder class, passing a data adapter to its constructor. For example, the following code creates a SQL Server command builder:

```
SqlDataAdapter da = new SqlDataAdapter();
SqlCommandBuilder cb = new SqlCommandBuilder(da);
```

Note For a command builder to work, the SelectCommand data adapter property must contain a query that returns either a primary key or a unique key for the database table. If none is present, an InvalidOperation exception is generated, and the commands aren't generated.

Try It Out: Using SqlCommandBuilder

Let's convert PersistAdds.cs in Listing 8-6 to use a command builder:

1. Add a new C# Console Application project named PersistAddsBuilder to your Chapter08 solution. Rename Program.cs to PersistAddsBuilder.cs.

2. Replace the code in PersistAddsBuilder.cs with the code in Listing 8-8.

Listing 8-8. PersistAddsBuilder.cs

```
using System;
using System.Data;
using System.Data.SqlClient;

namespace Chapter08
{
   class PersistAddsBuilder
   {
      static void Main(string[] args)
      {
         // connection string
         string connString = @"
            server = .\sqlexpress;
            integrated security = true;
            database = northwind
         ";

         // query
         string qry = @"
            select
               *
            from
               employees
```

```
    where
        country = 'UK'
";

// create connection
SqlConnection conn = new SqlConnection(connString);

try
{
    // create data adapter
    SqlDataAdapter da = new SqlDataAdapter();
    da.SelectCommand = new SqlCommand(qry, conn);

    // create command builder
    SqlCommandBuilder cb = new SqlCommandBuilder(da);

    // create and fill dataset
    DataSet ds = new DataSet();
    da.Fill(ds, "employees");

    // get data table reference
    DataTable dt = ds.Tables["employees"];

    // add a row
    DataRow newRow = dt.NewRow();
    newRow["firstname"] = "Roy";
    newRow["lastname"] = "Beatty";
    newRow["titleofcourtesy"] = "Sir";
    newRow["city"] = "Birmingham";
    newRow["country"] = "UK";
    dt.Rows.Add(newRow);

    // display rows
    foreach (DataRow row in dt.Rows)
    {
        Console.WriteLine(
            "{0} {1} {2}",
            row["firstname"].ToString().PadRight(15),
            row["lastname"].ToString().PadLeft(25),
            row["city"]);
    }
```

```
      // insert employees
      da.Update(ds, "employees");
   }
   catch(Exception e)
   {
      Console.WriteLine("Error: " + e);
   }
   finally
   {
      // close connection
      conn.Close();
   }
}
   }
}
```

3. Make this the startup project, and run it with Ctrl+F5. You should see the result shown in Figure 8-10. Roy Beatty is back in the Employees table.

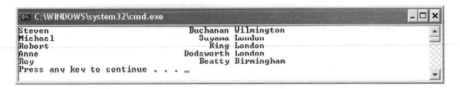

Figure 8-10. *Adding a row using a command builder*

How It Works

The most interesting thing to note isn't the line (yes, just one plus a comment) you added as much as what you replaced. The single statement

```
// create command builder
SqlCommandBuilder cb = new SqlCommandBuilder(da);
```

makes all the following code unnecessary:

```
// SQL to insert employees
string ins = @"
   insert into employees
```

```
            (
                firstname,
                lastname,
                titleofcourtesy,
                city,
                country
            )
            values
            (
                @firstname,
                @lastname,
                @titleofcourtesy,
                @city,
                @country
            )
        ";

        // create command
        SqlCommand cmd = new SqlCommand(ins, conn);
        //
        // map parameters
        cmd.Parameters.Add(
            "@firstname",
            SqlDbType.NVarChar,
            10,
            "firstname");
        cmd.Parameters.Add(
            "@lastname",
            SqlDbType.NVarChar,
            20,
            "lastname");
        cmd.Parameters.Add(
            "@titleofcourtesy",
            SqlDbType.NVarChar,
            25,
            "titleofcourtesy");
        cmd.Parameters.Add(
            "@city",
            SqlDbType.NVarChar,
            15,
            "city");
```

```
cmd.Parameters.Add(
    "@country",
    SqlDbType.NVarChar,
    15,
    "country");
//
// insert employees
da.InsertCommand = cmd;
```

Obviously, using command builders is preferable to coding SQL manually; however, remember that command builders work only on single tables and that the underlying database table must have a primary or unique key. Also, the data adapter SelectCommand property must have a query that includes the key columns.

■**Note** Though all five of the data providers in the .NET Framework Class Library have command builder classes, no class or interface exists in the System.Data namespace that defines them. So, if you want to learn more about command builders, the best place to start is the description for the builder in which you're interested. The System.Data.DataSet class and the System.Data.IDataAdapter interface define the underlying components that command builders interact with, and their documentation provides the informal specification for the constraints on command builders.

Concurrency

You've seen that updating a database with datasets and data adapters is relatively straightforward. However, we've oversimplified things; you've been assuming that no other changes have been made to the database while you've been working with disconnected datasets.

Imagine two separate users trying to make conflicting changes to the same row in a dataset and then trying to propagate these changes to the database. What happens? How does the database resolve the conflicts? Which row gets updated first, or second, or at all? The answer is unclear. As with so many real-world database issues, it all depends on a variety of factors. However, ADO.NET provides a fundamental level of concurrency control that's designed to prevent update anomalies. The details are beyond the scope of this book, but the following is a good conceptual start.

Basically, a dataset marks all added, modified, and deleted rows. If a row is propagated to the database but has been modified by someone else since the dataset was filled, the data manipulation operation for the row is ignored. This technique is known as *optimistic concurrency* and is essentially the job of the data adapter. When the Update method is called, the data adapter attempts to reconcile all changes. This works well in an environment where users seldom contend for the same data.

This type of concurrency is different from what's known as *pessimistic concurrency*, which *locks* rows upon modification (or sometimes even on retrieval) to avoid conflicts. Most database managers use some form of locking to guarantee data integrity.

Disconnected processing with optimistic concurrency is essential to successful multi-tiered systems. How to employ it most effectively given the pessimistic concurrency of DBMSs is a thorny problem. Don't worry about it now, but keep in mind that many issues exist, and the more complex your application, the more likely you'll have to become an expert in concurrency.

Using Datasets and XML

XML is the fundamental medium for data transfer in .NET. In fact, XML is a major foundation for ADO.NET. Datasets organize data internally in XML format and have a variety of methods for reading and writing in XML. For example:

- You can import and export the structure of a dataset as an XML schema using `System.Data.DataSet`'s `ReadXmlSchema` and `WriteXmlSchema` methods.

- You can read the data (and, optionally, the schema) of a dataset from and write it to an XML file with `ReadXml()` and `WriteXml()`. This can be useful when exchanging data with another application or making a local copy of a dataset.

- You can bind a dataset to an XML document (an instance of `System.Xml.XmlDataDocument`). The dataset and data document are *synchronized*, so you can use either ADO.NET or XML operations to modify it.

Let's look at one of these in action, copying a dataset to an XML file.

■**Note** If you're unfamiliar with XML, don't worry. ADO.NET doesn't require any detailed knowledge of it. Of course, the more you know, the better you can understand what's happening transparently, so we've provided a short primer on XML in Appendix A.

Try It Out: Extracting a Dataset to an XML File

You can preserve the contents and schema of a dataset in one XML file using the dataset's `WriteXml` method or in separate files using `WriteXml()` and `WriteXmlSchema()`. `WriteXml()` is overloaded, and in this example we'll show a version that extracts both data and schema:

1. Add a new C# Console Application project named WriteXML to your Chapter08 solution. Rename Program.cs to WriteXML.cs.

2. Replace the code in WriteXML.cs with the code in Listing 8-9.

Listing 8-9. WriteXML.cs

```csharp
using System;
using System.Data;
using System.Data.SqlClient;

namespace Chapter08
{
    class WriteXML
    {
        static void Main(string[] args)
        {
            // connection string
            string connString = @"
                server = .\sqlexpress;
                integrated security = true;
                database = northwind
            ";

            // query
            string qry = @"
                select
                    productname,
                    unitprice
                from
                    products
            ";

            // create connection
            SqlConnection conn = new SqlConnection(connString);

            try
            {
                // create data adapter
                SqlDataAdapter da = new SqlDataAdapter();
                da.SelectCommand = new SqlCommand(qry, conn);
```

```
            // open connection
            conn.Open();

            // create and fill dataset
            DataSet ds = new DataSet();
            da.Fill(ds, "products");

            // extract dataset to XML file
            ds.WriteXml(
                @"c:\bcs2005db\solutions\chapter08\productstable.xml"
            );
        }
        catch(Exception e)
        {
            Console.WriteLine("Error: " + e);
        }
        finally
        {
            // close connection
            conn.Close();
        }
    }
}
}
```

3. Make this the startup project, and run it with Ctrl+F5. You should see the result shown in Figure 8-11.

Figure 8-11. *Extracting a data table as XML*

4. Not much seems to have happened, but that's because you wrote to a file rather than to the screen. Open productstable.xml to see the XML. (One way in VCSE is to use File ➤ Open File... .) Figure 8-12 shows the XML extracted for the first five product rows.

■**Tip** By default, extracted XML documents are plain text files. You can open the productstable.xml file in any editor, or even use the type or more commands to view it.

```
productstable.xml   WriteXML.cs   Start Page                        ▼  ✕
 1    <?xml version="1.0" standalone="yes"?>
 2 ⊟ <NewDataSet>
 3 ⊟    <products>
 4        <productname>Chai</productname>
 5        <unitprice>18.0000</unitprice>
 6  -   </products>                            I
 7 ⊟    <products>
 8        <productname>Chang</productname>
 9        <unitprice>19.0000</unitprice>
10  -   </products>
11 ⊟    <products>
12        <productname>Aniseed Syrup</productname>
13        <unitprice>10.0000</unitprice>
14  -   </products>
15 ⊟    <products>
16        <productname>Chef Anton's Cajun Seasoning</productname>
17        <unitprice>22.0000</unitprice>
18  -   </products>
19 ⊟    <products>
20        <productname>Chef Anton's Gumbo Mix</productname>
21        <unitprice>21.3500</unitprice>
22  -   </products>
```

Figure 8-12. *Data table extracted as XML.*

How It Works

You replace a console display loop with a method call to write the XML file:

```
// extract dataset to XML file
ds.WriteXml(
    @"c:\bcs2005db\solutions\chapter08\productstable.xml"
);
```

You give the full path for the XML file to place it in the solution directory. Had you given only the filename, it would have been placed in the bin\Release subdirectory under the WriteXML project directory.

Note that the XML has simply mapped the dataset as a hierarchy. The first XML element <NewDataSet> is the dataset name (defaulted to NewDataSet, since you didn't specify one). The next element, <products>, uses the data table name (you have only one data table, since you used only one query to populate the dataset), and it's nested inside the dataset element. The data column elements, <productname> and <unitprice>, are nested inside this element.

The data for each column appears (as plain text) between the *start tag* (for example, <productname>) and the *end tag* (for example, </productname>) for each column element. Note that the <products> elements represent individual rows, not the whole table. So, the column elements are contained within the start tag <products> and end tag </products> for each row. If you scroll to the bottom of the XML file, you'll find the end tag </NewDataSet> for the dataset.

As we said, XML is fundamental to ADO.NET. You'll see more of it in Chapter 17.

Using Data Tables Without Datasets

As we mentioned in our first example, "Try It Out: Populating a Dataset with a Data Adapter," you can use data tables without datasets. Most of the time, this involves calling the same methods on data tables that you use for datasets. We'll give one example. You should then be able to analogize from it for other processing.

■**Note** You can also use datasets and data tables without data adapters. Such uses are beyond the scope of this book.

Try It Out: Populating a Data Table with a Data Adapter

This example is based on our first example, PopDataSet.cs (Listing 8-1). You'll create a data table, populate it with a data adapter, and then display its contents:

1. Add a new C# Console Application project named PopDataSet to your Chapter08 solution. Rename Program.cs to PopDataSet.cs.

2. Replace the code in PopDataSet.cs with the code in Listing 8-10. The lines changed from Listing 8-1 are highlighted.

Listing 8-10. PopDataTable.cs

```
using System;
using System.Data;
using System.Data.SqlClient;

namespace Chapter08
{
    class PopDataTable
    {
        static void Main(string[] args)
        {
            // connection string
            string connString = @"
                server = .\sqlexpress;
                integrated security = true;
                database = northwind
            ";
```

```csharp
// query
string sql = @"
   select
      productname,
      unitprice
   from
      products
   where
      unitprice < 20
";

// create connection
SqlConnection conn = new SqlConnection(connString);

try
{
   // open connection
   conn.Open();

   // create data adapter
   SqlDataAdapter da = new SqlDataAdapter(sql, conn);

   // create data table
   DataTable dt = new DataTable();

   // fill data table
   da.Fill(dt);

   // display data
   foreach (DataRow row in dt.Rows)
   {
      foreach (DataColumn col in dt.Columns)
         Console.WriteLine(row[col]);
      Console.WriteLine("".PadLeft(20, '='));
   }
}
catch(Exception e)
{
   Console.WriteLine("Error: " + e);
}
```

```
        finally
        {
            // close connection
            conn.Close();
        }
    }
  }
}
```

3. Run it with Ctrl+F5. You should see the same result as in Figure 8-3, for PopDataSet.cs. (Only the last ten rows are displayed.)

How It Works

Instead of creating a dataset

```
        // create dataset
        DataSet ds = new DataSet();
```

you create a data table:

```
        // create data table
        DataTable dt = new DataTable();
```

And instead of filling a dataset

```
        // fill dataset
        da.Fill(ds, "products");
```

you fill a data table:

```
        // fill data table
        da.Fill(dt);
```

Since a data table can hold only one table, notice that the Fill method doesn't accept the data table name as an argument. And, since you don't have to find a particular data table in a dataset, there was no need for this code:

```
        // get data table
        DataTable dt = ds.Tables["products"];
```

Otherwise, the code needs no changes.

> **Tip** Unless you really need to organize data tables in datasets so you can define relationships between them, using one or more data tables instead of one (or more) datasets is easier to code and takes up fewer runtime resources.

Understanding Typed and Untyped Datasets

Datasets can be *typed* or *untyped*. The datasets you've used so far have all been untyped. They were instances of System.Data.DataSet. An untyped dataset has no built-in schema. The schema is only implicit. It grows as you add tables and columns to the dataset, but these objects are exposed as collections rather than as XML schema elements. However, as we mentioned in passing in the previous section, you can explicitly export a schema for an untyped dataset with WriteXmlSchema (or WriteXml).

A typed dataset is one that's derived from System.Data.DataSet and uses an XML schema (typically in an .xsd file) in declaring the dataset class. Information from the schema (tables, columns, and so on) is extracted, generated as C# code, and compiled, so the new dataset class is an actual .NET type with appropriate objects and properties.

Either typed or untyped datasets are equally valid, but typed datasets are more efficient and can make code somewhat simpler. For example, using an untyped dataset, you'd need to write this

```
Console.WriteLine(ds.Tables[0].Rows[0]["CompanyName"]);
```

to get the value for the CompanyName column of the Customers table, assuming that the data table was the first in the dataset. With a typed dataset, you can access its data tables and data columns as class members. You could replace the previous code with this

```
Console.WriteLine(ds.Customers[0].CompanyName);
```

making the code more intuitive. In addition, VCSE has IntelliSense support for typed datasets.

Typed datasets are more efficient than untyped datasets, because typed datasets have a defined schema, and when they're populated with data, runtime type identification and conversion aren't necessary, since they are taken care of at compile time. Untyped datasets have a lot more work to do every time a result set is loaded.

However, typed datasets aren't always the best choice. If you're dealing with data that isn't basically well defined, whose definition changes dynamically, or that is only of temporary interest, the flexibility of untyped datasets can outweigh the benefits of typed ones.

This chapter is already long enough. Since we're not concerned with efficiency in our small sample programs, we won't use typed datasets and we don't need to cover creating them here.

Our emphasis in this book is explaining how C# works with ADO.NET by showing you how to code fundamental operations. If you can code them yourself, you'll have insight into what VCSE does when it generates things for you, as in the next chapter on using Windows Forms. This is invaluable for understanding how to configure generated components and debugging applications that use them.

Although you can code an .xsd file yourself (or export an XSL schema for an untyped dataset with System.Data.DataSet.WriteXmlSchema() and modify it) and then use the xsd.exe utility to create a class for a typed dataset, it's a lot of work, is subject to error, and is something you'll rarely (if ever) want or need to do. There's little advantage to seeing how to do it, even for insight, since creating a typed dataset in VCSE is easy. In fact, unlike the rest of the things we cover, the insight works in reverse. Seeing how to create a typed dataset in VCSE will help you understand what an .xsd requires (if you ever actually need to code one).

We won't leave you in the dark, though. You'll use a typed dataset in Chapter 18, in the last example program in the book, and we'll show you how to create one in VCSE there.

Summary

In this chapter, we covered the basics of datasets and data adapters. A dataset is a relational representation of data that has a collection of data tables, and each data table has collections of data rows and data columns. A data adapter is an object that controls how data is loaded into a dataset (or data table) and how changes to the dataset data are propagated back to the data source.

We presented basic techniques for filling and accessing datasets, demonstrated how to filter and sort data tables, and noted that though datasets are database-independent objects, disconnected operation isn't the default mode.

We discussed how to propagate data modifications back to databases with parameterized SQL and the data adapter's UpdateCommand, InsertCommand, and DeleteCommand properties, and how command builders simplify this for single-table updates.

We briefly mentioned the important issue of concurrency and then introduced XML, the fundamental technology behind ADO.NET. We provided an example of populating a data table without a dataset, and you should be able to analogize this for all the other operations on datasets that we covered.

Finally, we discussed typed and untyped datasets and pointed you to Chapter 18, if you want to look ahead and learn how to create typed datasets.

Now that you've seen the basics of using ADO.NET, we'll move from console applications to Windows applications.

■ ■ ■

Introducing Data Binding

Windows Forms controls can be *bound* to database data. Once bound, data can be displayed and updated with minimal coding. In this chapter, we'll cover:

- Simple and complex data binding

- How to bind database data to Windows Forms controls

- How to display and update database data with bound controls

What's Data Binding?

The term *data binding* refers to mapping elements of a data source to a graphical interface component so the component can work with the data automatically. For example, you can bind a column (but only one value at a time) to the Text property of a TextBox control or even bind an entire table to a data grid, such as the DataGridView control.

ADO.NET provides a neat data-binding infrastructure that VCSE uses to generate bindings. In fact, any class that implements the System.Windows.Forms.IBindableComponent interface, the System.Collections.IList interface, or the System.ComponentModel. IBindingList or IListSource interfaces is a *bindable component*.

You can bind Windows Forms controls to data in the following two ways:

- Simple data binding

- Complex data binding

You can also use a *binding source component* to simplify either type of binding.

■**Note** Chapter 8 of Matthew MacDonald's *Pro .NET 2.0 Windows Forms and Custom Controls in C#* (Berkeley, CA: Apress, 2005) provides a highly readable and detailed description of data binding.

Performing Simple Data Binding

Simple data binding is a one-to-one association between an individual control property and a single element of a data source. You can use it for controls that show only one value at a time. If the underlying data source is modified, then the control's Refresh method will update the bound value, reflecting any changes.

To get comfortable with the idea, let's code a small Windows application that uses simple data binding to bind two TextBox controls to two different columns of the Northwind Employees table.

Try It Out: Using Simple Data Binding

In this application, you'll bind two values to two text boxes to display the first and last names of an employee:

1. Create a new Windows Application project named Chapter09. When Solution Explorer opens, save the solution.

2. Rename the Chapter09 project SimpleBinding.

3. Change the Text property of Form1 to Simple Binding.

4. Add two text boxes to the form, as shown in Figure 9-1.

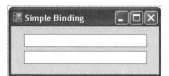

Figure 9-1. *Simple Binding form*

5. Double-click the form and add a using directive to Form1.cs for the System.Data.SqlClient namespace.

6. Insert the code in Listing 9-1 into the Form1_Load method.

Listing 9-1. Form1_Load()

```
string connString = @"
   server = .\sqlexpress;
   integrated security = true;
   database = northwind
";

string sql = @"
   select
       *
from
   employees
";

SqlConnection conn = new SqlConnection(connString);
SqlDataAdapter da = new SqlDataAdapter(sql, conn);
DataSet ds = new DataSet();
da.Fill(ds, "employees");

// Bind to FirstName column of the Employees table
textBox1.DataBindings.Add("text", ds, "employees.firstname");
// Bind to LastName column of the Employees table
textBox2.DataBindings.Add("text", ds, "employees.lastname");
```

7. Run the code with Ctrl+F5, and you should see the result shown in Figure 9-2.

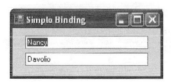

Figure 9-2. *Text boxes bound to column values*

How It Works

You fill a dataset with all columns from all rows in Employees:

```
string sql = @"
   select
      *
from
   employees
";

SqlConnection conn = new SqlConnection(connString);
SqlDataAdapter da = new SqlDataAdapter(sql, conn);
DataSet ds = new DataSet();
da.Fill(ds, "employees");
```

Once you fetch the data, you bind the Text property of the top text box to the FirstName column and that of the bottom text box to the LastName column, using the Add method of the ControlBindingsCollection that each text box's DataBindings property refers to:

```
// Bind to FirstName column of the Employees table
textBox1.DataBindings.Add("text", ds, "employees.firstname");
// Bind to LastName column of the Employees table
textBox2.DataBindings.Add("text", ds, "employees.lastname");
```

Each data-bound control in a Windows application maintains a collection of bindings for all its data-bound properties. This collection can contain a number of individual control property Binding objects. Although a text box is capable of displaying only one value at a time, you bind the Text properties to columns of the Employees table by the binding for it. The Add method has the following parameters:

- The name of the control property to bind to

- The data source

- The name of the data source member to bind to

Once bound, the data for the first row in the data table automatically displays in the text box controls. This is convenient, but not very useful. You'll see how to move through the rows of the bound table soon, in "Synchronizing Controls with a Data Source."

Performing Complex Data Binding

Complex data binding is an association between a control and one or more data elements of a data source. You can perform this type of binding with controls that allow more than one value to be displayed at a time, such as a data grid or a data list.

The next example uses a data grid (a DataGridView control) to display all rows and columns of the Northwind Customers table.

Try It Out: Using Complex Data Binding

To create the data grid application:

1. Add a Windows Application project named ComplexBinding to the Chapter09 solution.

2. Change the Text property of Form1 to Complex Binding.

3. Add a DataGridView control from the Toolbox. A series of windows will prompt you for binding information. The first is shown in Figure 9-3.

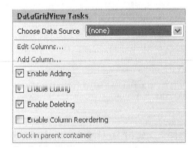

Figure 9-3. *DataGridView Tasks*

4. Open the drop-down list, and you'll see the window shown in Figure 9-4.

Figure 9-4. *No data sources yet defined*

5. Click Add Project Data Source… . The Data Source Configuration Wizard will appear, as shown in Figure 9-5.

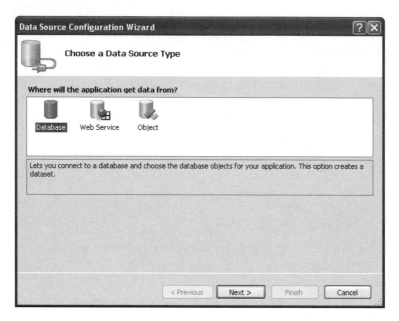

Figure 9-5. *Data Source Configuration Wizard*

6. Click the Database icon, then click Next. The Choose Your Data Connection window will appear, as shown in Figure 9-6.

7. The connection you created in Chapter 2 should appear in the drop-down list. If you're curious, click the plus sign to view the connection string, as shown in Figure 9-7.

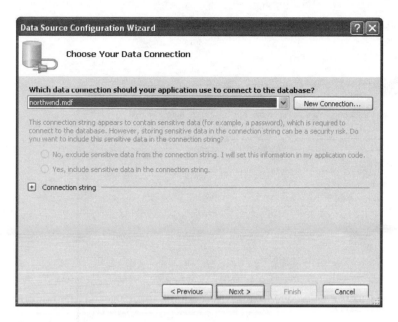

Figure 9-6. *Choose Your Data Connection window*

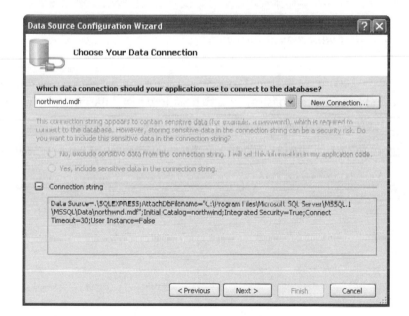

Figure 9-7. *Viewing a connection string*

8. Click Next, and you'll be prompted to save the connection string, as shown in Figure 9-8.

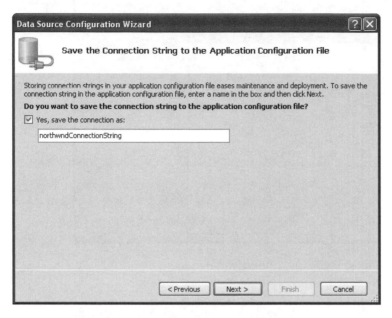

Figure 9-8. *Save the Connection String window*

9. For our purposes, it doesn't matter if you save it or not, so just click Next. You'll be prompted to choose the database objects to be stored in a dataset, as shown in Figure 9-9.

10. Expand the Tables node and check the Customers table, as shown in Figure 9-10.

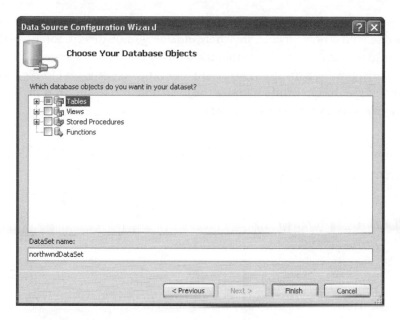

Figure 9-9. *Choose Your Database Objects window*

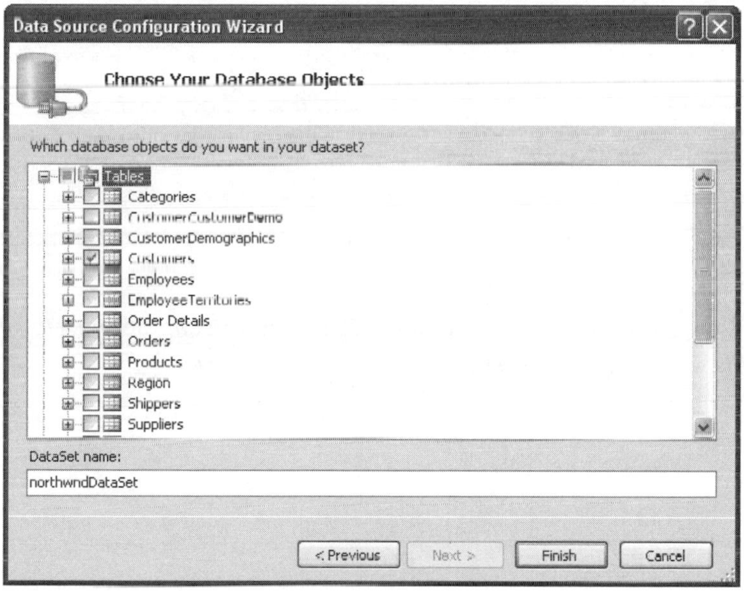

Figure 9-10. *Choose a database table*

11. Click Finish, and you'll go back to the window in Figure 9-3. You don't need to do anything else with it now, so click anywhere outside it to dismiss it. You'll see the screen shown in Figure 9-11. Notice that the data grid now shows a row of column headings and a row for data on the form and that three icons appear in the tray at the bottom of the Design window. Resize the form and grid to suit your preference for how many rows and columns to display.

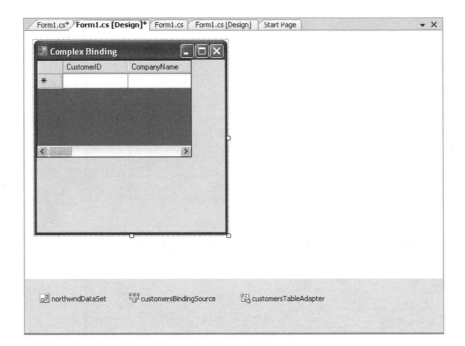

Figure 9-11. *Data grid view and three tray icons*

12. Make this the startup project, and run it with Ctrl+F5. You should see a result similar to the one shown in Figure 9-12.

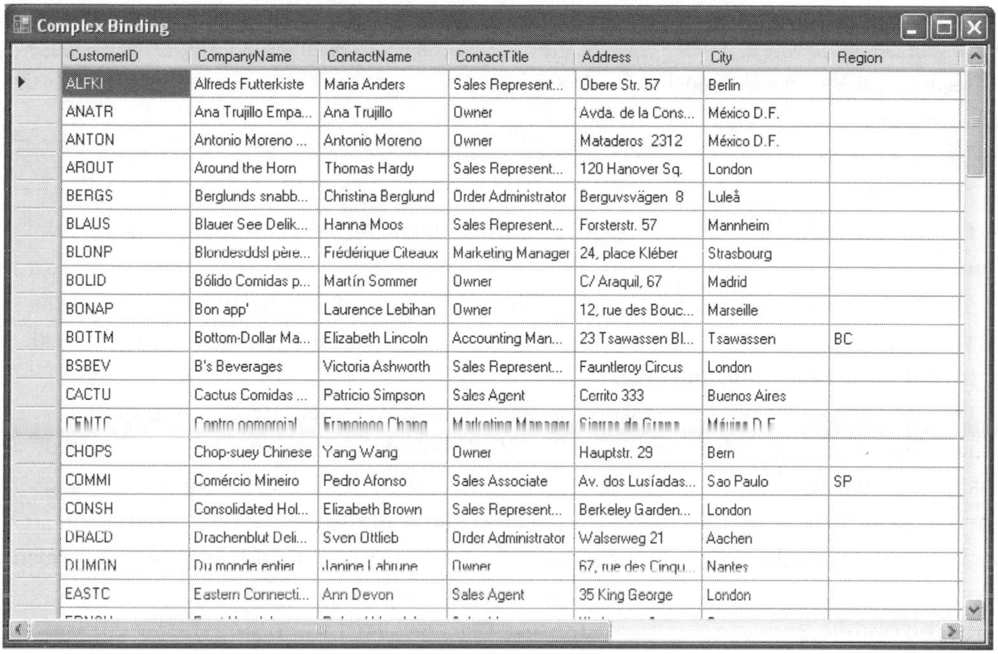

Figure 9-12. *Displaying customers bound to a data grid view*

How It Works

It works like magic. You went through lots of screens, but wrote no code at all. Pretty cool!

The magic happens because of the objects created for you, represented by the icons in the tray. Most of the details are well beyond the scope of this book, but if you look at Form1.Designer.cs, you'll find four lines that define private variables used for the data grid view, dataset, binding source, and table adapter:

```
private System.Windows.Forms.DataGridView dataGridView1;
private northwndDataSet northwndDataSet;
private System.Windows.Forms.BindingSource customersBindingSource;
private ComplexBinding.northwndDataSetTableAdapters.CustomersTableAdapter
        customersTableAdapter;
```

If you're really curious, look at the 1,476 lines of northwndDataSet.Designer.cs code that VCSE generated to implement the bindings.

■**Note** For details on how to customize DataGridView, for use with any data source including databases, see Chapter 15 of Matthew MacDonald's *Pro .NET 2.0 Windows Forms and Custom Controls in C#* (Berkeley, CA: Apress, 2005).

Let's look at some of the basic aspects of the objects in the tray and how they work together.

On the left, northwndDataSet is exactly that—a dataset (implemented as a partial class that derives from System.Data.DataSet) where the data from the database will be loaded. It's the data source for the data grid.

On the right, customersTableAdapter is also what you'd expect (from Chapter 8)— a data adapter. To be precise, it's not itself a data adapter (it's implemented as a partial class that derives from System.ComponentModel.Component), but it includes a SqlDataAdapter as one of its private fields and uses the data adapter to fill the dataset. As you'll see in "Updating from a Data Grid," since customersTableAdapter uses a data adapter, it can also propagate changes from the dataset to the database.

In the middle, customersBindingSource is a Windows Forms binding source control (an instance of System.Windows.Forms.BindingSource). It intermediates the binding between the data-grid control and the dataset. Method calls on the binding source handle all interaction between the control and the dataset. You can use binding sources for both simple and complex data binding.

Understanding Data Binding: Behind the Scenes

You've now programmed both simple and complex data binding, but how does all this work? How do controls bind themselves to data sources? To answer these questions, we'll give you some insight into the data-binding mechanism and show how it works.

The Windows data-bound controls are able to bind to data because of the functionality made available by the Binding class (in the System.Windows.Forms namespace). This class is responsible for creating a simple binding between a single control property and a data element in a data source.

The DataBindings property of a control (any class that derives from System.Windows. Forms.Control) returns a ControlBindingsCollection object, which is a collection of Binding objects, each of which you can add to the collection with its Add method. A data-bound control can have a collection of bindings, each associated with a different property of the control. For example, you can bind the Text property of a Label control to a single column in a table and at the same time bind its ForeColor property to an array of different color values, completely unrelated to the table.

The Add method has two overloads: one that takes a single Binding object and another that implicitly creates an instance of a Binding object by calling the Binding class constructor (which is what you used in the SimpleBinding application).

The Binding class constructor takes three parameters. The first parameter can be the name of a property of a control, such as the Text property of a TextBox control. The second parameter can be an instance of a DataSet, DataTable, or any class that implements the System.Collections.IList interface (among others). The third parameter describes a data member from the data source. It's a string literal that must resolve into a scalar value, such as a data column name in a data table.

If you'd rather declare a Binding object explicitly, you can do it. The following code shows how to bind the FirstName column when explicitly creating a Binding object (try it in SimpleBinding and you'll see it works):

```
Binding newBind = new Binding("text", ds, "employees.firstname");
textBox1.DataBindings.Add(newBind);
```

This approach could be useful in situations where you'd like to bind two or more controls to the same data element. For example, if you have a Label control and a TextBox control in a Windows application and you'd like to bind both of these controls to the same column in a table, for whatever reason, you could create one Binding object and add that to the ControlBindingsCollection of each of the controls with the Add method.

The following code is an example of binding the Text property of two controls to the same column in the Employees table, assuming you already have a Label control and a TextBox control on your form:

```
Binding newBind = new Binding("text", ds, "employees.firstname");
textBox1.DataBindings.Add(newBind);
Label1.DataBindings.Add(newBind);
```

■**Note** When you use a dataset as a data source for binding, the control is actually bound to a data view, behind the scenes. Data views are designed to provide different views of the data stored in an underlying data table, so they're useful when it comes to data binding. A data view can allow two or more controls to be bound to the same data source, thus allowing each bound control to have a different view of data altogether. For instance, one control could display all available rows in a table, and another could display selected rows or columns. Similarly, a bound DataRow object is actually a DataRowView object that provides a customizable view.

Synchronizing Controls with a Data Source

Data binding is a powerful feature, allowing your application to make the most of rendering data dynamically and making it simple to synchronize bound controls with the underlying data source.

Suppose you build a Windows application that uses a couple of text boxes to bind to the same data source, where each control is bound to a different column in a table. Realistically, the data source will probably have more than one row. In the first example, of simple data binding, you bound a couple of text boxes to a data source and displayed only one row. To navigate back and forth through the available rows, your controls need to be synchronized so that they display the correct data from the same row, since they're bound to two different columns.

The System.Windows.Forms namespace includes an abstract class for this purpose. A *binding manager* is an instance of a class that derives from the abstract BindingManagerBase class. The binding manager enables greater control over the data being displayed by controls, binding data to the same data source by maintaining the current position (the *row pointer*) in the data source. The binding manager supervises and keeps track of the ordinal position of the current row and fires events to notify the application if the position has changed.

The two fundamental properties of a binding manager are Position and Current. Position is a zero-based integer value that describes an ordinal position of the rows being read in the data source. With the Position property, you can programmatically advance the row pointer to move to the next row and vice versa. The Current property returns the data object at the current position in the data source.

The two concrete binding managers are CurrencyManager and PropertyManager. CurrencyManager is specifically designed for data sources that implement IList (or interfaces based on it). PropertyManager is designed for a data source that's neither a list nor a collection but is a single property of another object or is a single value. You can use it only for maintaining the Current property of the object. Trying to use the Position property will have no effect, since the data source isn't a list but a single value.

You can't create an instance of the BindingManagerBase class directly, because it's an abstract base class, but you can obtain instances of its derived classes by calling the BindingContext property of a Windows form, which returns an instance of an appropriate binding manager type, depending on the type of data source being used.

Every Windows form groups all bindings defined by its child controls into a collection called BindingContext. This collection returns an appropriate binding manager for the specified data source and data member.

Let's now look at a simple example that illustrates how to use a binding manager. The application will extend our use of a couple of our two simply bound TextBox controls by adding two buttons to navigate through the table.

Try It Out: Using a Binding Manager

Let's do an example that uses a binding manager:

1. Add a Windows Application project named BindingManagers to the Chapter09 solution. Change the form's Text property to Binding Managers.

2. Drag two TextBox controls and two Button controls from the Toolbox onto the form. Change the Text property of the left button to << Back. Change the text of right button to Next >>. Your form should look like that in Figure 9-13.

Figure 9-13. *Adding navigation to simple bindings*

3. Drag a DataSet control onto the form. You should see the window shown in Figure 9-14.

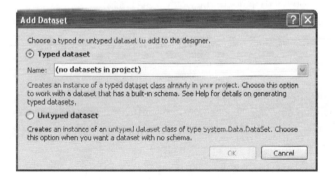

Figure 9-14. *Adding a dataset to a form*

4. Click "Untyped dataset," then click OK. This will add a dataset to the component tray.

5. Press F7 to edit the Form1.cs code. Add the following using directive:

```
using System.Data.SqlClient;
```

6. Add the following field to the Form1 class declaration:

```
// Declare a binding manager field
private BindingManagerBase bMgr;
```

7. Go back to the form and double-click it, then insert the code in Listing 9-2 into the Form1_Load method.

Listing 9-2. Form1_Load()

```
string connString = @"
    server = .\sqlexpress;
    integrated security = true;
    database = northwind
";

string sql = @"
    select
        *
    from
        employees
";

SqlConnection conn = new SqlConnection(connString);
SqlDataAdapter da = new SqlDataAdapter(sql, conn);
da.Fill(dataSet1, "employees");

// Bind text boxes to data columns
textBox1.DataBindings.Add("text", dataSet1, "employees.firstname");
textBox2.DataBindings.Add("text", dataSet1, "employees.lastname");

// Create the binding manager (CurrencyManager)
bMgr = this.BindingContext[dataSet1, "employees"];
```

8. Go back to the form and double-click the Next >> button. Insert the following code into the button2_Click method:

```
// Point to the next row and refresh the contents of the text box
bMgr.Position += 1;
```

9. Go back to the form and double-click the << Back button. Insert the following code into the button1_Click method:

```
// Point to the previous row and refresh contents of the text box
bMgr.Position -= 1;
```

10. Make this the startup project, and run it with Ctrl+F5. You should see the form shown in Figure 9-15. Use the buttons to move back and forth in the table.

Figure 9-15. *Navigating through a table with a binding manager*

How It Works

This application is similar to SimpleBinding, but you use a binding manager to navigate through the data table. You declare a BindingManagerBase field:

```
// Declare a binding manager field
private BindingManagerBase bMgr;
```

After you bind the text boxes and columns, you get a suitable binding manager from the BindingContext property of the form:

```
// Create the binding manager (CurrencyManager)
bMgr = this.BindingContext[dataSet1, "employees"];
```

In this case, BindingContext returns an instance of a CurrencyManager, since a DataSet implements the IListSource interface. With a binding manager at hand, you could now manage all data bindings in the Windows form.

■Tip In steps 4 and 5, you add a dataset to the form with a control instead of code. You could also use a control to add the binding manager. Exploiting the full power of VCSE to simplify development of Windows database applications is well beyond our scope here, but we hope to have piqued your curiosity and that you'll investigate and experiment on your own. See Sahil Malik's excellent *Pro ADO.NET 2.0* (Berkeley, CA: Apress, 2005) for more information. It claims to be "The only ADO.NET book you will ever need," and we believe it very well might be, after you've read ours.

You then implement the logic for the navigational buttons. The `button2_Click` method is called every time the Next >> button is clicked. The body of the method comprises a single line of code

```
bMgr.Position += 1;
```

that moves the position of the current row in the data table forward by incrementing the `Position` property of the binding manager.

Similarly, the `button1_Click` method is called every time the << Back button is clicked. It decrements the `Position` property of the binding manager:

```
bMgr.Position -= 1;
```

Updating from a Data Grid

The `DataGridView` control is one of the most powerful Windows Forms controls. In "Performing Complex Data Binding," you bound a `DataGridView` to all the columns of the `Customers` table and displayed a scrollable grid of its rows. In "Try It Out: Using a Binding Manager," you saw how to take advantage of simple binding to move back and forth in a table. We'll now show you some more features (and there are many more) of `DataGridView`—in particular, how easy it is to add more sophisticated navigation to it and to update a table with it.

■Note `DataGridView` has a counterpart Web Forms control, `GridView`, and the same data-binding principles apply to ASP.NET 2.0 programming. Visual Web Developer 2005 Express Edition is the free IDE for developing Web applications with C# or Visual Basic.

Try It Out: Updating a Table Using a Data Grid

There's usually more than one way to accomplish something in VCSE, so instead of modifying the ComplexBinding project, we'll create a similar but more powerful project in a slightly different way to expand your techniques for developing Windows database applications:

1. Add a Windows Application project named GridUpdate to the Chapter09 solution. Make the project the startup project. (Yes, now, not later.)

2. Change the Text property of Form1 to Customer Maintenance.

3. On the VCSE menu, click Data ➤ Add New Data Source…. You'll see the same window as in Figure 9-5, in "Try It Out: Using Complex Data Binding." Follow the same steps you did there to create a data source for the whole Customers table. Note that when you eventually click Finish, the data source will be created, but, unlike Figure 9-11, nothing will change on your form and no tray will appear at the bottom of the screen. However, look in Solution Explorer and you'll find that northwndDataSet.xsd has been added to the GridUpdate project (see Figure 9-16).

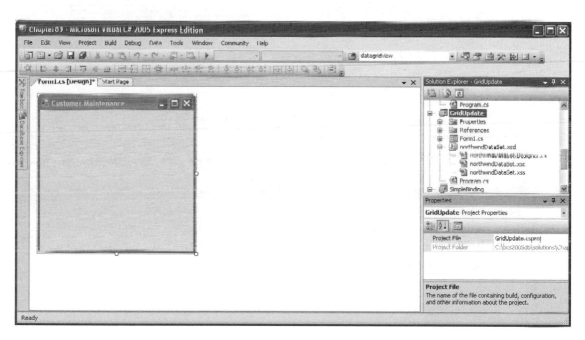

Figure 9-16. *GridUpdate after adding a new data source*

4. On the VCSE menu, click Data ➤ Show Data Sources. The Data Sources window will appear, as shown in Figure 9-17.

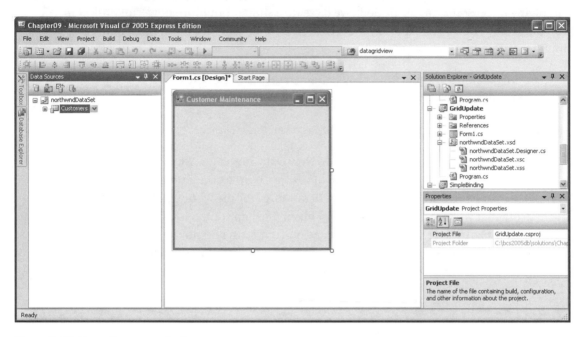

Figure 9-17. *Data Sources window*

■**Note** You set GridUpdate as the startup project in step 1, because the Data Sources window displays the data sources for the current startup project.

---

5. Click the check that appears to the right of Customers node (if there's no check, click the Customers node to make it appear), and then click DataGridView. This chooses the control to use with the data source. Drag the Customers node onto the form, and you'll see the screen shown in Figure 9-18. It's similar to Figure 9-11, but it includes an extra control at the top of the form (an instance of System. Windows.Forms.BindingNavigator) and an icon for it in the component tray.

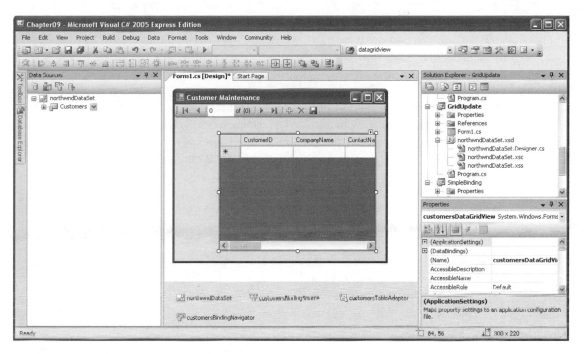

Figure 9-18. *Data grid with a control bar*

6. Resize the form and data grid to suit your tastes, and run the project with Ctrl+F5. You'll see the screen shown in Figure 9-19.

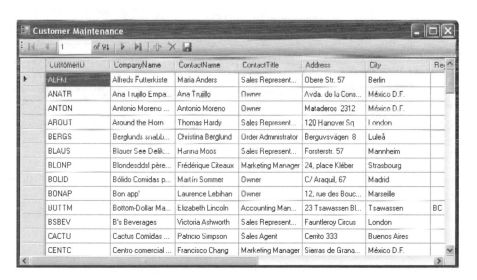

Figure 9-19. *A navigable and updatable customer data grid*

7. Play around with the data grid to see how the navigation control works and how you can you can use it to insert and delete rows in the data grid. **BUT DON'T CLICK THE Save Data BUTTON.** Once you're comfortable with the control, just close the window.

8. Add a new row. To keep things very simple, just enter zzz for both the customer and company names. Change the city for customer WOLZA from Warszawa to Gdansk. Now click the Save Data button. The new row is now inserted into the Customers table in the database, and the city for WOLZA has been updated too. Close the window and rerun the project to prove this.

9. Put Customers back the way it was by changing WOLZA's city back to Warszawa and deleting customer zzz. Click Save Data to propagate the changes to the database.

Once again, you didn't write any code to access Customers, not even to perform navigation or propagate updates. Very cool!

How It Works

The key is adding the binding navigator, and in particular, the Save Data button it provides.

Behind the scenes, the following code is generated for you in the event handler for the button (customersBindingNavigatorSaveItem_Click):

```
this.Validate();
this.customersBindingSource.EndEdit();
this.customersTableAdapter.Update(this.northwndDataSet.Customers);
```

The first line fires the Validating and Validated events for the DataGridView, where you could handle validation of the data grid changes before propagating them to the database.

The second line applies the pending changes in the data grid to the data source. Keep in mind that the data source *isn't* the Customers database table. It's the northwndDataSet dataset.

The third line simply does the same kind of thing you did in Chapter 8 to propagate changes to a dataset to the database. It calls the Update method on a data adapter. Here, since there is only one data table in the dataset (DataGridView cannot be bound to multiple tables), the second argument to Update()—the table in the dataset to update—is not required.

As you also saw in Chapter 8, data adapters need to have commands to execute appropriate SQL for insertions, changes, and deletions, and all three commands are generated for northwndDataSet. To see them, click on the dataset in the component tray, click the small box with the right arrow that appears, and click Edit in Dataset Designer… . You'll see the screen shown in Figure 9-20.

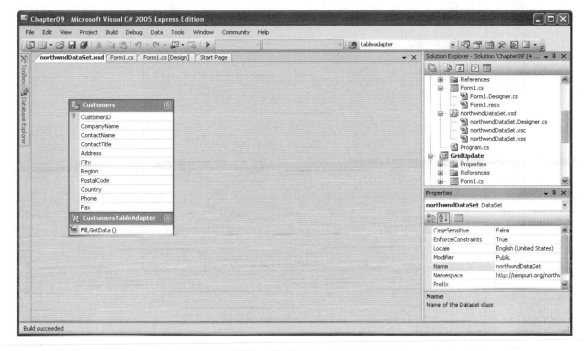

Figure 9-20. *northwndDataSet.xsd in Dataset Designer*

■**Tip** You could have simply double-clicked northwndDataSet.xsd in Solution Explorer to get to Dataset Designer, but we wanted you to see an alternative. VCSE is full (perhaps too full) of them.

Click CustomersTableAdapter in the diagram and look at the Properties window. All four commands are listed. Expand any of them, and you'll see the SQL that was generated. For example, expand the UpdateCommand property, click on the CommandText label, and click on the ellipsis that appears over the command text value. You'll see the Query Builder window, as shown in Figure 9-21. You can customize the SQL for any command with Query Builder.

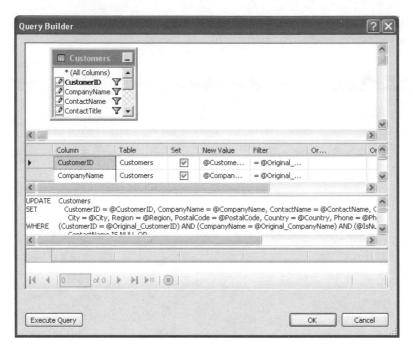

Figure 9-21. *Viewing SQL in Query Builder*

■**Tip** Many (perhaps most) professional Windows application developers believe that the best practice is to minimize reliance on generated code, especially for updates. More precise management of how a control interacts with a database is often desirable and sometimes essential. That's why we focus on console applications in this book. They force you to write your own code, so you can code whatever you need, even for Windows applications. At any rate, it gives you insight into what the code generated for a control has to do, so you can dig into it and see what it's doing when things don't work as expected.

Summary

This chapter covered the fundamentals of data binding and showed you how to use both simple and complex data binding. It then focused on data grids to display and update database data. This was only a start, and you'll find plenty of other things to study about data binding as you advance in C# database programming, but we hope you're now comfortable with the concepts and can clearly see that knowing how to code data access and update logic yourself for console programs is still extremely important, even when all code is generated for you by Windows Forms (and Web Forms) controls.

In the next chapter, you'll return to T-SQL and see how to create tables and relationships between tables.

Understanding Tables and Relationships

In this chapter we'll discuss tables and relationships between tables. These issues are fundamental database design issues, but this isn't a tutorial on the art database design, which is one of the most challenging tasks in computing, a task that is seldom done all that well. Our goal here is to familiarize you with some concepts and terminology that are essential for *navigating* a relational database—that is, moving from table to table to access related data, which we'll do in Chapter 11.

In this chapter, we'll cover:

- Creating and dropping tables

- Relationships among tables

- Primary and foreign keys

- Data (entity and referential) integrity

- Normalization and denormalization

Managing Tables

Tables are the fundamental components of a relational database. In fact, both data and relationships are stored simply as data in tables.

Tables (called *relations* in the relational model) are composed of *rows* (*tuples*, which rhymes with *couples*, in the relational model) and *columns* (*attributes* in the relational model). Each column represents a piece of information. For example, the LastName column in Northwind's Employees table represents the last name for each employee. A table must have one or more columns. In the Employees table, each row is an instance of an employee. A table can have zero or more rows.

Each column in a table is strongly typed, just like every variable in C#, but a difference (called *impedance*) exists between SQL data types and C# types. In Chapters 3 and 7 we described how SQL data types are mapped to .NET types to handle this difference.

Creating Tables

Creating your own tables to experiment with is an easy, and often convenient, thing to do. You can create a table in two ways:

- Using a visual tool that generates a CREATE TABLE statement

- Manually coding a CREATE TABLE statement

Creating a Table with SSMSE

Let's use SSMSE to create a table named test_Employees in the Northwind database, using some of the columns of the Employees table. Note that this table name is prefixed with test_ to distinguish it from the Employees table.

Try It Out: Creating a Table with SSMSE

SSMSE provides a GUI for creating tables. Let's create test_Employees with it.

1. In Object Explorer, expand the Northwind node, right-click the Tables node, and click New Table… .

2. In the window that opens, enter the information shown in Figure 10-1. We've specified three columns: EmployeeId of type int, LastName of type nvarchar(30), and BirthDate of type datetime. You can choose the data type by clicking a Data Type cell and picking it from the drop-down list. Note that the BirthDate column has Allow Nulls checked. This means that rows can be inserted without birth date values (in other words, you may not know the birth date, but you can still insert a row).

3. Click the Save icon on the toolbar. When prompted for a name for the table, enter test_Employees and then click OK (see Figure 10-2). Note that the definition window is now named Table – dbo.test_Employees.

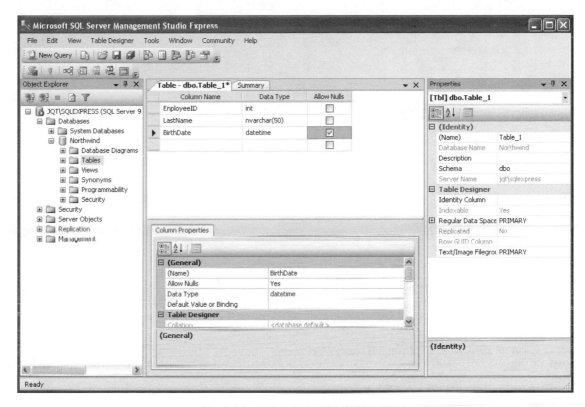

Figure 10-1. *Defining the test_Employees table*

Figure 10-2. *Creating the test_Employees table*

How It Works

SSMSE has created a new table. To verify that the table was created, expand the
test_Employees node in Object Explorer. It should appear as in Figure 10-3, with the
column names you specified.

Figure 10-3. *Checking the test_Employees table*

Creating a Table with SQL

Behind the scenes, SSMSE actually generated SQL to create test_Employees. The simplest form of the CREATE TABLE statement is:

```
CREATE TABLE tablename
    (
    column1 datatype1 nullspec1,
    column2 datatype2 nullspec2,
    ...,
    columnn datatypen nullspecn
    )
```

where tablename is the name of the table you want to create, column1 is the name of the first column, datatype1 is the data type of column1, and nullspec1 specifies whether the column should allow null values.

While most parts of this syntax are intuitive, notice that the null specifications for columns are either NULL or NOT NULL. And, though not apparent from the syntax, table names must be unique within *schemas* (e.g., dbo is the schema in Northwind to which all the tables we're working with belong) within a database.

Note Actually, table names in SQL Server are composed of three parts, and it's the combination that must be unique within a database. For simplicity we've avoided the issue by using unique table names. Further, though you can use mixed case for table and column names, and SQL Server accepts this as the spelling for these database objects, SQL references to database objects aren't case sensitive. For example, you can refer to table test_Employees as test_employees (or even Test_employeeS); this also applies to column names.

Try It Out: Creating a Table with SQL

SSMSE can be used to edit and submit SQL, so let's submit a CREATE TABLE statement with it. To create a table similar to the one you saw in the previous section using the CREATE TABLE statement, use the following SQL to create a test_Employees2 table.

```
create table test_Employees2
    (
    EmployeeID int          not null,
    LastName   nvarchar(50) not null,
    BirthDate  datetime     null
    )
```

1. Click the Northwind node in Object Explorer. This makes Northwind the context in which you'll execute your SQL. Click New Query. An edit window opens as in Figure 10-4.

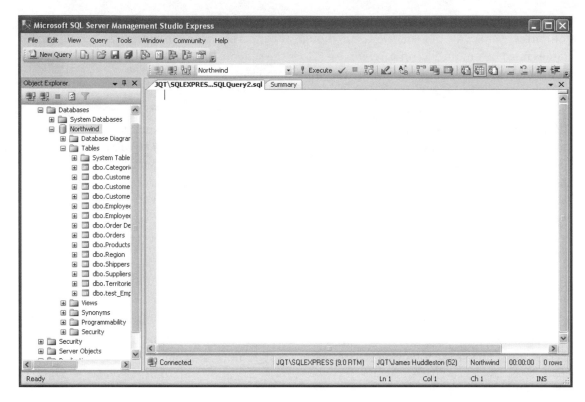

Figure 10-4. *SQL edit window*

2. Enter the CREATE TABLE statement for test_Employees2 and click Execute. The screen should appear as in Figure 10-5.

Note In yet another bit of confusing database terminology, you used New Query to submit a statement! Despite its name, the SQL edit window can handle both queries and statements.

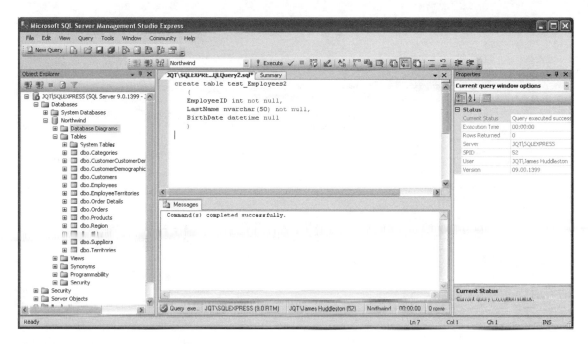

Figure 10-5. *Creating test_Employees2*

How It Works

The CREATE TABLE statement was submitted and executed without error. To check this, right-click the Tables node under Northwind in Object Explorer and click Refresh. You'll see the new table, as in Figure 10-6.

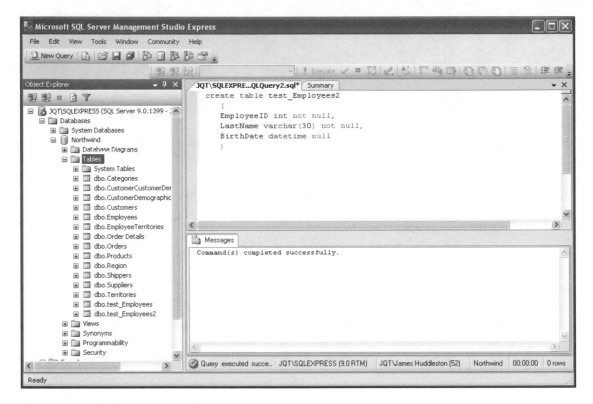

Figure 10-6. *Checking test_Employees2*

Dropping Tables

Dropping a table from a database completely removes its definition and data. You can drop a table with SSMSE's Object Explorer by right-clicking the table and selecting Delete. You can also drop a table with the SQL DROP TABLE statement:

```
DROP TABLE tablename
```

where tablename is the name of the table to drop.

Dropping a Table with SSMSE

Let's use SSMSE to drop test_Employees2.

Try It Out: Dropping a Table with SSMSE

As stated earlier, you can use Object Explorer to drop tables.

1. In Object Explorer, right-click the node for `test_Employees2` and click Delete.

2. In the Delete Object (a table is just one kind of database object) window, click OK. See Figure 10-7. Notice that the table immediately disappears from Object Explorer.

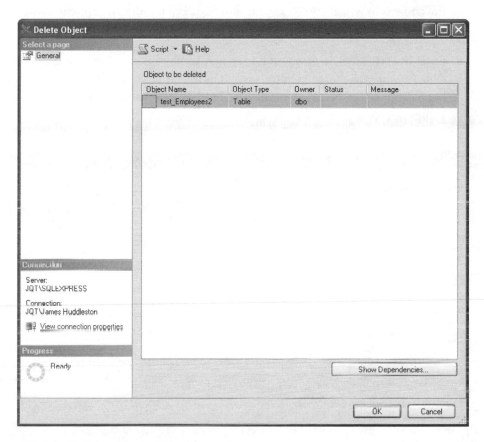

Figure 10-7. *Dropping test_Employees2*

How It Works

SSMSE transparently generated and submitted a SQL `DELETE TABLE` statement.

Dropping a Table with SQL

Let's use a SQL `DROP TABLE` statement to drop `test_Employees`.

Try It Out: Dropping a Table with SQL

We'll once again use the SSMSE SQL edit window.

1. If you don't have the edit window open in the Northwind context, click the North-wind node in Object Explorer and then click New Query. Northwind should still be the context in which you'll execute your SQL, but if it doesn't appear in the edit window status bar, click New Query.

2. Enter the DROP TABLE statement for test_Employees as shown in Figure 10-8 and click Execute. The screen should appear as in Figure 10-8. Note that although it's been dropped, test_Employees remains in Object Explorer until you refresh the Tables node.

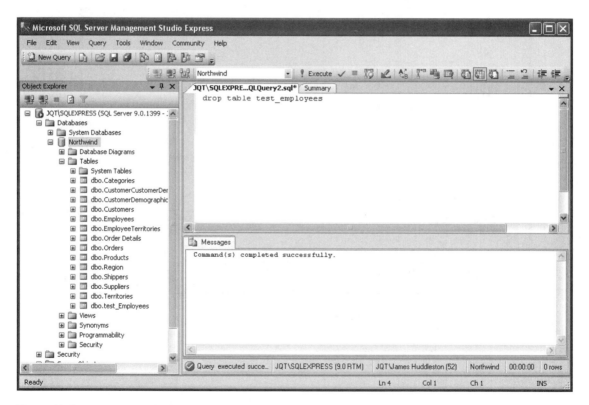

Figure 10-8. *Dropping test_Employees*

3. Right-click the Tables node under Northwind in Object Explorer and click Refresh. You'll see the new table, as in Figure 10-8.

How It Works

The DROP TABLE statement was submitted and executed without error.

Relationships Between Tables

Different tables quite often contain related data. For example, one sales rep in a company may take many orders, which were placed by many customers. The products ordered may come from different suppliers, and chances are that each supplier can supply more than one product. All of these relationships exist in the Northwind database, and can be classified as:

One-to-One (1:1): For each row in Table A there is at most only one related row in Table B, and vice versa. This relationship is typically used to separate data by frequency of use, to optimally organize data physically. There are no 1:1 table relationships in the Northwind database, but we'll create one ourselves later, in "Try It Out: Defining a Table with a Foreign Key."

One-to-Many (1:M): For each row in Table A there are zero or more related rows in Table B, but for each row in Table B there is at most one row in Table A. This is a commonly found relationship. An example in Northwind is given in Figure 10-9, where many orders can belong to one customer. Here, Customers is referred to as the "parent" table and Orders as the "child" table in the relationship.

Figure 10-9. *A one-to-many relationship*

Many-to-Many (M:M): For each row in Table A there are zero or more related rows in Table B, and vice versa (see Figure 10-10). This is implemented by using a third table (often referred to as a *junction table*) that serves as the path between the related tables. Again, this is a very commonly found relationship. An example in Northwind is given in Figure 10-10, where an order can have many products and a product can belong to many orders. The Order Details table not only represents the M:M relationship but also contains data about each particular order-product combination.

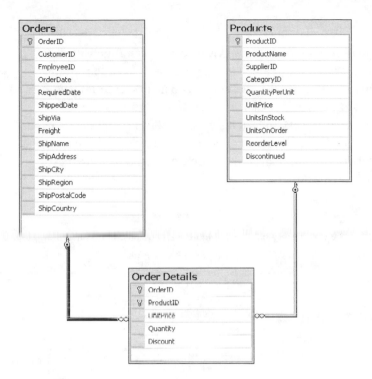

Figure 10-10. *A many-to-many relationship*

Note Though relationships among tables are extremely important, the term *relational database* has nothing to do with this. Relational databases are (to varying extents) based on the *relational model of data* invented by Dr. Edgar F. (Ted) Codd at IBM in the 1970s. Codd based his model on the mathematical (set-theoretic) concept of a *relation*. Relations are sets of tuples that can be manipulated with a well-defined— and well-behaved—set of mathematical operations, in fact, two sets, *relational algebra* and *relational calculus*. You don't have to know or understand the mathematics to work with relational databases, but if you hear it said that a database is relational because it "relates data" you'll know that whoever said it doesn't understand relational databases.

Understanding Keys

Relationships are represented by data in tables. To establish a relationship between two tables, you need to have data in one table that enables you to find a row or rows in another table. That's where *keys* come in, specifically *primary* and *foreign* keys.

Primary Keys

A *primary key* is a column or combination of columns whose values uniquely identify rows in a table. No column of a primary key can be null. Let's take a closer look at the Employees table in the Northwind database (see Figure 10-11). The first column is EmployeeID. It's marked as PK (primary key) and not null. EmployeeID uniquely identifies each employee (i.e., each row in Employees). In fact, it's the only column that does so and it doesn't need to be combined with any other columns to do it. For example, the LastName column, even though it's not null, can't be the primary key since more than one employee could have the same last name.

■**Note** The Order Details table has a *composite* (composed of more than one column) primary key, because two columns, OrderID and ProductID, are required to uniquely identify each row.

Figure 10-11. *The primary key of Employees*

Foreign Keys

A *foreign key* is a column or combination of columns (i.e., it can be composite) that matches the primary key (or, in most DBMSs, including SQL Server, any unique key) of a table, which is typically another table but may be the same table. For example, in

Figure 10-11 the ReportsTo column is marked FK, since it's a foreign key to the Employees table itself, representing the relationship of what employees work for what other employees.

Figure 10-10 is a classic example of how foreign keys affect relationships. The primary key of Order Details is the composite of OrderID and ProductID, the primary keys of Orders and Products, respectively. So, Order Details can be considered to be on the "many" end of a 1:M relationship with Orders and also a separate 1:M relationship with Products. Since each row in Order Details represents a unique combination of an order and a product, each row connects a row in Orders with a row in Products to embody the M:M relationship between Orders and Products.

Data Integrity

Data integrity means that data values in a database are correct and consistent. There are two aspects to data integrity: *entity integrity* and *referential integrity*.

Entity Integrity

We mentioned earlier in the section "Primary Keys" that no part of a primary key can be null. This is to guarantee that primary key values exist for all rows. The requirement that primary key values exist and that they be unique is known as *entity integrity*. To establish entity integrity, we need to define primary keys so that the DBMS can enforce their uniqueness. When we created the test_Employees table earlier, we didn't define its primary key, so we didn't provide for entity integrity.

Try It Out: Defining a Table with a Primary Key

Since we've already dropped test_Employees, let's re-create it, this time with a primary key. There are several ways to do this. We'll use the simplest way and do it with SQL. Just add the keywords primary key to the EmployeeID column definition:

```
create table test_Employees
  (
  EmployeeID int        not null primary key,
  LastName   nvarchar(50) not null,
  BirthDate  datetime     null
  )
```

1. Click the Northwind node in Object Explorer. This makes Northwind the context in which you'll execute your SQL. Click New Query. Enter the SQL as in Figure 10-12, then click Execute.

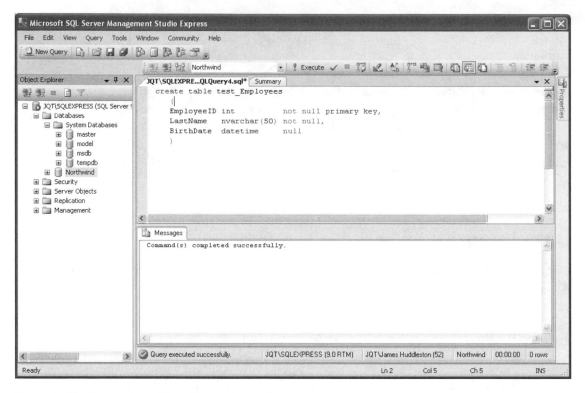

Figure 10-12. *Creating a table with a primary key*

How It Works

Since the CREATE TABLE statement specified that EmployeeID is a primary key, SQL Server created test_Employees with a primary key. Refresh the Northwind display in Object Explorer and expand the Columns node for test_Employees. You'll find that EmployeeID is now marked PK, as in Figure 10-13.

Figure 10-13. *EmployeeID is the primary key of test_Employees.*

Referential Integrity

Once a relationship is defined between tables with foreign keys, the key data must be managed to maintain the correct relationships, that is, to enforce *referential integrity* (RI). RI requires that all foreign key values in a child table either match primary key values in a parent table or (if permitted) be null. This is also known as satisfying a *foreign key constraint.*

As with primary keys, SQL Server doesn't know about foreign keys unless they are explicitly defined.

Try It Out: Defining a Table with a Foreign Key

Since we've just defined test_Employees, let's define another table to reference it with a foreign key. There are several ways to do this. We'll do it expediently with the following SQL:

```
create table test_EmployeesResumes
  (
  EmployeeID int  not null primary key
                    references test_employees,
  Resume    text null
  )
```

1. Click the Northwind node in Object Explorer. This makes Northwind the context in which you'll execute your SQL. Click New Query. Enter the SQL as in
   Figure 10-14, then click Execute.

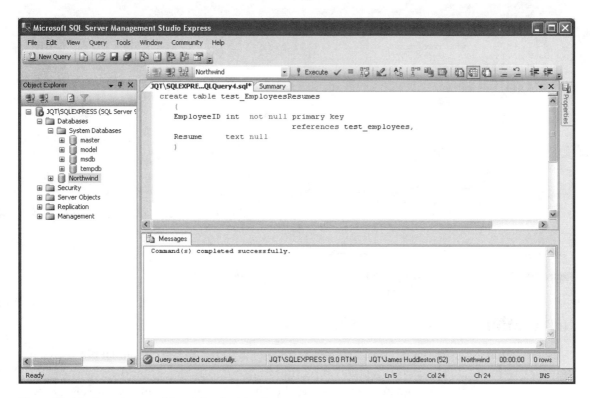

Figure 10-14. *Creating a table with a foreign key*

How It Works

In addition to specifying that EmployeeID is the primary key, the CREATE TABLE statement
specified that EmployeeID *references* test_Employees, so SQL Server created test_
EmployeesResumes with a primary key that is also a foreign key to the primary key of
test_Employees. Refresh the Northwind display in Object Explorer and expand the
Columns node for test_Employees. You'll find that EmployeeID is marked PK, FK, as
in Figure 10-15.

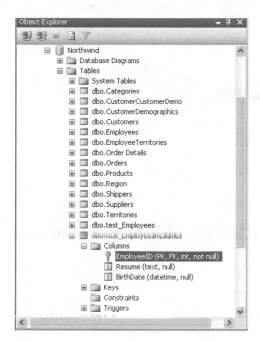

Figure 10-15. *EmployeeID is a foreign key to test_Employees.*

Testing Entity and Referential Integrity

Now that you've established a foreign key relationship from test_EmployeesResumes to test_Employees, let's see how SQL Server enforces both entity and referential integrity.

Try It Out: Testing Entity Integrity

Essentially, entity integrity forbids duplicate rows, that is, rows with the same primary key. Let's see how SSE handles this:

1. In Object Explorer, right-click test_Employees and click Open Table. A window with a data grid should appear. Enter the data in Figure 10-16. Two rows are added as you type.

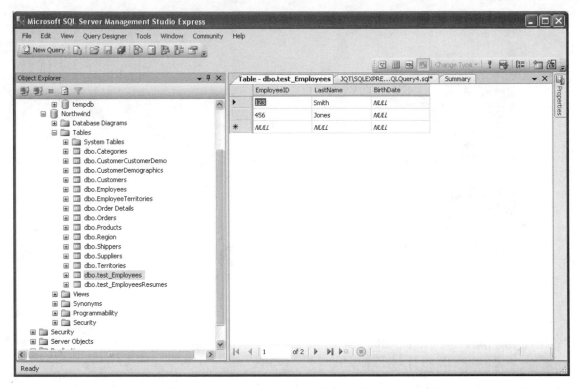

Figure 10-16. *Adding unique rows to test_Employees*

2. Now attempt to add a third row, with the same EmployeeID as the first row, as in Figure 10-17.

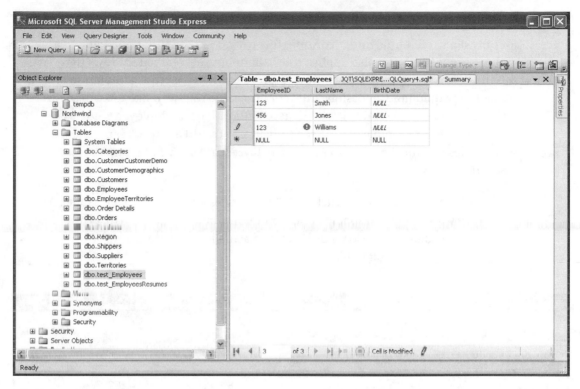

Figure 10-17. *Adding a duplicate row to test_Employees*

A message box appears, as in Figure 10-18.

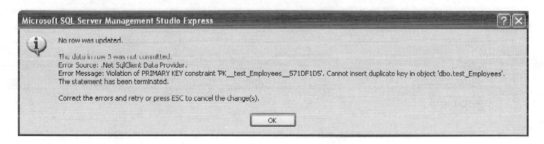

Figure 10-18. *Enforcing entity integrity*

How It Works

Since you defined EmployeeID as the primary key of test_Employees, SQL Server prevents insertion of rows with duplicate key values, and SSMSE displays a message box informing you of the attempt to violate entity integrity.

Try It Out: Testing Referential Integrity

Not only does referential integrity forbid inserting child rows that don't match a unique parent key, but it also applies rules about how to treat parent rows that have child rows. Let's add a child row in test_EmployeesResumes, a crude simulation of a table that would hold a possibly large column value that we'd like to keep separate from the test_Employees table itself but associate with each employee who has a resume. This is an example of a 1:1 relationship. Let's add a row to test_EmployeesResumes for the first row in test_Employees and see what it implies for referential integrity.

1. In Object Explorer, right-click test_EmployeesResumes and click Open Table. A window with a data grid should appear. Enter the data in Figure 10-19. (The Resume column allows nulls, so we don't need to actually enter a resume.) One row is added when you hit Enter.

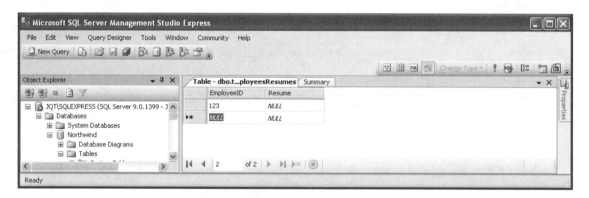

Figure 10-19. *Adding a row to test_EmployeeResumes*

2. Now go back to the test_Employees grid (or reopen it if it's closed) and try to delete the first row by right-clicking in it and selecting Delete. A message box will appear as in Figure 10-20.

3. Try to delete the second row by right-clicking in it and selecting Delete. This deletion works.

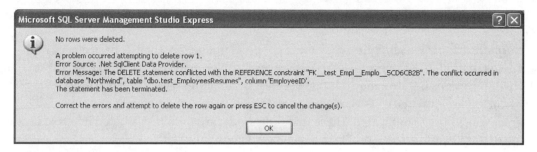

Figure 10-20. *Attempting to delete a parent row with children*

How It Works

You added a row to `test_EmployeesResumes` whose foreign key matches the primary key of the first row in `test_Employees`. Since you defined a foreign key constraint and didn't specify what to do when a parent row is deleted, when you attempt to delete a parent row that has a child, SQL Server by default takes `NO ACTION` and prevents the deletion.

You can specify that parent deletions `CASCADE`, causing all child rows to be deleted. We don't cover the syntax here, but be aware that the "rules" for what happens when deleting rows that participate in foreign key relationships are part of the table definition for child tables. You need to know what rule the table's creator used, so you can understand the implications of deleting parents.

Note SQL Server provides for four referential integrity constraints for both deletes of parent rows and updates of foreign keys: `NO ACTION`, `CASCADE`, `SET NULL`, and `SET DEFAULT`. See BOL for details.

Since there was no child row in `test_EmployeesResumes` for the second row in `test_Employees`, there was no referential integrity issue in deleting it, regardless of the referential integrity constraint defined.

Note We've talked about the "first" and "second" rows of `test_Employees`, because it was convenient to do so, but it's not really precise. Rows in tables have no definite order. To be precise, when referring to the "first" row, we should have said "the `test_Employees` row with primary key value 123," since the only way to uniquely identify any row in a table is by its primary key value, not by its position in the table.

Normalization

Normalization is a technique for avoiding potential update anomalies, basically by minimizing redundant data in a logical database design. Normalized designs are in a sense "better" designs because they (ideally) keep each data item in only one place. Normalized database designs usually reduce update processing costs but can make query processing more complicated. These trade-offs must be carefully evaluated in terms of the required performance profile of a database. Often, a database design needs to be *denormalized* to adequately meet operational needs.

Normalizing a logical database design involves a set of formal processes to separate the data into multiple, related tables. The result of each process is referred to as a *normal form*. Five normal forms have been identified in theory, but most of the time third normal form (3NF) is as far as one needs to go in practice. To be in 3NF, a *relation* (the formal term for what SQL calls a table and the precise concept on which the mathematical theory of normalization rests) must already be in second normal form (2NF), and 2NF requires a relation to be in first normal form (1NF). Let's look briefly at what these normal forms mean.

First normal form (1NF) means that all column values are *scalar*, in other words, they have a single value that can't be further decomposed in terms of the data model. For example, although individual characters of a string can be accessed through a procedure that decomposes the string, only the full string is accessible *by name* in SQL, so, as far as the data model is concerned, they aren't part of the model. Likewise, in a table with a manager column and a column containing a list of employees who work for a given manager, the manager and the list would be accessible by name but the individual employees in the list wouldn't be. All relations—and SQL tables— are by definition in 1NF since the lowest level of accessibility (known as the table's *granularity*) is the column level, and column values are scalars in SQL.

Second normal form (2NF) requires that *attributes* (the formal term for SQL columns) that aren't parts of keys be *functionally dependent* on a key that uniquely identifies them. Functional dependence basically means that for a given key value only one value exists in a table for a column or set of columns. For example, if a table contained employees and their titles, and more than one employee could have the same title (very likely), a key that uniquely identified employees wouldn't uniquely identify titles, so the titles wouldn't be functionally dependent on a key of the table. To put the table into 2NF, you'd create a separate table for titles—with its own unique key—and replace the title in the original table with a foreign key to the new table. Note how this reduces data redundancy. The titles themselves now appear only once in the database. Only their keys appear in other tables, and key data isn't considered redundant (though, of course, it requires columns in other tables and data storage).

Third normal form (3NF) extends the concept of functional dependence to *full functional dependence*. Essentially, this means that all nonkey columns in a table are uniquely identified by the whole, not just part of, the primary key. For example, if you revised our hypothetical 1NF managers-employees table to have three columns (managername, employeeid, and employeename) instead of two, and you defined the composite primary key as managername + employeeid, the table would be in 2NF (since employeename, the nonkey column, is dependent on the primary key), but it wouldn't be in 3NF since employeename is uniquely identified by part of the primary key (employeeid). Creating a separate table for employees and removing employeename from managers-employees would put the table into 3NF. Note that even though this table is now normalized to 3NF, the database design is still not as normalized as it should be. Creating another table for managers, using an ID shorter than the manager's name, though not required for normalization here, is definitely a better approach that would probably be advisable for a real-world database.

Database design (even of small databases) is an art more than a science, and applying normalization wisely is always important. On the other hand, normalization inherently increases the number of tables and therefore the number of operations (called *joins*) required to retrieve data. *Denormalizing* one or more tables, by intentionally providing redundant data to reduce the number or complexity of joins to get quicker query response times, may be necessary. With either normalization or denormalization, the goal is to control redundancy so that the database design adequately (and ideally, optimally) supports the actual use of the database.

Summary

In this chapter you furthered your understanding of relational databases, particularly how data in tables represents relationships between tables. Among the things we covered were:

- How to create and drop tables

- The different types of relationships between tables

- What primary keys and foreign keys are

- What entity and referential integrity mean and how they are defined and enforced

- What normalization and denormalization mean

In the next chapter we'll revisit SQL queries and experiment with more advanced query facilities, including how to combine data from multiple tables.

■ ■ ■

Learning More About Queries

In Chapter 3, you learned about queries and the INSERT, UPDATE, and DELETE statements. In Chapter 10, you learned how to create tables and define relationships between them. Now you'll look at more SQL for coding queries. SQL has a wide variety of functions and constructs for querying, so it's impossible to cover all permutations of them in one chapter. You'll look at the more frequently used ones.

In this chapter, we'll cover:

- The DISTINCT keyword

- Subqueries

- The GROUP BY clause

- Aggregate functions

- Datetime functions

- CASE expressions

- Joins

As in Chapter 10, we'll use SSMSE to submit SQL.

More SQL Query Syntax

It's important for any serious database programmer to master SQL, so let's expand your knowledge of SQL query syntax. For the rest of this chapter, you'll query the Northwind database in a variety of ways.

DISTINCT

You use the DISTINCT keyword as a query to exclude duplicate values from the result set. You can use it only once in the select list of a query. If multiple columns are selected, DISTINCT eliminates rows where the combination of all the column values is identical.

Try It Out: Querying Using DISTINCT

Say you want to find a discrete list of ProductIDs against which orders have been placed. DISTINCT handles this type of query:

1. Open a SQL edit window in SSMSE (remember to make Northwind your query context). Enter the following query and click Execute:

```
select
    productid
from
    [order details]
```

2. All the product IDs that have an order placed against them are returned (see Figure 11-1). Note that there are 2,155 rows in the result set.

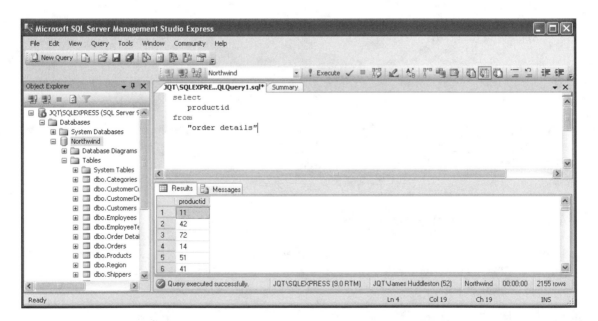

Figure 11-1. *Products with orders*

3. Now change the query to include DISTINCT:

```
select distinct
    productid
from
    [order details]
```

4. The product IDs are returned but without duplicates (see Figure 11-2). There are 77 rows in the result set.

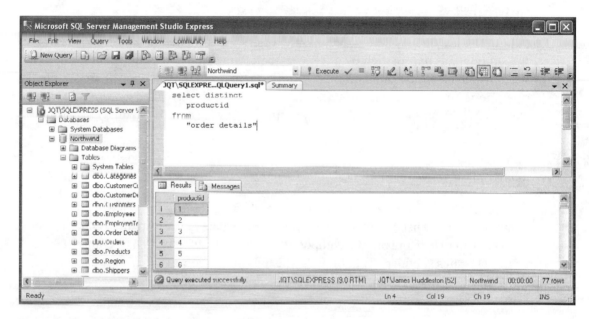

Figure 11-2. *Products with orders, without duplicates*

How It Works

DISTINCT eliminates duplicate rows from the result set. It also seems to have sorted the rows, and it probably did, since it internally sorts them to eliminate duplicates. But, if you absolutely must rely on rows being sorted, use an ORDER BY clause, to be sure, as in:

```
select distinct
    productid
from
    [order details]
order by
    productid
```

Notice that the table name is enclosed in double quotes. This is necessary because the name has an embedded blank.

■**Note** Standard SQL uses double quotes to enclose names with embedded blanks (or other special characters). In SQL Server, you can also use brackets ([ ]).

Subqueries

Subqueries are queries embedded in other queries or statements that use the result of the subquery as part of their own retrieval logic. You can use subqueries in many contexts to create sophisticated queries. If you keep in mind that all queries are simply operations on tables that produce a single table (a result set, called a *derived table* in standard SQL), subqueries will be easy to understand. Let's look at some of their typical uses.

IN

The IN operator (the IN predicate in standard SQL) determines if the value of a specific column matches a list of values. The list must be of a data type compatible with the column to be matched and may be composed of either literals separated by commas or the result set from a subquery, but not both. The following is some example syntax:

```
SELECT
    column1, column2, ..., columnN
FROM
    table1
WHERE
    columnX IN (1, 10, 14)
```

Here, the list contains three integer literals. The matching column (columnX, which is some column in the table but not necessarily one in the select list) must be of a numeric data type for this list to be compatible. Only the rows in table1 whose columnX value is 1, 10, or 14 will be selected:

```
SELECT
    column1, column2, ..., columnN
FROM
    table1
```

```
WHERE
  columnX IN
    (
    SELECT
      column1
    FROM
      table2
    )
```

This query accomplishes much the same result as the first, but instead of a list of literals, it uses the values from a column in another table to populate the list. If column1 of table2 had only the values 1, 10, and 14, this would have the same effect as the first query. Of course, if other values occurred in table2, they would also occur in the list, and the outer query probably wouldn't produce the same result set as the first query. (A subquery is sometimes referred to as an *inner query*, and the query that contains it is referred to as an *outer query*.)

You have many, many variations on how you can code subqueries. Since they *are* queries, all the clauses and other keywords available for queries can be used in them. Our goal here is to simply show the straightforward pattern they follow and, in this case, to demonstrate how you can use them to replace a list of literals.

Try It Out: Using the IN Predicate

Now let's look more closely at the IN predicate itself. For example, you may want to get a list of all orders entered by employees with IDs of 1 and 6:

1. Enter the following query into SSMSE and execute it. You should see the results shown in Figure 11-3. Scroll down, and you'll see that only rows where EmployeeID equals 1 or 6 are selected:

```
select
  *
from
  orders
where
  employeeid in (1, 6)
order by
  employeeid
```

■**Tip** Recall that SELECT * is actually bad practice in real-world programming. Best practice is to specify explicitly the columns to select. We'll use SELECT * for simplicity, but you should use a select list in production applications.

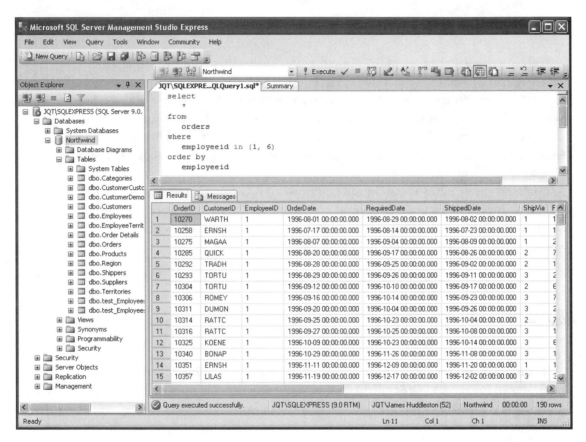

Figure 11-3. *Selecting with the IN predicate*

How It Works

Here, you use a list of literal values with the IN operator. The WHERE clause specifies that only rows where EmployeeID equals either 1 or 6 should be retrieved:

```
where
    employeeid in (1, 6)
```

Try It Out: Using the NOT IN Predicate

The keyword NOT, used in conjunction with IN, selects rows that don't match any value in a list. Let's say you need to get a list of all orders that have been entered by employees other than the ones with IDs of 1 or 6:

1. Enter the following query into SSMSE and execute it. You should see the results shown in Figure 11-4:

```
select
    *
from
    orders
where
    employeeid not in (1, 6)
order by
    employeeid
```

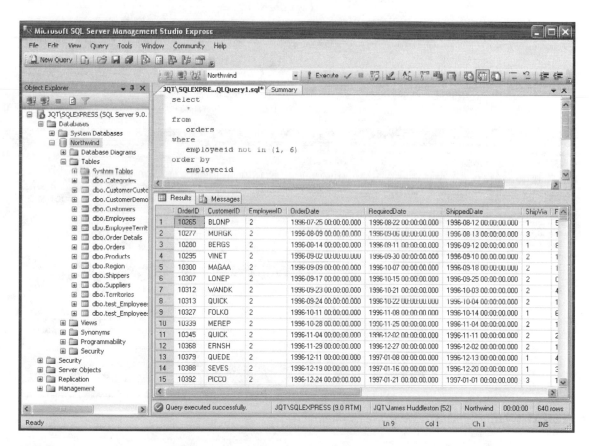

Figure 11-4. *Selecting with the NOT IN predicate*

How It Works

Here, you use the same list of literal values with the `IN` predicate. The `WHERE` clause specifies that only rows where `EmployeeID` doesn't equal either 1 or 6 should be retrieved:

```
where
    employeeid not in (1, 6)
```

Try It Out: Using a Function with the IN Predicate

You can use functions along with the `IN` predicate. For example, the `SUBSTRING` function
returns a portion of a string. You could use this instead of the `LIKE` predicate if you need
to find all the employees whose last name begins with a *D* or an *S*:

1. Enter the following query into SSMSE and execute it. You should see the results
   shown in Figure 11-5:

```
select
    *
from
    employees
where
    substring(lastname, 1, 1) in ('D', 'S')select
```

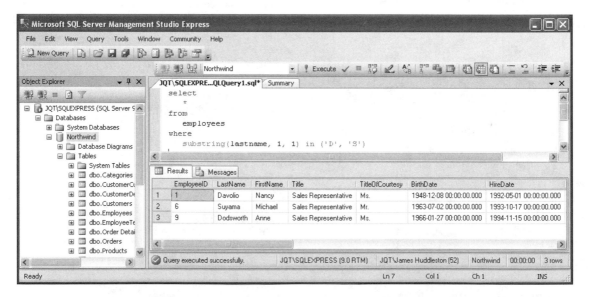

Figure 11-5. *Using a function with the IN predicate*

How It Works

Here, you use a list of literal values with the IN predicate, but instead of matching a column against them, you match the result of a function applied against a column value. The WHERE clause specifies that only rows where the first character of the employee's last name is either *D* or *S* should be retrieved:

```
where
   substring(lastname, 1, 1) in ('D', 'S')
```

In the SUBSTRING function, the first argument specifies the character data type column (or other string expression) from which you want to extract a substring. The second argument specifies the position where you want to begin extracting the substring. In this case, by specifying 1, you start the extract at the first character. The third argument specifies the number of characters you want to extract. In this case, by specifying 1, you extract one character.

The net effect of this function is that, for each row in the table, the first character of the LastName column is extracted by the function. Then the substring is compared to the list. If it matches an entry in the list, the row is selected.

GROUP BY

The GROUP BY clause groups rows sharing common values for the purpose of calculating an aggregate. Often you'll want to generate reports from the database with summary figures for a particular column or set of columns. For example, you may want to find out the total quantity for each order from the Order Details table.

Try It Out: Using the GROUP BY Clause

The Order Details table contains the list of products for each order and the quantity of each product ordered. You need to total the quantity of all products in each order:

1. Enter the following query into SSMSE and execute it. You should see the results shown in Figure 11-6:

```
select
   orderid        'Order ID',
   sum(quantity) 'Total Quantity Ordered'
from
   "order details"
group by
   orderid
```

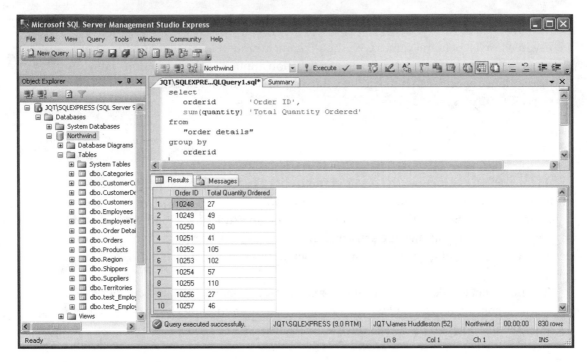

Figure 11-6. *Using ORDER BY to aggregate*

■ **Tip** The literals Order ID and Total Quantity Ordered provide *aliases* for the columns. (In SQL Server, you can use brackets instead of the standard SQL single quotes.) Neither alias is required, but when using functions, it's typical to specify an alias. Otherwise, the column heading would either have been blank (or sum(quantity), depending on your RDBMS). We added the alias for OrderID to demonstrate how you can specify explicit column names in SQL. This is better practice than relying on whatever spelling may automatically be used based on the column name in the database or the query.

How It Works

You use the SUM function to total the Quantity column of the Order Details table by OrderID. The alias provides a custom column header for the total:

```
sum(quantity) 'Total Quantity Ordered'
```

Other Aggregates

SQL has several built-in functions that aggregate the values of a column. Aggregate functions return a single value. For example, you can use the aggregate functions to calculate the total number or average value of orders placed. You can find the order with the least value or the most expensive order. Aggregate functions, as their name indicates, work on a set of records and then calculate the appropriate aggregated value. SUM, MIN, MAX, AVG, and COUNT are frequently used aggregate functions.

Try It Out: Using the MIN, MAX, and AVG Functions

Let's find the minimum, maximum, and average number of items of each product from the Order Details table:

1. Enter the following query into SSMSE and execute it. You should see the results shown in Figure 11-7.

```
select
    productid      'Product ID',
    min(quantity) 'Minimum',
    max(quantity) 'Maximum',
    avg(quantity) 'Average'
from
    "order details"
group by
    productid
order by
    productid
```

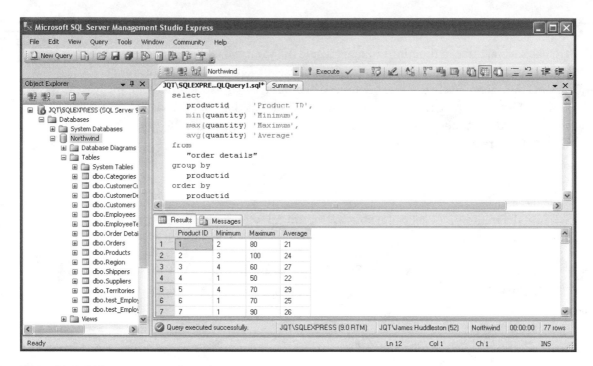

Figure 11-7. *Using aggregate functions*

How It Works

You use the MIN and MAX functions to find the minimum and maximum values, and you use the AVG function to calculate the average value:

```
min(quantity) 'Minimum',
max(quantity) 'Maximum',
avg(quantity) 'Average'
```

Since you want the results listed by product, you use the GROUP BY clause. From the result set, you see that product 1 has a minimum order quantity of 2, a maximum order quantity of 80, and an average order quantity of 21.

■Note You use an ORDER BY clause to assure the results are in product ID sequence. As with DISTINCT, some DBMSs would have inferred this sequence from the GROUP BY clause. But, in general, unless you explicitly use ORDER BY, you can't predict the sequence of the rows in a result set.

Datetime Functions

Although the SQL standard defines a DATETIME data type and its components YEAR, MONTH, DAY, HOUR, MINUTE, and SECOND, it doesn't dictate how a DBMS makes this data available. Each DBMS offers a suite of functions that extract parts of DATETIMEs. Let's look at some examples of T-SQL datetime functions.

Try It Out: Using Transact-SQL Date and Time Functions

Follow these steps to practice with Transact-SQL date and time functions:

1. Enter the following query into SSMSE and execute it. You should see the results shown in Figure 11-8:

```
select
    current_timestamp          'standard datetime',
    getdate()                  'Transact-SQL datetime',
    datepart(year, getdate())  'datepart year',
    year(getdate())            'year function',
    datepart(hour, getdate())  'hour'
```

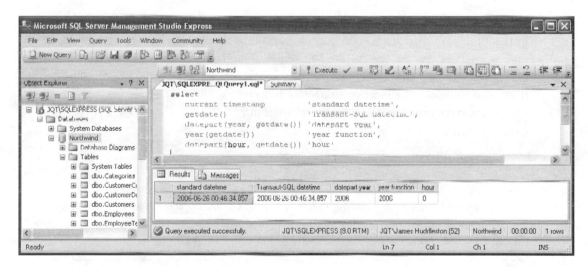

Figure 11-8. *Using date and time functions*

How It Works

You use a nonstandard version of a query, omitting the FROM clause, to display the current date and time and individual parts of them. The first two columns in the select list give the complete date and time:

```
current_timestamp          'standard datetime',
getdate()                  'Transact-SQL datetime',
```

The first line uses the CURRENT_TIMESTAMP value function of standard SQL; the second uses the GETDATE function of T-SQL. They're equivalent in effect, both returning the complete current date and time. (Note that the output format is specific to each DBMS.)

The next two lines each provide the current year. The first uses the T-SQL DATEPART function; the second uses the T-SQL YEAR function. Both take a datetime argument and return the integer year. The DATEPART function's first argument specifies what part of a datetime to extract. Note that T-SQL doesn't provide a date specifier for extracting a complete date, and it doesn't have a separate DATE function:

```
datepart(year, getdate()) 'datepart year',
year(getdate())           'year function',
```

The final line gets the current hour. You must use the T-SQL DATEPART function here, since no HOUR function is analogous to the YEAR function. Note that T-SQL doesn't provide a time specifier for extracting a complete time, and it doesn't have a separate TIME function:

```
datepart(hour, getdate()) 'hour'
```

You can format dates and times and alternative functions for extracting and converting them in various ways. You can also add, subtract, increment, and decrement dates and times. How this is done is DBMS-specific, though all DBMSs comply to a reasonable extent with the SQL standard in how they do it. Whatever DBMS you use, you'll find that dates and times are the most complicated data types to use. But, in all cases, you'll find that functions (sometimes a richer set of them than in T-SQL) are the basic tools for working with dates and times.

Tip When providing date and time input, character string values are typically expected; for example, 6/28/2004 would be the appropriate way to specify the value for a column holding the current date from the example. However, DBMSs store datetimes in system-specific encodings. When you use date and time data, read the SQL manual for your database carefully to see how to best handle it.

CASE Expressions

The CASE expression allows an alternative value to be displayed depending on the value of a column. For example, a CASE expression can provide *Texas* in a result set for rows that have the value *TX* in the state column. Let's take a look at the syntax of the CASE expression. It has two different forms: the simple CASE and the searched CASE.

Simple CASE Expressions

This is the simple CASE syntax, where the ELSE part is optional:

```
CASE <case operand>
    WHEN <when operand> THEN
        <when result>
    ELSE
        <else result>
END
```

The CASE keyword is followed by a column name or an expression that's to be tested against the operand (a scalar value) following the WHEN keyword. If <case operand> has the same value as <when operand>, <when result> is used; otherwise, <else result> is used as the selection list value.

Try It Out: Using a Simple CASE Expression

Let's use a simple CASE expression:

1. Enter the following query into SSMSE and execute it. You should see the results shown in Figure 11-9:

```
select distinct
    year(orderdate) NumYear,
    case year(orderdate)
        when 1998 then
            'Last year'
        else
            'Prior year'
    end LabYear
from
    orders
```

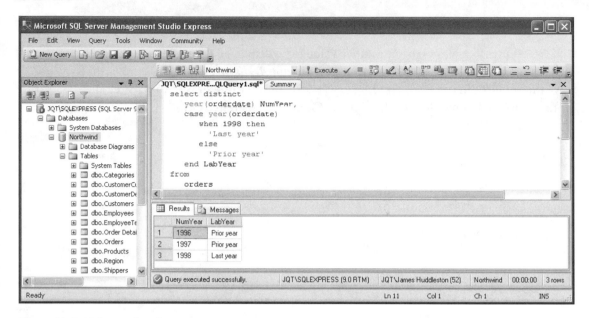

Figure 11-9. *Using a simple CASE expression*

How It Works

You simply label years as either *Last year* or *Prior year* depending on whether they were 1998 (the last year for orders in this version of the Northwind database) or earlier (in this database, none are later than 1998). The first two lines get a list of the distinct years (in the Orders table):

```
select distinct
    year(orderdate) NumYear,
```

Note that you specify an alias NumYear, but since it doesn't include blanks, you don't have to enclose it in single quotes (or brackets).

The next item in the select list (note that a CASE expression is used just like a column name or function call) is a simple CASE expression, where you provide the result of the YEAR function applied to the order date as the <case operand>, the numeric literal 1998 as the <when operand>, and two strings to label the last year and the prior year, depending on whether the year is 1998 (in other words, whether it matches the <when operand>):

```
    case year(orderdate)
        when 1998 then
            'Last year'
        else
            'Prior year'
    end LabYear
```

Note that since a CASE expression is merely another member of a select list, you can (and do) give it an alias, LabYear.

Try It Out: Using a More Complex Simple CASE Expression

Let's modify this CASE expression to get an idea of how flexible it can be:

1. Enter the following query into SSMSE and execute it. You should see the results shown in Figure 11-10:

```
select distinct
    year(orderdate) NumYear,
    case year(orderdate)
        when 1998 then
            str(year(orderdate))
        else
            case year(orderdate)
                when 1997 then
                    'Prior'
                else
                    'Earlier'
            end
    end LabYear
from
    orders
```

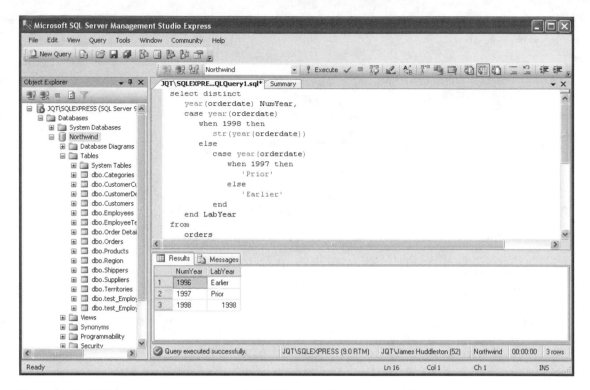

Figure 11-10. *Using a more complex simple CASE expression*

How It Works

You do a couple interesting things here. First, you change the label for the last year to the year itself rather than a string, showing that the <when operand> can be a data value (here, in fact, the result of a function applied to a column):

```
when 1998 then
    str(year(orderdate))
```

Note that you use the STR function to convert the integer returned by YEAR to a string, since you're planning to use strings for the alternative labels, and a CASE expression must return values of a single data type.

You then nest a CASE expression inside the original ELSE (they can also be nested in the WHEN part) to support labeling the other years separately. You label 1997 as *Prior* and all others as *Earlier*.

```
else
   case year(orderdate)
      when 1997 then
         'Prior'
      else
         'Earlier'
   end
```

Many other variations are possible. The simple CASE expression can be quite complex. Exploit it to achieve query results that would otherwise require a lot more work—for both you and the database! Now, let's examine the searched CASE.

Searched CASE Expressions

The following is the searched CASE syntax, where the ELSE part is optional:

```
CASE
   WHEN <search condition> THEN
      <when result>
   ELSE
      <else result>
END
```

Note the differences between the searched and simple CASEs. The searched CASE has no <case operand>, and the <when operand> is replaced by a <search condition>. These seemingly minor changes add an enormous amount of power.

Try It Out: Using a Searched CASE Expression

Let's modify the simple CASE example to demonstrate searched CASE:

1. Enter the following query into SSMSE and execute it. You should see the results shown in Figure 11-11:

```
select distinct
   year(orderdate) NumYear,
   case
      when
         year(orderdate) =
```

```
            (
            select
                max(year(orderdate))
            from
                orders
            )
        then
          'Last year'
        else
          'Prior year'
      end LabYear
    from
      orders
```

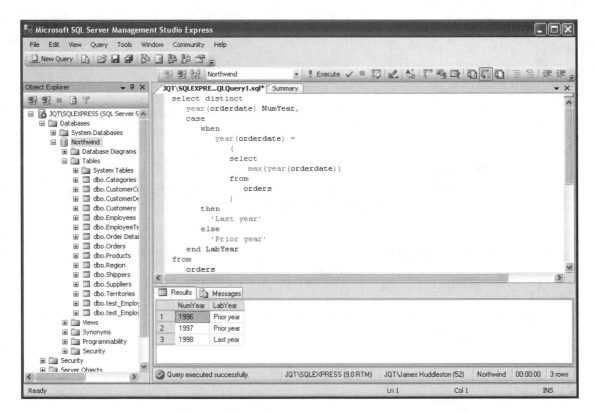

Figure 11-11. *Using a searched CASE expression*

How It Works

The original query, though it works, is severely limited in that it works correctly only if 1998 is really the last year for orders. You correct this flaw with a searched CASE. Now the query does the right thing whatever years are in the Orders table. You replace the numeric literal <when operand>, 1998, with a predicate (which can be just as complex as any predicate in a WHERE clause):

```
year(orderdate) =
   (
   select
      max(year(orderdate))
   from
      orders
   )
```

This predicate includes a subquery. Remember, subqueries are simply queries embedded in other queries. Here, one is embedded in a CASE expression rather than in an IN predicate (as demonstrated earlier in the chapter). The value returned by the subquery is the maximum year in the Orders table, so whenever you run the query, you'll get the correct last year—without ever having to know what it is.

Note Complex queries are a normal part of database applications. The more you learn about SQL, the better you'll be able to exploit its considerable power. All major DBMSs have query optimizers that can find efficient access paths for even complex queries. You should code whatever complexity you need, relying on the optimizer to do its job; however, even simple queries can sometimes be inefficient, depending on how they're coded. In addition to learning SQL, learn whatever tool your DBMS offers to analyze query access paths.

You've merely scratched the surface of the many, many facilities SQL offers for coding complex, highly sophisticated queries. Let's now look at the most important one.

Joins

Most queries require information from more than one table. A *join* is a relational operation that produces a table by retrieving data from two (not necessarily distinct) tables and matching their rows according to a *join specification.*

Different types of joins exist, which you'll look at individually, but keep in mind that every join is a *binary* operation—that is, one table is joined to another, which may be the same table, since tables can be joined to themselves. The join operation is a rich and somewhat complex topic. The next sections will cover the basics.

Inner Joins

An inner join is the most frequently used join. It returns only rows that satisfy the join specification. Although in theory any relational operator (such as > or <) can be used in the join specification, almost always the equality operator (=) is used. Joins using the equality operator are called *natural joins*.

The basic syntax for an inner join is as follows:

```
select
   <select list>
from
   left-table INNER JOIN right-table
   ON
   <join specification>
```

Notice that INNER JOIN is a binary operation, so it has two operands, left-table and right-table, which may be base tables or anything (for example, a table produced by a subquery or by another join) that can be queried. The ON keyword begins the join specification, which can contain anything that could be used in a WHERE clause.

Try It Out: Writing an Inner Join

Let's retrieve a list of orders, the IDs of the customers who placed them, and the last name of the employees who took them:

1. Enter the following query into SSMSE and execute it. You should see the results shown in Figure 11-12:

```
select
   orders.orderid,
   orders.customerid,
   employees.lastname
from
   orders inner join employees
   on
   orders.employeeid = employees.employeeid
```

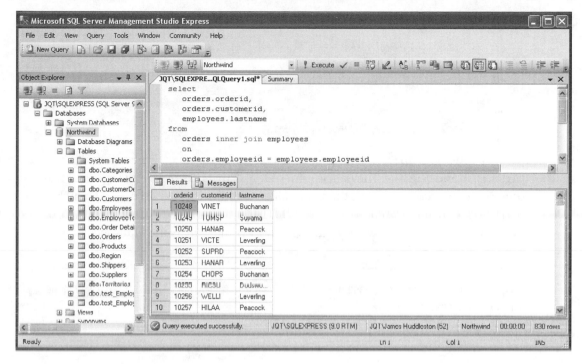

Figure 11-12. *Using INNER JOIN*

How It Works

Let's start with the select list:

```
select
    orders.orderid,
    orders.customerid,
    employees.lastname
```

Since you're selecting columns from two tables, you need to identify which table a
column comes from. You do this by prefixing the table name and a dot (.) to the column
name. This is known as *disambiguation,* or removing ambiguity so the database manager
knows which column to use. Though this has to be done only for columns that appear in
both tables, the best practice is to qualify all columns with their table names.

The following FROM clause specifies both the tables you're joining and the kind of join
you're using:

```
from
    orders inner join employees
    on
    orders.employeeid = employees.employeeid
```

It specifies an inner join of the Orders and Employees tables:

```
orders inner join employees
```

It also specifies the criteria for joining them:

```
on
orders.employeeid = employees.employeeid
```

The inner join on EmployeeID produces a table composed of three columns: OrderID, CustomerID, and LastName. The data is retrieved from rows in Orders and Employees where their EmployeeID columns have the same value. Any rows in Orders that don't match rows in Employees are ignored and vice versa. (This isn't the case here, but you'll see an example soon.) An inner join always produces only rows that satisfy the join specification.

Tip Columns used for joining don't have to appear in the select list. In fact, EmployeeID isn't in the select list of the example query.

Try It Out: Writing an Inner Join Using Correlation Names

Joins can be quite complicated. Let's revise this one to simplify things a bit:

1. Enter the following query into SSMSE and execute it. You should see the results shown in Figure 11-13:

```
select
    o.orderid,
    o.customerid,
    e.lastname
from
    orders o inner join employees e
    on
    o.employeeid = e.employeeid
```

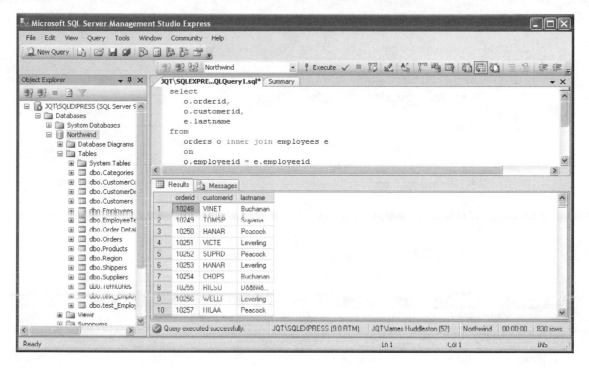

Figure 11-13. *Using correlation names*

How It Works

You simplify the table references by providing a *correlation name* for each table. (This is somewhat similar to providing column aliases, but correlation names are intended to be used as alternative names for tables. Column aliases are used more for labeling than for referencing columns.) You can now refer to Orders as o and to Employees as e. Correlation names can be as long as table names and can be in mixed case, but obviously the shorter they are, the easier they are to code.

You use the correlation names in both the select list

```
select
    o.orderid,
    o.customerid,
    e.lastname
```

and the ON clause:

```
on
o.employeeid = e.employeeid
```

Let's do another variation, so you can see how to use correlation names and aliases together.

Try It Out: Writing an Inner Join Using Correlation Names and Aliases

Let's do another variation, using correlation names and aliases together:

1. Enter the following query into SSMSE and execute it. You should see the results shown in Figure 11-14:

```
select
    o.orderid    OrderID,
    o.customerid CustomerID,
    e.lastname   Employee
from
    orders o join employees e
    on
    o.employeeid = e.employeeid
```

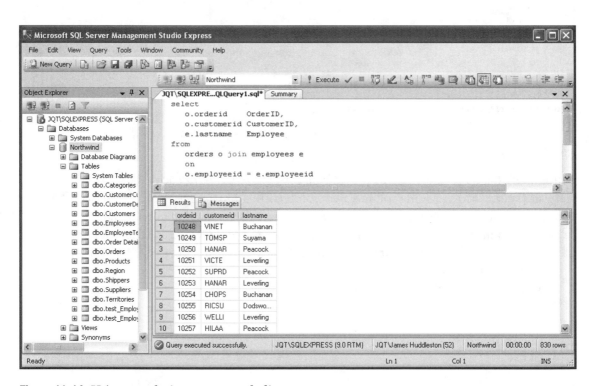

Figure 11-14. *Using correlation names and aliases*

How It Works

You simply add aliases for each column in the select list. This produces more customized column headings. It has no effect on the rest of the query:

```
select
    o.orderid   OrderID,
    o.customerid CustomerID,
    e.lastname   Employee
```

You also remove the keyword INNER from the join operator, just to prove that it's optional. It's better practice to use it, since it clearly distinguishes inner joins from *outer joins*, which you'll look at soon:

```
    orders o join employees e
```

In the next example of inner joins, you'll look at their original—but deprecated—syntax. You may see this frequently in legacy code, and it still works with most DBMSs, but the SQL standard may not allow it in the future.

Try It Out: Coding an Inner Join Using Original Syntax

To write an inner join using the original syntax:

1. Enter the following query into SSMSE and execute it. You should see the results shown in Figure 11-15:

   ```
   select
       o.orderid     OrderID,
       o.customerid CustomerID,
       e.lastname    Employee
   from
       orders o, employees e
       where
           o.employeeid = e.employeeid
   ```

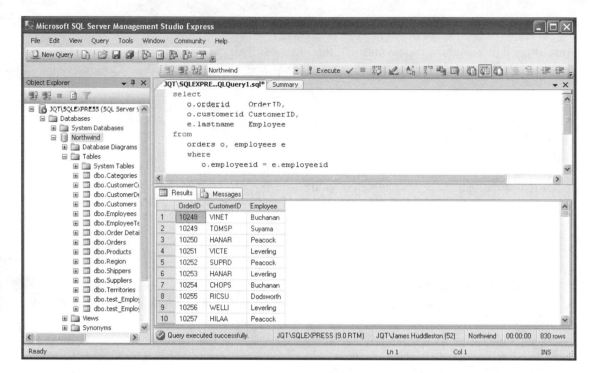

Figure 11-15. *Coding an INNER JOIN using original syntax*

How It Works

Note the differences in how you specify the join operator with a comma instead of INNER JOIN, and how you use a WHERE instead of an ON clause:

```
from
    orders o, employees e
    where
        o.employeeid = e.employeeid
```

This syntax was the only one available until the 1992 SQL standard. Any number of tables could be specified, separated by commas. All join predicates had to be specified in a single WHERE clause. Although you haven't seen an example, in the new syntax each join is a distinct operation on two tables and has its own ON clause, so joining more than two tables requires multiple join operators, each with its own ON clause. The new syntax is not only preferred because the old may someday be unsupported, but also because it forces you to specify precisely (and think clearly about) what joins you need.

As the final inner join example, you'll see how to perform joins on more than two tables with the new syntax.

Try It Out: Writing an Inner Join of Three Tables

You'll replace the customer ID with the customer name. To get it, you have to access the Customers table. Enter the following query into SSMSE and execute it. If you widen the CustomerName column, you should see the results shown in Figure 11-16:

```
select
    o.orderid     OrderID,
    c.companyname CustomerName,
    e.lastname    Employee
from
    orders o
    inner join
    employees e
    on
        o.employeeid = e.employeeid
    inner join
    customers c
    on
        o.customerid = c.customerid
```

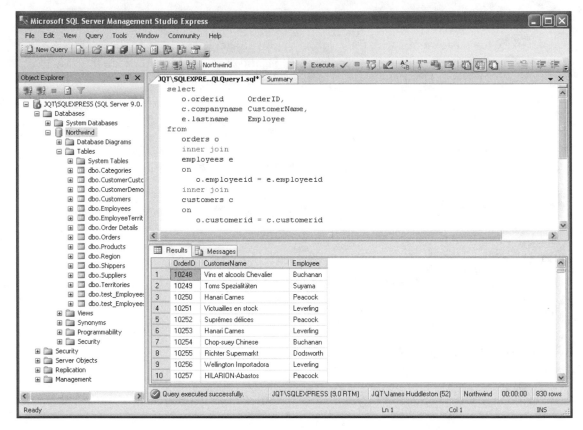

Figure 11-16. *Coding an INNER JOIN of three tables*

How It Works

First, you modify the select list, replacing CustomerID from the Orders table with CompanyName from the Customers table:

```
select
    o.orderid      OrderID,
    c.companyname  CustomerName,
    e.lastname     Employee
```

Second, you add a second inner join, as always with two operands: the table produced by the first join, and the base table Customers. You reformat the first join operator, splitting it across three lines simply to make it easier to distinguish the tables and joins. You can also use parentheses to enclose joins, and you can make them clearer when you use multiple joins (further, since joins produce tables, you can also associate their results with correlation names, for reference in later joins and even in the select list, but such complexity is beyond the scope of this discussion):

```
from
   orders o
   inner join
   employees e
   on
      o.employeeid = e.employeeid
   inner join
   customers c
   on
      o.customerid = c.customerid
```

The result of the first join, which matches orders to employees, is matched against the Customers table from which the appropriate customer name is retrieved for each matching row from the first join. Since referential integrity exists between Orders and both Employees and Customers, all Orders rows have matching rows in the other two tables.

How the database actually satisfies such a query depends on a number of things, but joins are such an integral part of relational database operations that query optimizers are themselves optimized to find efficient access paths among multiple tables to perform multiple joins. However, the fewer joins needed, the more efficient the query, so plan your queries carefully. Usually, you have several ways to code a query to get the same data, but almost always only one of them is the most efficient.

Now you know how to retrieve data from two or more tables—when the rows match. What about rows that don't match? That's where outer joins come in.

Outer Joins

Outer joins return *all* rows from (at least) one of the joined tables, even if rows in one table don't match rows in the other. Three types of outer joins exist: left outer join, right outer join, and full outer join. The terms *left* and *right* refer to the operands on the left and right of the join operator. (Refer to the basic syntax for the inner join, and you'll see why we called the operands left-table and right-table.) In a left outer join, all rows from the left table will be retrieved whether they have matching rows in the right table. Conversely, in a right outer join, all rows from the right table will be retrieved whether they have matching rows in the left table. In a full outer join, all rows from both tables are returned.

■Tip Left and right outer joins are logically equivalent. It's always possible to convert a left join into a right join by changing the operator and flipping the operands, or a right join into a left with a similar change. So, only one of these operators is actually needed. Which one you choose is basically a matter of personal preference, but a useful rule of thumb is to use either left or right, but not both, in the same query. The query optimizer won't care, but humans find it much easier to follow a complex query if the joins always go in the same direction.

When is this useful? Quite frequently. In fact, whenever a parent-child relationship exists between tables, despite the fact that referential integrity is maintained, some parent rows may not have related rows in the child table, since child rows may be allowed to have null foreign key values and therefore not match any row in the parent table. This situation doesn't exist in the original Orders and Employees data, so you'll have to add some data before you can see the effect of outer joins.

You need to add an employee so that you have a row in the Employees table that doesn't have related rows in Orders. To keep things simple, you'll provide data only for the columns that aren't nullable.

Try It Out: Adding an Employee with No Orders

To add an employee with no orders:

1. Enter the following SQL into SSMSE and execute it. You should see the result shown in Figure 11-17:

```
insert into employees
(
    firstname,
    lastname
)
values ('Amy', 'Abrams')
```

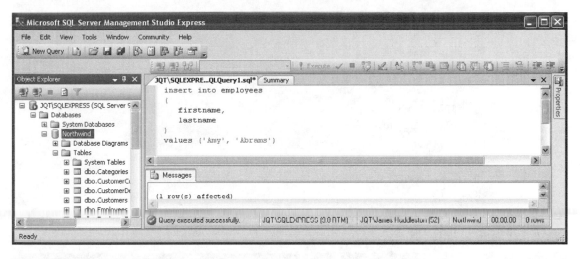

Figure 11-17. *Adding an employee with no orders*

How It Works

You submit a single INSERT statement, providing the two required columns. The first column, EmployeeID, is an IDENTITY column, so you can't provide a value for it, and the rest are nullable, so you don't need to provide values for them:

```
insert into employees
(
    firstname,
    lastname
)
values ('Amy', 'Abrams')
```

You now have a new employee, Amy Abrams, who has never taken an order.

Now, let's say you want a list of all orders taken by all employees—but this list must include *all* employees, even those who haven't taken any orders.

Try It Out: Using LEFT OUTER JOIN

To list all employees, even those who haven't taken any orders:

1. Enter the following SQL into SSMSE and execute it. You should see the results shown in Figure 11-18:

```
select
   e.firstname,
   e.lastname,
   o.orderid
from
   employees e
   left outer join
   orders o
   on
   e.employeeid = o.employeeid
order by
   2, 1
```

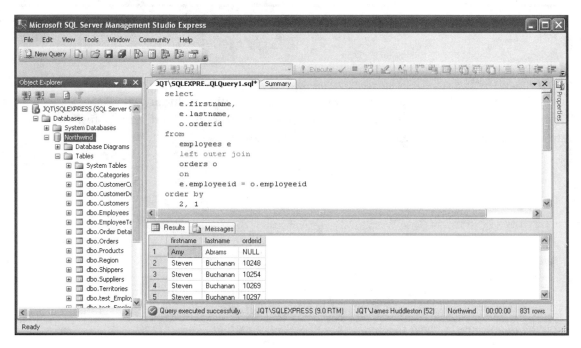

Figure 11-18. *Using LEFT OUTER JOINs*

How It Works

Had you used an inner join, you would have missed the row for the new employee. (Try it for yourself.) The only new SQL in the FROM clause is the join operator itself:

```
left outer join
```

You also add an ORDER BY clause, to sort the result set by first name within last name, to see that the kind of join has no effect on the rest of the query, and to see an alternate way to specify columns, by position number within the select list rather than by name. This technique is convenient (and may be the only way to do it for columns that are produced by expressions—for example, by the SUM function):

```
order by
    2, 1
```

Note that the OrderID column for the new employee is NULL, since no value exists for it. The same holds true for any columns from the table that don't have matching rows (in this case, the right table).

You can obtain the same result by placing the Employees table on the right and the Orders table on the left of the join operator and changing the operator to RIGHT OUTER JOIN. (Try it!) Remember to flip the correlation names, too.

The keyword OUTER is optional and is typically omitted. Left and right joins are *always* outer joins.

Other Joins

The SQL standard also provides for FULL OUTER JOIN, UNION JOIN, and CROSS JOIN (and even NATURAL JOIN, which is basically an inner join using equality predicates), but these are much less used and beyond the scope of this book. We won't provide examples, but this section contains a brief summary of them.

A FULL OUTER JOIN is like a combination of both the LEFT and RIGHT OUTER JOINs. All rows from both tables are retrieved, even if they have no related rows in the other table.

A UNION JOIN is unlike outer joins in that it doesn't match rows. Instead, it creates a table that has all the rows from both tables. For two tables, it's equivalent to the following query:

```
select
    *
from
    table1
union all
select
    *
from
    table2
```

The tables must have the same number of columns, and the data types of corresponding columns must be compatible (that is, able to hold the same types of data).

A CROSS JOIN combines all rows from both tables. It doesn't provide for a join specification, since this would be irrelevant. It produces a table with all columns from both tables and as many rows as the product of the number of rows in each table. The result is also known as a *Cartesian product*, since that's the mathematical term for associating each element (row) of one set (table) with all elements of another set. For example, if there are five rows and five columns in table A and ten rows and three columns in table B, the cross join of A and B would produce a table with fifty rows and eight columns. This join operation is not only virtually inapplicable to any real-world query, but it's also a potentially very expensive process for even small real-world databases. (Imagine using it for production tables with thousands or even millions of rows.)

Summary

In this chapter, we covered how to construct more sophisticated queries using the following SQL features:

- The DISTINCT keyword to eliminate duplicates from the result set

- Subqueries, which are queries embedded in other queries

- The IN predicate, using lists of literals and lists returned by subqueries

- Aggregate functions, such as MIN, MAX, SUM, and AVG

- The GROUP BY clause for categorizing aggregates

- Functions for accessing the components of the datetime data type

- CASE expressions for providing column values based on logical tests

- Correlation names

- Inner, outer, and other joins

In the next chapter, you'll learn about another important database object, the stored procedure.

■ ■ ■

Using Stored Procedures

Stored procedures are programs run on the database server that allow you to package SQL in an optimal fashion for reuse. Writing stored procedures is a major study in itself. Our goal here is to introduce you to the rudiments of stored procedures so you understand how C# programs need to interact with them. In this chapter, we cover:

- How to create, modify, and delete stored procedures in SSMSE

- How to use stored procedures in C# programs

Creating Stored Procedures

Stored procedures can have *parameters* that can be used for input or output. They also have a single integer *return value* (which defaults to zero), and they can return zero or more result sets. They can be called from client programs or other stored procedures. They are powerful indeed and are becoming the preferred mode for much database programming, particularly for multi-tier applications and Web services, since (among their many benefits) they can dramatically reduce network traffic between clients and database servers.

You'll create three stored procedures (two of which you'll access from C#): one that is about as trivial as it can get, one that introduces you to parameters, and one that exhibits the common traits you typically handle when calling a stored procedure from C#.

Try It Out: Creating and Executing a Trivial Stored Procedure

Let's create a stored procedure that produces a list of the names of employees in the Northwind database. It requires no input and doesn't need to set a return value.

1. In Object Explorer, expand the Northwind node, expand the Programmability node, right-click the Stored Procedures node, and click New Stored Procedure.... (See Figure 12-1.)

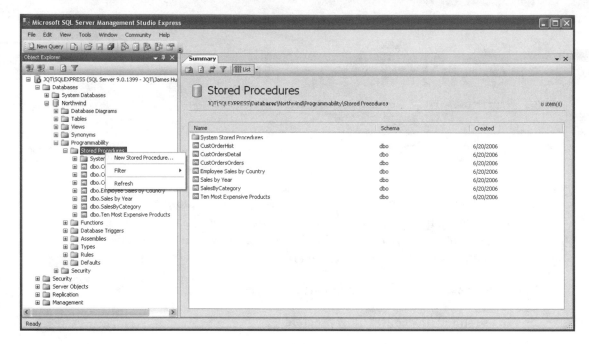

Figure 12-1. *Creating a stored procedure in Object Explorer*

2. You'll be presented with a SQL edit window as in Figure 12-2.

3. It has some comments and a bit of SQL already generated, which provide a skeleton for stored procedure code, but we don't need any of this, so replace it all with the following SQL:

```
create procedure sp_Select_All_Employees
as
    select
        employeeid,
        firstname,
        lastname
    from
        employees
```

4. Execute the SQL. You should see the screen in Figure 12-3.

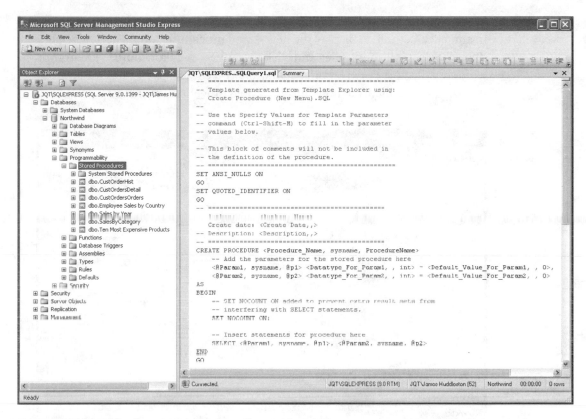

Figure 12-2. *SSMSE edit window for stored procedures*

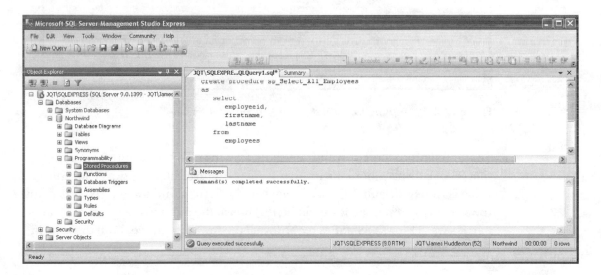

Figure 12-3. *Creating a stored procedure in SSMSE*

5. To execute the stored procedure, expand the Stored Procedures node, right-click it, and click Refresh, to display the new stored procedure node. Then right-click dbo.sp_Select_All_Employees and click Execute Stored Procedure… . A prompt window will appear as in Figure 12-4, where you could enter values for input parameters, but there are none for this stored procedure, so just click OK.

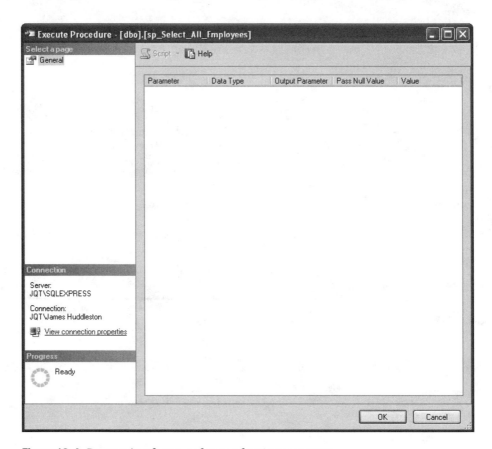

Figure 12-4. *Prompting for stored procedure parameters*

6. The stored procedure runs, and you should get the results in Figure 12-5. Note that SSMSE displays both the result set and the return value in grids. The return value is zero by default. Now scroll down in the Results window and see how many rows are in the result set. It should be 10. Look at the rightmost entry in the status bar. It says "11 rows". SSMSE is reporting all the rows it returned, both the rows in Results and the row in Return Value.

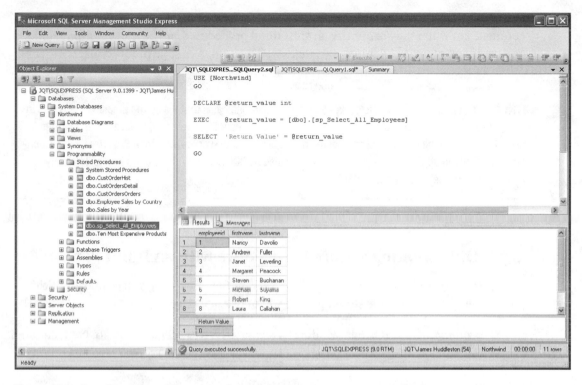

Figure 12-5. *Results of running a stored procedure*

How It Works

The CREATE PROCEDURE statement creates stored procedures. The AS keyword separates the signature (the procedure's name and parameter list, but here you define no parameters) of the stored procedure from its body (the SQL that makes up the procedure).

```
create procedure sp_Select_All_Employees
as
```

After AS, the procedure body has just one component, a simple query:

```
select
    employeeid,
    firstname,
    lastname
from
    employees
```

All this stored procedure does is run a query. SSMSE submitted the CREATE PROCEDURE statement and once the stored procedure was created, you ran it from Object Explorer.

That's it. There's nothing complicated about creating stored procedures. The challenge is coding them when they're nontrivial, and stored procedures can be quite complicated and can do very powerful things, but that's well beyond the scope of this book.

Note The prefix sp_ is a T-SQL convention that typically indicates that the stored procedure is coded in SQL. The prefix xp_ (extended procedure) is also used to indicate that the stored procedure isn't written in SQL. (However, not all sp_ stored procedures provided by SQL Server are written in SQL.) By the way, hundreds of sp_ (and other) stored procedures are provided by SQL Server 2005 to perform a wide variety of common tasks. See BOL for details.

Try It Out: Creating a Stored Procedure with an Input Parameter

Let's create a stored procedure that produces a list of orders for a given employee. We'll pass the employee ID to the stored procedure for use in a query.

1. Reopen the first SQL edit window (see Figure 12-3) by clicking its tab. Replace the SQL there with

```
create procedure sp_Orders_By_EmployeeId
    @employeeid int
as
    select
        orderid,
        customerid
    from
        orders
    where
        employeeid = @employeeid;
```

   and execute it to create the stored procedure.

2. To execute the stored procedure, refresh the Stored Procedures node, right-click dbo.sp_Orders_By_EmployeeId, and click Execute Stored Procedure… . Enter 2 in the Value column of the prompt window and click OK. You should get the result in Figure 12-6.

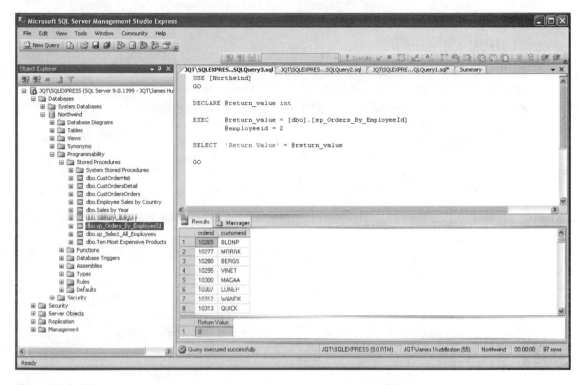

Figure 12-6. *Using an input parameter*

How It Works

The CREATE PROCEDURE statement created a stored procedure that has one input parameter. Parameters are specified between the procedure name and the AS keyword. Here you specified only the parameter name and data type, so by default it is an input parameter. Parameter names start with @.

```
create procedure sp_Orders_By_EmployeeId
   @employeeid int
as
```

This parameter is used in the WHERE clause of the query:

```
where
   employeeid = @employeeid;
```

■**Note** We've used a semicolon to terminate the query. It's optional here, but we'll see when it needs to be used in our next example.

Try It Out: Creating a Stored Procedure with an Output Parameter

Output parameters are typically used to pass values between stored procedures, but sometimes they need to be accessed from C#, so let's write a stored procedure with an output parameter so we can use it in a C# program later. We'll also show how to return a value other than zero.

1. Reopen the first SQL edit window (see Figure 12-3). Replace the SQL there with

```
create procedure sp_Orders_By_EmployeeId2
   @employeeid int,
   @ordercount int = 0 output
as
   select
      orderid,
      customerid
   from
      orders
   where
      employeeid = @employeeid;

   select
      @ordercount = count(*)
   from
      orders
   where
      employeeid = @employeeid

   return @ordercount
```

and execute it to create the stored procedure.

2. To execute the stored procedure, refresh the Stored Procedures node, right-click dbo.sp_Orders_By_EmployeeId2, and click Execute Stored Procedure… . Enter 2 in the Value column for @employeeid and click OK. You should get the result in Figure 12-7. Note that both the @ordercount and Return Value rows show 96. These two rows plus the 96 in Results explain why "98 rows" is displayed in the status bar.

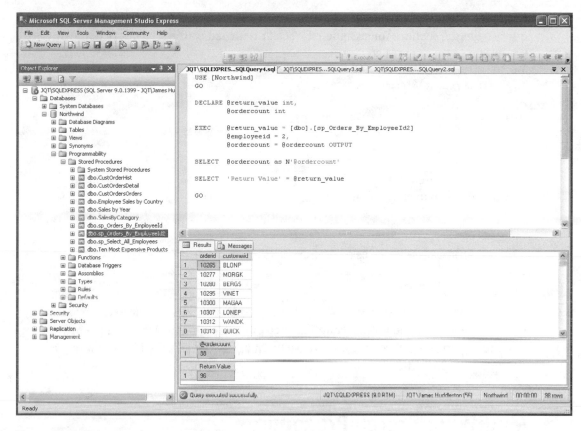

Figure 12-7. *Using an output parameter*

How It Works

You added an output parameter, @ordercount,

```
create procedure sp_Orders_By_EmployeeId2
    @employeeid int,
    @ordercount int = 0 output
as
```

assigning a default value of zero. The keyword output marks it as an output parameter.
   You also added an additional query:

```
select
    @ordercount = count(*)
from
    orders
where
    employeeid = @employeeid
```

and that's why we used a semicolon in `sp_Orders_By_EmployeeId`, to separate the first query from the second. You assigned the scalar returned by the new query to the output parameter in the `SELECT` list:

```
@ordercount = count(*)
```

then you returned the same value:

```
return @ordercount
```

The `COUNT` function returns an integer, so this was a convenient way to demonstrate how to use the `RETURN` statement.

Tip Input parameters can also be assigned default values.

There are other ways to do these (and many other) things with stored procedures. We've done all we need for this chapter, since our main objective is not learning how to write stored procedures but how to use them in C#. But let's see how to modify and delete stored procedures.

Modifying Stored Procedures

SSMSE makes it easy to retrieve and modify stored procedures.

Try It Out: Modifying Our Trivial Stored Procedure

Let's retrieve our first stored procedure and change it to sort employees by name.

1. In Object Explorer, right-click dbo.sp_Select_All_Employees and click Modify. The code will be displayed in an edit window, embedded in an `ALTER PROCEDURE` statement. (See Figure 12-8.)

2. Add an `ORDER BY` clause to the query and execute the `ALTER PROCEDURE` statement:

   ```
   order by
       lastname,
       firstname
   ```

3. Execute the stored procedure in Object Explorer. You should see the screen in Figure 12-9. Notice the employee names are now sorted.

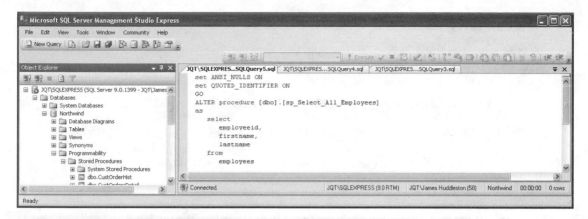

Figure 12-8. *Retrieving a stored procedure with Object Explorer*

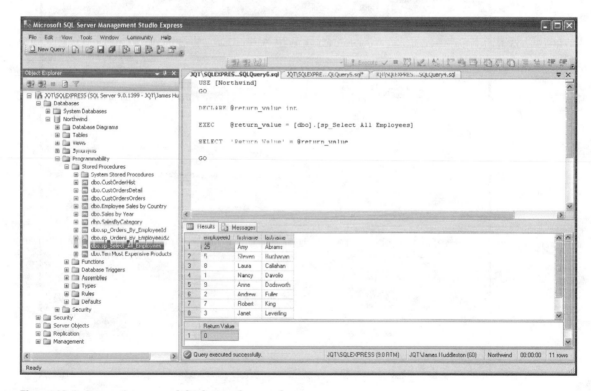

Figure 12-9. *Executing a modified stored procedure*

How It Works

It works very simply. SSMSE retrieves the source code for the stored procedure so you can conveniently edit it. After you've executed the ALTER PROCEDURE statement, the stored procedure is updated in the database. There is no need to refresh the Stored Procedures node. You just right-clicked on the procedure and executed it.

Deleting Stored Procedures

SSMSE makes it easy to delete stored procedures.

Try It Out: Deleting Our Trivial Stored Procedure

Let's delete our first stored procedure for retrieving a specific employee's orders.

1. In Object Explorer, right-click dbo.sp_Order_By_EmployeeID and click Delete.
   When the confirmation window appears (see Figure 12-10), click OK.

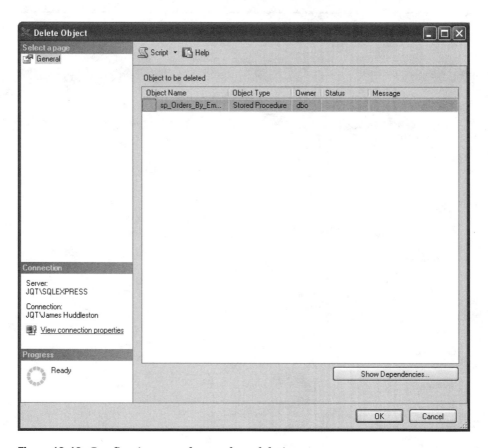

Figure 12-10. *Confirming stored procedure deletion*

2. Note that the dbo.sp_Order_By_EmployeeID node immediately disappears from
   Object Explorer. See Figure 12-11.

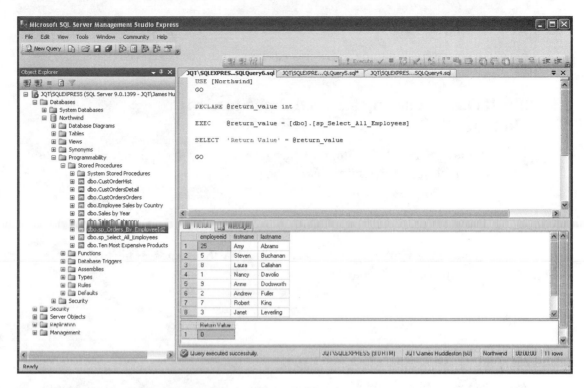

Figure 12-11. *Object Explorer after deleting a stored procedure*

How It Works

There's nothing simpler. You just right-clicked on the procedure and deleted it.

Tip You don't need to use Object Explorer to delete stored procedures. You can execute a DELETE
PROCEDURE statement yourself, but it's more work.

Working with Stored Procedures in C#

Now that you've created some stored procedures, you can use them with C#.

Try It Out: Executing a Stored Procedure with No Input Parameters

Let's execute sp_Select_All_Employees, which takes no input and returns only a result set, a list of all employees sorted by name.

1. Create a new Console Application project named Chapter12. When Solution Explorer opens, save the solution.

2. Rename the Chapter12 project CallSp1. Rename the Program.cs file to CallSp1.cs, and replace the generated code with the code in Listing 12-1.

Listing 12-1. CallSp1.cs

```
using System;
using System.Data;
using System.Data.SqlClient;

namespace Chapter12
{
   class CallSp1
   {
      static void Main()
      {

         // create connection
         SqlConnection conn = new SqlConnection(@"
            server = .\sqlexpress;
            integrated security = true;
            database = northwind
         ");

         try
         {
            // open connection
            conn.Open();
```

```
        // create command
        SqlCommand cmd = conn.CreateCommand();

        // specify stored procedure to execute
        cmd.CommandType = CommandType.StoredProcedure;
        cmd.CommandText = "sp_select_all_employees";

        // execute command
        SqlDataReader rdr = cmd.ExecuteReader();

        // Process the result set
        while (rdr.Read())
        {
            Console.WriteLine(
                "{0} {1} {2}"
            , rdr[0].ToString().PadRight(5)
            , rdr[1].ToString()
            , rdr[2].ToString()
            );
        }
        rdr.Close();
    }
    catch (SqlException ex)
    {
        Console.WriteLine(ex.ToString());
    }
    finally
    {
        conn.Close();
    }
}
}
}
```

3. Build and run the solution by pressing Ctrl+F5. You should see the result in Figure 12-12.

Figure 12-12. *Running a stored procedure with C#*

How It Works

This wasn't much different from CommandReader.cs in Chapter 6. The biggest difference is how you created and configured the command:

```
// create command
SqlCommand cmd = conn.CreateCommand();

// specify stored procedure to execute
cmd.CommandType = CommandType.StoredProcedure;
cmd.CommandText = "sp_select_all_employees";
```

Instead of using new to create a command (and pass a query and a connection to its constructor), you used the connection's CreateCommand method. You then specified the command type was for a stored procedure call rather than a query. Finally, you set the command text to the stored procedure name.

The rest of the code changed only trivially, to handle displaying the extra column. You used ExecuteReader just as you would for a query, which makes sense, since the stored procedure simply executes a query and returns a result set.

Try It Out: Executing a Stored Procedure with Parameters

You'll call the sp_Orders_By_EmployeeId2 stored procedure, supplying the employee ID as an input parameter and displaying the result set, the output parameter, and the return value.

1. Add a new C# Console Application project named CallSp2 to your Chapter12 solution. Rename Program.cs to CallSp2.cs.

2. Replace the code in CallSp2.cs with the code in Listing 12-2.

Listing 12-2. `CallSp2.cs`

```csharp
using System;
using System.Data;
using System.Data.SqlClient;

namespace Chapter12
{
    class CallSp2
    {
        static void Main()
        {

            // create connection
            SqlConnection conn = new SqlConnection(@"
                server = .\sqlexpress;
                integrated security = true;
                database = northwind
            ");

            try
            {
                // open connection
                conn.Open();

                // create command
                SqlCommand cmd = conn.CreateCommand();

                // specify stored procedure to execute
                cmd.CommandType = CommandType.StoredProcedure;
                cmd.CommandText = "sp_orders_by_employeeid2";

                // create input parameter
                SqlParameter inparm = cmd.Parameters.Add(
                    "@employeeid"
                  , SqlDbType.Int
                );
                inparm.Direction = ParameterDirection.Input;
                inparm.Value = 2;
```

```
// create output parameter
SqlParameter ouparm = cmd.Parameters.Add(
   "@ordercount"
 , SqlDbType.Int
);
ouparm.Direction = ParameterDirection.Output;

// create return value parameter
SqlParameter retval = cmd.Parameters.Add(
   "return_value"
 , SqlDbType.Int
);
retval.Direction = ParameterDirection.ReturnValue;

// execute command
SqlDataReader rdr = cmd.ExecuteReader();

// Process the result set
while (rdr.Read())
{
   Console.WriteLine(
      "{0} {1}"
    , rdr[0].ToString().PadRight(5)
    , rdr[1].ToString()
    );
}
rdr.Close();

// display output parameter value
Console.WriteLine(
   "The output parameter value is {0}"
 , cmd.Parameters["@ordercount"].Value
);

// display return value
Console.WriteLine(
   "The return value is {0}"
 , cmd.Parameters["return_value"].Value
);
}
```

```
        catch (SqlException ex)
        {
            Console.WriteLine(ex.ToString());
        }
        finally
        {
            conn.Close();
        }
    }
  }
}
```

3. Make this the startup project and run it by pressing Ctrl+F5. You should see the result in Figure 12-13.

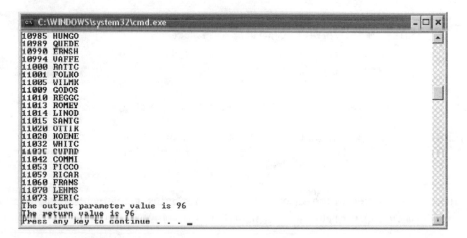

Figure 12-13. *Using parameters and the return value with C#*

How It Works

This is very much like the previous example. The main difference was that you added three command parameters, specifying the kind of parameter with the Direction property:

```
// create input parameter
SqlParameter inparm = cmd.Parameters.Add(
    "@employeeid"
  , SqlDbType.Int
);
inparm.Direction = ParameterDirection.Input;
inparm.Value = 2;

// create output parameter
SqlParameter ouparm = cmd.Parameters.Add(
    "@ordercount"
  , SqlDbType.Int
);
ouparm.Direction = ParameterDirection.Output;

// create return value parameter
SqlParameter retval = cmd.Parameters.Add(
    "return_value"
  , SqlDbType.Int
);
retval.Direction = ParameterDirection.ReturnValue;
```

You set the input parameter value to 2 before the call

```
inparm.Value = 2;
```

and retrieved the values for the output parameter and return value by indexing into the
command's parameters collection after the stored procedure returned:

```
// display output parameter value
Console.WriteLine(
    "The output parameter value is {0}"
  , cmd.Parameters["@ordercount"].Value
);

// display return value
Console.WriteLine(
    "The return value is {0}"
  , cmd.Parameters["return_value"].Value
);
```

You can create as many input and output parameters as you need. You *must* provide
command parameters for all input parameters that don't have default values. You don't

have to provide command parameters for any output parameters you don't need to use. Input and output parameter names must agree with the parameter names in the stored procedure, except for case (remember that T-SQL is not case sensitive).

Though it's handled in ADO.NET as a command parameter, there is always only one return value. As with output parameters, you don't need to create a command parameter for the return value unless you intend to use it. But unlike with input and output parameters, you can give it whatever parameter name you choose.

Summary

In this chapter you created simple stored procedures to get a feel for the kind of input and output they provide, as a basis for understanding what's involved in calling stored procedures from C#. You saw that calling stored procedures isn't inherently different from executing queries and statements. You simply create appropriate command parameters for the stored procedure parameters you need to use.

You applied the same techniques that you practiced in earlier chapters. We didn't cover handling multiple result sets from stored procedures, because you use the same technique as for queries, which you used in Chapter 7.

Now you'll extend your database programming skills to handle ADO.NET and database exceptions.

CHAPTER 13

■ ■ ■

Handling Exceptions

Up to now, we've been rather relaxed in our handling of database exceptions. Robust database applications demand more careful attention to this important issue. Structured exception handling is both elegant and robust. In database programming, errors come from three sources: application programs, ADO.NET, and database servers. We assume you're familiar with handling application exceptions in C# with try statements, so we'll focus on the last two sources.

In this chapter, we'll cover:

- Handling ADO.NET exceptions

- Handling SQL Server exceptions

Handling ADO.NET Exceptions

First, let's see how to handle exceptions thrown by ADO.NET. These exceptions arise when ADO.NET is trying to communicate with SQL Server, before the database server responds. We'll use a Windows application, since it makes generating and viewing error situations and messages more convenient. To generate an exception expediently, you'll try to execute a stored procedure without specifying the CommandText property. You'll do this first without handling the exception, then you'll modify things to handle it.

Try It Out: Handling an ADO.NET Exception (Part 1)

To handle an ADO.NET exception:

1. Create a new Windows Application project named Chapter13. When Solution Explorer opens, save the solution.

2. Rename the Chapter13 project AdoNetExceptions.

3. Change the Text property of Form1 to ADO.NET Exceptions.

4. Add a tab control to the form. Change the Text property of tabPage1 to ADO.NET. Add a button to the tab page, and change its Text property to ADO.NET Exception-1. Add a label to the right of this button, and change its Text property to Incorrect ADO.NET code will cause an exception. Add a second button to the tab page, and change its Text property to ADO.NET Exception-2. Add a label to the right of this button, and change its Text property to Accessing a nonexistent column will cause an exception.

5. Change the second tab page's Text property to Database. The layout should look like Figure 13-1.

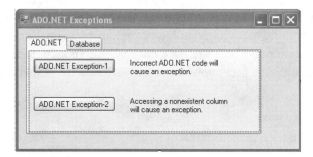

Figure 13-1. *ADO.NET tab page*

6. Add the following using directive for the SQL Server data provider namespace to Form1.cs:

```
using System.Data.SqlClient;
```

7. Insert the code in Listing 13-1 to the click event handler for button1. This will provide the first exception.

Listing 13-1. button1_Click()

```
// Create connection
SqlConnection conn = new SqlConnection(@"
    data source = .\sqlexpress;
    integrated security = true;
    database = northwind
");

// Create command
SqlCommand cmd = conn.CreateCommand();
```

```
// Specify that a stored procedure is to be executed
cmd.CommandType = CommandType.StoredProcedure;

// Deliberately fail to specify the procedure
// cmd.CommandText = "sp_Select_All_Employees";

// Open connection
conn.Open();
// Create data reader
SqlDataReader dr = cmd.ExecuteReader();
// Close reader
dr.Close();

if (conn.State == ConnectionState.Open)
{
    MessageBox.Show ("Finally block closing the connection", "Finally");
    conn.Close();
}
```

8. Run the program with Ctrl+F5. Click the ADO.NET Exception 1 button, and you'll see the message box shown in Figure 13-2. Click Quit.

Figure 13-2. *Unhandled exception message*

9. Modify the button1_Click event handler with the bold code shown in Listing 13-2. (We've indented unchanged code as required, but haven't highlighted it.)

Listing 13-2. *Modifications to* button1_Click()

```
// Create connection
SqlConnection conn = new SqlConnection(@"
    data source = .\sqlexpress;
    integrated security = true;
    database = northwind
");
```

```
    // Create command
    SqlCommand cmd = conn.CreateCommand();

    // Specify that a stored procedure is to be executed
    cmd.CommandType = CommandType.StoredProcedure;

    // Deliberately fail to specify the procedure
    // cmd.CommandText = "sp_Select_All_Employees";

    try
    {
        // Open connection
        conn.Open();
        // Create data reader
        SqlDataReader dr = cmd.ExecuteReader();
        // Close reader
        dr.Close();
    }
    catch (System.Data.SqlClient.SqlException ex)
    {
        string str;
        str = "Source: " + ex.Source;
        str += "\n" + "Exception Message: " + ex.Message;
        MessageBox.Show (str, "Database Exception");
    }
    catch (System.Exception ex)
    {
        string str;
        str = "Source: " + ex.Source;
        str += "\n" + "Exception Message: " + ex.Message;
        MessageBox.Show (str, "Non-Database Exception");
    }
    finally
    {
        if (conn.State == ConnectionState.Open)
        {
            MessageBox.Show ("Finally block closing the connection", "Finally");
            conn.Close();
        }
    }
```

10. Run the program with Ctrl+F5. Click the ADO.NET Exception-1 button, and you'll see the message box shown in Figure 13-3. Click OK.

Figure 13-3. *Handled exception message*

11. When the message box in Figure 13-4 appears, click OK, then close the window.

Figure 13-4. *Message from finally block*

How It Works

It would be highly unusual to miss setting the CommandText property. However, this is an expedient way to cause an ADO.NET exception. You specify the command for a stored procedure call, but you don't specify the stored procedure to call

```
// Specify that a stored procedure is to be executed
cmd.CommandType = CommandType.StoredProcedure;

// Deliberately fail to specify the procedure
// cmd.CommandText = "sp_Select_AllEmployees";
```

so when you call the ExecuteReader method, you get an exception, as shown in Figure 13-2. Though it's an unhandled exception, it still gives you an accurate diagnostic

```
ExecuteReader: CommandText property has not been intiailized.
```

and it even gives you the option to continue or quit. However, leaving this decision to users isn't a very good idea.

After seeing what happens without handling the exception, you place the call in a try block:

```
try
{
    // Open connection
    conn.Open();
    // Create data reader
    SqlDataReader dr = cmd.FxecuteReader();
    // Close reader
    dr.Close();
}
```

To handle the exception yourself, you code two `catch` clauses:

```
catch (System.Data.SqlClient.SqlException ex)
{
    string str;
    str = "Source:" + ex.Source;
    str += "\n" + "Exception Message:" + ex.Message;
    MessageBox.Show (str, "Database Exception");
}
catch (System.Exception ex)
{
    string str;
    str = "Source:" + ex.Source;
    str += "\n" + "Exception Message:" + ex.Message;
    MessageBox.Show (str, "Non-Database Exception");
}
```

In the first `catch` clause, you specify a database exception type. The second `catch` clause, which produces the message box in Figure 13-3, is a generic block that catches all types of exceptions. Note the caption of the message box in this `catch` block. It says *Non-Database Exception*. Although you may think that a failure to specify a command string is a database exception, it's actually an ADO.NET exception; in other words, this error is trapped before it gets to the database server.

When the button is clicked, since the `CommandText` property isn't specified, an exception is thrown and caught by the second `catch` clause. Even though a `catch` clause for `SqlException` is provided, the exception is a `System.InvalidOperationException`—a common exception thrown by the CLR, not a database exception.

The exception message indicates where the problem occurred: in the `ExecuteReader` method. The `finally` block checks if the connection is open and, if it is, closes it and gives a message to that effect. Note that in handling the exception, you don't terminate the application:

```
finally
{
    if (conn.State == ConnectionState.Open)
    {
        MessageBox.Show ("Finally block closing the connection", "Finally");
        conn.Close();
    }
}
```

Try It Out: Handling an ADO.NET Exception (Part 2)

Let's try another example of an ADO.NET exception. You'll execute a stored procedure and then reference a nonexistent column in the returned dataset. This will throw an ADO.NET exception. This time, you'll code a specific catch clause to handle the exception:

1. Use the sp_Select_All_Employees stored procedure you created in Chapter 12. If you haven't created it already, please go to Chapter 12 and follow the steps in "Try It Out: Creating and Executing a Trivial Stored Procedure."

2. Insert the code in Listing 13-3 into the body of the button2_Click method.

Listing 13-3. button2_Click()

```
// Create connection
SqlConnection conn = new SqlConnection(@"
    data source = .\sqlexpress,
    integrated security = true;
    database = northwind
");

// Create command
SqlCommand cmd = conn.CreateCommand();

// Specify that a stored procedure is to be executed
cmd.CommandType = CommandType.StoredProcedure;
cmd.CommandText = "sp_Select_All_Employees";
```

```
try
{
  // Open connection
  conn.Open();

  // Create data reader
  SqlDataReader dr = cmd.ExecuteReader();

  // Access nonexistent column
  string str = dr.GetValue(20).ToString();

  // Close reader
  dr.Close();
}
catch (System.InvalidOperationException ex)
{
  string str;
  str = "Source: " + ex.Source;
  str += "\n" + "Message: "+ ex.Message;
  str += "\n" + "\n";
  str += "\n" + "Stack Trace: " + ex.StackTrace;
  MessageBox.Show (str, "Specific Exception");
}
catch (System.Data.SqlClient.SqlException ex)
{
  string str;
  str = "Source: " + ex.Source;
  str += "\n" + "Exception Message: " + ex.Message;
  MessageBox.Show (str, "Database Exception");
}
catch (System.Exception ex)
{
  string str;
  str = "Source: " + ex.Source;
  str += "\n" + "Exception Message: " + ex.Message;
  MessageBox.Show (str, "Non-Database Exception");
}
```

```
finally
{
    if (conn.State == ConnectionState.Open)
    {
        MessageBox.Show ("Finally block closing the connection", "Finally");
        conn.Close();
    }
}
```

Tip Testing whether a connection is open before attempting to close it isn't actually necessary. The Close method doesn't throw any exceptions, and calling it multiple times on the same connection, even if it's already closed, causes no errors.

3. Run the program with Ctrl+F5. Click the ADO.NET Exception-2 button, and you'll see the message box shown in Figure 13-5. Click OK. When the finally block message appears, click OK, then close the window.

Figure 13-5. *Handling a specific ADO.NET exception*

4. For a quick comparison, now generate a SQL Server exception, an error that occurs within the database. Alter the name of the stored procedure in the code to a name that doesn't exist within the Northwind database. For example:

```
cmd.CommandText = "sp_Select_No_Employees";
```

5. Run the program with Ctrl+F5. Click the ADO.NET Exception-2 button, and you'll see the message box shown in Figure 13-6. Click OK. When the `finally` block message appears, click OK, then close the window.

Figure 13-6. *Handling a SQL Server exception*

How It Works

First you create the data reader and try to access an invalid column:

```
// Create data reader
SqlDataReader dr = cmd.ExecuteReader();

// Access nonexistent column
string str = dr.GetValue(20).ToString();
```

An exception is thrown, because you tried to get the value of column 20, which doesn't exist. You add a new `catch` clause to handle this kind of ADO.NET error:

```
catch (System.InvalidOperationException ex)
{
    string str;
    str = "Source: " + ex.Source;
    str += "\n" + "Message: "+ ex.Message;
    str += "\n" + "\n";
    str += "\n" + "Stack Trace: " + ex.StackTrace;
    MessageBox.Show (str, "Specific Exception");
}
```

When an exception of type `System.InvalidOperationException` is thrown, this `catch` clause executes, displaying the source, message, and stack trace for the exception. Without this specific `catch` clause, the generic `catch` clause would have handled the exception. (Try commenting out this `catch` clause and reexecuting the code to see which `catch` clause handles the exception.)

Next, you run the program for a nonexistent stored procedure:

```
// Specify that a stored procedure is to be executed
cmd.CommandType = CommandType.StoredProcedure;
cmd.CommandText = "sp_Select_No_Employees";
```

You catch your (first) database exception with

```
catch (System.Data.SqlClient.SqlException ex)
```

which leads into the next topic: handling exceptions thrown by the database manager.

Handling Database Exceptions

An exception of type System.Data.SqlClient.SqlException is thrown when SQL Server returns a warning or error. This class is derived from System.SystemException and is sealed so it can't be inherited, but it has several useful members that you can interrogate to obtain valuable information about the exception.

An instance of SqlException is thrown whenever the .NET data provider for SQL Server encounters an error or warning from the database. Table 13-1 describes the properties of this class that provide information about the exception.

Table 13-1. SqlException *Properties*

Property Name	Description
Class	Gets the severity level of the error returned from the SqlClient data provider. The severity level is a numeric code that's used to indicate the nature of the error. Levels 1 to 10 are informational errors; 11 to 16 are user-level errors; and 17 to 25 are software or hardware errors. At level 20 or greater, the connection is usually closed.
Data	Gets a collection of key-value pairs that contain user-defined information.
ErrorCode	The HRESULT of the error.
Errors	Contains one or more SqlError objects that have detailed information about the exception. This is a collection that can be iterated through.
HelpLink	The help file associated with this exception.
InnerException	Gets the exception instance that caused the current exception.
LineNumber	Gets the line number within the Transact-SQL command batch or stored procedure that generated the exception.
Message	The text describing the exception.
Number	The number that identifies the type of exception.

Continued

Table 13-1. *Continued*

Property Name	Description
Procedure	The name of the stored procedure that generated the exception.
Server	The name of the computer running the instance of SQL Server that generated the exception.
Source	The name of the provider that generated the exception.
StackTrace	A string representation of the call stack when the exception was thrown.
State	Numeric error code from SQL Server that represents an exception, warning, or "no data found" message. For more information, see SQL Server Books Online.
TargetSite	The method that throws the current exception.

When an error occurs within SQL Server, it uses a T-SQL `RAISERROR` statement to raise an error and send it back to the calling program. A typical error message looks like the following:

```
Server: Msg 2812, Level 16, State 62, Line 1
Could not find stored procedure 'sp_DoesNotExist'
```

In this message, 2812 represents the error number, 16 represents the severity level, and 62 represents the state of the error.

You can also use the `RAISERROR` statement to display specific messages within a stored procedure. The `RAISERROR` statement in its simplest form takes three parameters. The first parameter is the message itself that needs to be shown. The second parameter is the severity level of the error. Any users can use severity levels 11 through 16. They represent messages that can be categorized as information, software, or hardware problems. The third parameter is an arbitrary integer from 1 through 127 that represents information about the state or source of the error.

Let's see how a SQL error, raised by a stored procedure, is handled in C#. You'll create a stored procedure and use the following T-SQL to raise an error when the number of orders in the Orders table exceeds ten:

```
if @orderscount > 10
   raiserror (
      'Orders Count is greater than 10 - Notify the Business Manager',
      16,
      1
   )
```

Note that in this `RAISERROR` statement, you specify a message string, a severity level of 16, and an arbitrary state number of 1. When a `RAISERROR` statement that you write contains a message string, the error number is given automatically as 50000. When

SQL Server raises errors using RAISERROR, it uses a predefined dictionary of messages to give out the corresponding error numbers. (See SQL Server Books Online to learn how to add your own messages to SQL Server's predefined messages.)

Try It Out: Handling a Database Exception (Part 1): RAISERROR

Let's raise a database error and handle the exception:

1. Add a button to the Database tab page and change its Text property to Database Exception-1. Add a label to the right of this button, and change its Text property to Calls a stored procedure that uses RAISERROR.

2. Add a second button to the tab page, and change its Text property to Database Exception-2. Add a label to the right of this button, and change its Text property to Calls a stored procedure that encounters an error.

3. Add a third button to the tab page, and change its Text property to Database Exception-3. Add a label to the right of this button, and change its Text property to Creates multiple SqlError objects. The layout should look like Figure 13-7.

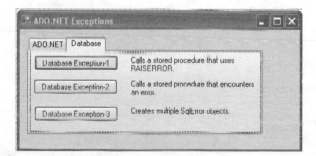

Figure 13-7. *Database tab page*

4. Using SSMSE, create a stored procedure in Northwind named sp_DbException_1, as follows:

```
create procedure sp_DbException_1
as
    set nocount on

    declare @ordercount int
```

```
select
    @ordercount = count(*)
from
    orders

if @ordercount > 10
    raiserror (
        'Orders Count is greater than 10 - Notify the Business Manager',
        16,
        1
    )
```

5. Add the code in Listing 13-4 to the button3_Click method.

Listing 13-4. button3_Click()

```
// Create connection
SqlConnection conn = new SqlConnection(@"
    data source = .\sqlexpress;
    integrated security = true;
    database = northwind
");

// Create command
SqlCommand cmd = conn.CreateCommand();

// Specify that a stored procedure to be executed
cmd.CommandType = CommandType.StoredProcedure;
cmd.CommandText = "sp_DbException_1";

try
{
    // Open connection
    conn.Open();

    // Execute stored procedure
    cmd.ExecuteNonQuery();
}
catch (System.Data.SqlClient.SqlException ex)
{
    string str;
    str = "Source: " + ex.Source;
```

```
      str += "\n"+ "Number: "+ ex.Number.ToString();
      str += "\n"+ "Message: "+ ex.Message;
      str += "\n"+ "Class: "+ ex.Class.ToString ();
      str += "\n"+ "Procedure: "+ ex.Procedure.ToString();
      str += "\n"+ "Line Number: "+ex.LineNumber.ToString();
      str += "\n"+ "Server: "+ ex.Server.ToString();

      MessageBox.Show (str, "Database Exception");
   }
   catch (System.Exception ex)
   {
      string str;
      str = "Source: " + ex.Source;
      str += "\n" + "Exception Message: " + ex.Message;
      MessageBox.Show (str, "General Exception");
   }
   finally
   {
      if (conn.State == ConnectionState.Open)
      {
         MessageBox.Show(
            "Finally block closing the connection",
            "Finally"
         );
         conn.Close();
      }
   }
}
```

6. Run the program with Ctrl+F5, then click the Database Exception-1 button. You'll see the message box shown in Figure 13-8. Click OK to close the message box, then OK to close the next one, then close the window.

Figure 13-8. *RAISERROR Database Exception message*

Observe the caption and contents of the message box. The source, message, name of the stored procedure, exact line number where the error was found, and name of the server are all displayed. You obtain this detailed information about the exception from the SqlException object.

How It Works

In the sp_DBException_1 stored procedure, you first find the number of orders in the Orders table and store the number in a variable called @ordercount:

```
select
    @ordercount = count(*)
from
    orders
```

Then, if @ordercount is greater than ten, you raise an error using the RAISERROR statement:

```
if @ordercount > 10
    raiserror (
        'Orders Count is greater than 10 - Notify the Business Manager',
        16,
        1
    )
```

Then, in the button3_Click method, you execute the stored procedure using the ExecuteNonQuery method within a try block:

```
try
{
    // Open connection
    conn.Open();

    // Create data reader
    cmd.ExecuteNonQuery();
}
```

When the stored procedure executes, the RAISERROR statement raises an error, which is converted to an exception by ADO.NET. The following code handles the exception:

```
catch (System.Data.SqlClient.SqlException ex)
{
    string str;
    str = "Source: " + ex.Source;
    str += "\n"+ "Number: "+ ex.Number.ToString();
    str += "\n"+ "Message: "+ ex.Message;
    str += "\n"+ "Class: "+ ex.Class.ToString ();
    str += "\n"+ "Procedure: "+ ex.Procedure.ToString();
    str += "\n"+ "Line Number: "+ex.LineNumber.ToString();
    str += "\n"+ "Server: "+ ex.Server.ToString();

    MessageBox.Show (str, "Database Exception");
}
```

Try It Out: Handling a Database Exception (Part 2): Stored Procedure Error

Now let's see what happens when a statement in a stored procedure encounters an error. You'll create a stored procedure that attempts an illegal INSERT, and then you'll extract information from the SqlException object:

1. Using SSMSE, create a stored procedure in Northwind named sp_DbException_2, as follows:

```
create procedure sp_DBException_2
as
    set nocount on

    insert into employees
    (
        employeeid,
        firstname
    )
    values (50, 'Cinderella')
```

2. Insert the code in Listing 13-5 into the button4_Click method:

Listing 13-5. button4_Click()

```
// Create connection
SqlConnection conn = new SqlConnection(@"
   data source = .\sqlexpress;
   integrated security = true;
   database = northwind
");

// Create command
SqlCommand cmd = conn.CreateCommand();

// Specify stored procedure to be executed
cmd.CommandType = CommandType.StoredProcedure;
cmd.CommandText = "sp_DbException_2";

try
{
   // Open connection
   conn.Open();

   // Execute stored procedure
   cmd.ExecuteNonQuery();
}
catch (System.Data.SqlClient.SqlException ex)
{
   string str;
   str = "Source: " + ex.Source;
   str += "\n"+ "Number: "+ ex.Number.ToString();
   str += "\n"+ "Message: "+ ex.Message;
   str += "\n"+ "Class: "+ ex.Class.ToString ();
   str += "\n"+ "Procedure: "+ ex.Procedure.ToString();
   str += "\n"+ "Line Number: "+ex.LineNumber.ToString();
   str += "\n"+ "Server: "+ ex.Server.ToString();

   MessageBox.Show (str, "Database Exception");
}
catch (System.Exception ex)
```

```
    {
        string str;
        str = "Source: " + ex.Source;
        str += "\n" + "Exception Message: " + ex.Message;
        MessageBox.Show (str, "ADO.NET Exception");
    }
    finally
    {
        if (conn.State == ConnectionState.Open)
        {
            MessageBox.Show(
                "Finally block closing the connection",
                "Finally"
            );
            conn.Close();
        }
    }
}
```

3. Run the program with Ctrl+F5, and then click the Database Exception-2 button. You'll see the message box shown in Figure 13-9. Click OK to close the message box, then OK to close the next one, then close the window.

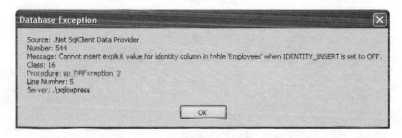

Figure 13-9. *Stored procedure Database Exception message*

How It Works

The stored procedure tries to insert a new employee into the Employees table:

```
insert into employees
(
    employeeid,
    firstname
)
values (50, 'Cinderella')
```

However, since the EmployeeID column in the Employees table is an IDENTITY column, you can't explicitly assign a value to it.

■**Tip** Actually, you can—as the message indicates—if you use SET IDENTITY INSERT employees OFF in the stored procedure before you attempt the INSERT. This would allow you to insert explicit EmployeeID values, but this seldom is, or should be, done.

When this SQL error occurs, the specific SqlException catch clause traps it and displays the information. The finally block then closes the connection.

It's possible for stored procedures to encounter several errors. You can trap and debug these using the SqlException object, as you'll see next.

Try It Out: Handling a Database Exception (Part 3): Errors Collection

The SqlException class has an Errors collection property. Each item in the Errors collection is an object of type SqlError. When a database exception occurs, the Errors collection is populated. For example, let's try to establish a connection to a nonexistent database and investigate the SqlException's Errors collection:

1. Insert the code in Listing 13-6 into the button5_Click method. Note that you're intentionally misspelling the database name.

Listing 13-6. button5_Click()

```
// Create connection
SqlConnection conn = new SqlConnection(@"
    data source = .\sqlexpress;
    integrated security = true;
    database = northwnd
");

// Create command
SqlCommand cmd = conn.CreateCommand();

// Specify stored procedure to be executed
cmd.CommandType = CommandType.StoredProcedure;
cmd.CommandText = "sp_DbException_2";
```

```csharp
try
{
    // Open connection
    conn.Open();

    // Execute stored procedure
    cmd.ExecuteNonQuery();
}
catch (System.Data.SqlClient.SqlException ex)
{
    string str ="";
    for (int i - 0; i < ex.Errors.Count; i++)
    {
        str +=
            "\n" + "Index #" + i + "\n"
          + "Exception: " + ex.Errors[i].ToString() + "\n"
          + "Number: " + ex.Errors[i].Number.ToString() + "\n"
        ;
    }
    MessageBox.Show (str, "Database Exception");
}
catch (System.Exception ex)
{
    string str;
    str = "Source: " + ex.Source;
    str += "\n" + "Exception Message: " + ex.Message;
    MessageBox.Show (str, "ADO.NET Exception");
}
finally
{
    if (conn.State == ConnectionState.Open)
    {
        MessageBox.Show(
            "Finally block closing the connection",
            "Finally"
        );
        conn.Close();
    }
}
```

2. Run the program with Ctrl+F5, and then click the `Database Exception-2` button. You'll see the message box shown in Figure 13-10.

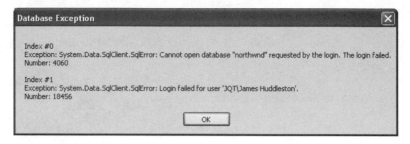

Figure 13-10. *Handling multiple database errors*

Observe that two items are found in the `Errors` collection, and their error numbers are different.

How It Works

In the connection string, you specify a database that doesn't exist on the server; here you misspell `Northwind` as `Northwnd`:

```
// Create connection
SqlConnection conn = new SqlConnection(@"
    data source = .\sqlexpress;
    integrated security = true;
    database = northwnd
");
```

When you try to open the connection, an exception of type `SqlException` is thrown, and you loop through the items of the `Errors` collection and get each `Error` object using its indexer:

```
catch (System.Data.SqlClient.SqlException ex)
{
    string str ="";
    for (int i = 0; i < ex.Errors.Count; i++)
```

```
        {
            str +=
                "\n" + "Index #" + i + "\n"
              + "Exception: " + ex.Errors[i].ToString() + "\n"
              + "Number: " + ex.Errors[i].Number.ToString() + "\n"
            ;
        }
        MessageBox.Show (str, "Database Exception");
    }
```

This example shows that the SqlException object carries detailed information about every SQL error in its Errors collection.

Summary

In this chapter, you saw how to handle exceptions thrown by ADO.NET and by SQL Server. In particular, you learned how to handle both single and multiple database errors with the System.Data.SqlClient.SqlException class.

In the next chapter, you'll look at transactions and how to maintain database integrity when multiple users are working concurrently.

CHAPTER 14

■■■

Using Transactions

A *transaction* is a set of operations performed so all operations are guaranteed to succeed or fail as one unit.

A common example of a simple transaction is transferring money from a checking account to a savings account. This involves two operations: deducting money from the checking account and adding it to the savings account. Both must succeed together and be *committed* to the accounts, or both must fail together and be *rolled back* so that the accounts are maintained in a consistent state. Under no circumstances should money be deducted from the checking account but not added to the savings account (or vice versa). By using a transaction, both operations can be guaranteed to succeed or fail together.

Transactions may comprise many individual operations and even other transactions. Transactions are essential for maintaining data integrity, both for multiple related operations and when multiple users update the database concurrently.

In this chapter, we'll cover:

- When to use transactions

- The ACID properties of a transaction

- How to code transactions

When to Use Transactions

You should use transactions when several operations must succeed or fail as a unit. The following are some frequent scenarios where you must use transactions:

- In batch processing, where multiple rows must be inserted or deleted as a single unit

- Whenever a change to one table requires that other tables be kept consistent

- When modifying data in two or more databases, concurrently

- In distributed transactions, where data is manipulated in databases on different servers

When you use transactions, you place locks on data pending permanent change to the database. No other operations can take place on locked data until you lift the lock. You could lock anything from a single row up to the whole database. This is called *concurrency*; that is, concurrency is how the database handles multiple updates at one time.

In the bank example, locks ensure that two separate transactions don't access the same accounts at the same time. If they did, either deposits or withdrawals could be lost.

■Note It's important to keep transactions pending for the shortest period of time. A lock stops others from accessing the locked database resource. Too many locks, or locks on frequently accessed resources, can seriously degrade performance.

Understanding ACID Properties

A transaction is characterized by four properties, often referred to as the *ACID properties*: atomicity, consistency, isolation, and durability.

Atomicity: A transaction is atomic if it's regarded as a single action rather than a collection of separate operations. So, a transaction succeeds and is committed to the database only when all the separate operations succeed. On the other hand, if a single operation fails during the transaction, everything is considered to have failed and must be undone (rolled back) if it has already taken place. In the case of the order-entry system of the Northwind database, when you enter an order into the Orders and Order Details tables, data will be saved together in both tables, or it won't be saved at all.

Consistency: The transaction should leave the database in a consistent state— whether or not it completed successfully. The data modified by the transaction must comply with all the constraints placed on the columns in order to maintain data integrity. In the case of Northwind, you can't have rows in the Order Details table without a corresponding row in the Orders table, as this would leave the data in an inconsistent state.

Isolation: Every transaction has a well-defined boundary. One transaction shouldn't affect other transactions running at the same time. Data modifications made by one transaction must be isolated from the data modifications made by all other transactions. A transaction sees data in the state it was in before another concurrent transaction modified it, or it sees the data after the second transaction has completed, but it doesn't see an intermediate state.

Durability: Data modifications that occur within a successful transaction are kept permanently within the system regardless of what else occurs. Transaction logs are maintained so that should a failure occur the database can be restored to its original state before the failure. As each transaction is completed a row is entered in the database transaction log. If you have a major system failure that requires the database to be restored from a backup, you could then use this transaction log to insert (roll forward) any successful transactions that had taken place.

Every database server that offers support for transactions enforces these four properties automatically. All you need to do is create the transactions in the first place, which is what you'll look at next.

How to Code Transactions

The following three T-SQL statements control transactions in SQL Server:

BEGIN TRANSACTION: This marks the beginning of a transaction.

COMMIT TRANSACTION: This marks the successful end of a transaction. It signals the database to save the work.

ROLLBACK TRANSACTION: This denotes that a transaction hasn't been successful and signals the database to roll back to the state it was in prior to the transaction.

Note that there is no END TRANSACTION statement. Transactions end on (explicit or implicit) commits and rollbacks.

■**Note** All our example programs to this point have run in SQL Server's default *autocommit mode*, i.e., SQL Server implicitly committed or rolled back each statement depending on its success or failure. Auto-commit mode can't provide atomicity and consistency for multiple statements. It's also a potentially prohibitively expensive way to do things if you need to perform many (thousands or millions, but sometimes even just hundreds) of inserts. How to design transactions to handle such heavy loads is beyond the scope of this book, but what you learn here forms the basis for designing solutions for all transactional situations.

Coding Transactions in T-SQL

We'll use a stored procedure to practice coding transactions in SQL. It's an intentionally artificial example but representative of transaction processing fundamentals. It keeps things simple so you can focus on the important issue of what can happen in a transaction. That's what you really need to understand, especially when you later code the same transaction in C#.

■**Warning** Using ROLLBACK and COMMIT inside stored procedures typically requires careful consideration of what transactions may already be in progress and led to the stored procedure call. Our example runs by itself, so we're not concerned with this here, but you should always consider whether it's a potential issue.

Try It Out: Coding a Transaction in T-SQL

Let's code a transaction to both add a customer to and delete one from the Northwind Customers table. Customers has eleven columns, but only two, CustomerID and CompanyName, don't allow nulls, so we'll use just those columns for insertion. We'll also use arbitrary customer IDs to make it easy to find the rows we manipulate when viewing customers sorted by ID.

1. In SSMSE, create a stored procedure named sp_Trans_Test, using the code in Listing 14-1. Note that you're using several new SQL statements for stored procedure programming. We don't explain the ones not involved in transactions, but their meaning and usage should be obvious.

Listing 14-1. sp_Trans_Test

```
create procedure sp_Trans_Test
    @newcustid nchar(5),
    @newconame nvarchar(40),
    @oldcustid nchar(5)
as
    declare @inserr int
    declare @delerr int
    declare @maxerr int

    set @maxerr = 0
```

```
begin transaction

-- Add a customer
insert into customers
(
    customerid,
    companyname
)
values(@newcustid, @newconame)

-- Save error number
set @inserr = @@error
if @inserr > @maxerr
    set @maxerr = @inserr

-- Delete a customer
delete from customers
where
    customerid = @oldcustid

-- Save error number
set @delerr = @@error
if @delerr > @maxerr
    set @maxerr = @delerr

-- If an error occurred, roll back
if @maxerr <> 0
    begin
        rollback
        print 'Transaction rolled back'
    end
else
    begin
        commit
        print 'Transaction committed'
    end

print 'INSERT error number:' + cast(@inserr as nvarchar(8))
print 'DELETE error number:' + cast(@delerr as nvarchar(8))

return @maxerr
```

2. Run the stored procedure from Object Explorer. When prompted, enter just a for both @newcustid and @newconame and z for @oldcustid. A new edit window will appear, displaying your input values. The Results window should show a Return Value of zero. Click on the Messages tab and you should see the same messages as in Figure 14-1.

Figure 14-1. *Rows inserted (but not deleted) in a transaction*

3. Look at the table with Object Explorer (right-click dbo.Customers and click Open Table) and you'll see that customer aaa has been inserted. (See Figure 14-2.)

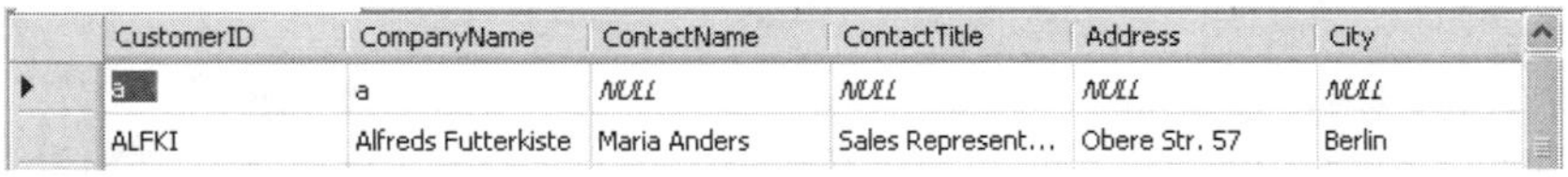

Figure 14-2. *Row inserted in a transaction*

4. Add another customer, with aa for both @newcustid and @newconame and z for @oldcustid.

How It Works

We'll discuss the T-SQL first, then the results. You defined three input parameters:

```
create procedure sp_Trans_Test
    @newcustid nchar(5),
    @newconame nvarchar(40),
    @oldcustid nchar(5)
as
```

and declared three local variables:

```
declare @inserr int
declare @delerr int
declare @maxerr int
```

that you used to instrument the stored procedure, so you can capture and display the error numbers from the INSERT and DELETE statements.

You marked the beginning of the transaction with a BEGIN TRANSACTION statement and followed it with the INSERT and DELETE statements that are part of the transaction. After each statement, you saved the return number for it.

```
begin transaction

-- Add a customer
insert into customers
(
    customerid,
    companyname
)
values(@newcustid, @newconame)

-- Save error number
set @inserr = @@error
if @inserr > @maxerr
    set @maxerr = @inserr

-- Delete a customer
delete from customers
where
    customerid = @oldcustid

-- Save error number
set @delerr = @@error
if @delerr > @maxerr
    set @maxerr = @delerr
```

Error handling is important at all times in SQL Server, and it's never more so than inside transactional code. When you execute any T-SQL statement, there's always the possibility that it may not succeed. The T-SQL @@ERROR function returns the error number for the last T-SQL statement executed. If no error occurred, @@ERROR returns zero.

@@ERROR is reset after *every* T-SQL statement (even SET and IF) is executed, so if you want to save an error number for a particular statement you must store it before the next statement executes. That's why you declared the local variables. You used @maxerr to simplify the test, but you could have tested the others instead.

If @@ERROR returns any value other than 0, an error has occurred, and you want to roll back the transaction. You also include PRINT statements to report that a rollback or commit has occurred.

```
-- If an error occurred, roll back
if @maxerr <> 0
   begin
      rollback
      print 'Transaction rolled back'
   end
else
   begin
      commit
      print 'Transaction committed'
   end
```

■**Tip** T-SQL (and standard SQL) supports various alternative forms for keywords and phrases. We've used just ROLLBACK and COMMIT here.

Then you added some more instrumentation, so you could see what error numbers were encountered during the transaction:

```
print 'INSERT error number:' + cast(@inserr as nvarchar(8))
print 'DELETE error number:' + cast(@delerr as nvarchar(8))

return @maxerr
```

Now let's look at what happened when you executed the stored procedure. You ran it twice, and added a new customer each time, but you also entered the same nonexistent customer to delete each time. If all statements in a transaction are supposed to succeed or fail as one unit, why did the INSERT succeed when the DELETE didn't delete anything?

Figure 14-2 should make everything clear. Both the INSERT and DELETE had zero error numbers. (When a DELETE doesn't find any rows to delete, T-SQL doesn't treat that as an error.) In fact, that's why you used a nonexistent customer. The rest of the Customers (well, all but two) have child Orders, and you can't delete customers before you delete their orders.

Now that you have a couple customers we can delete at will, let's explore some of the essential features of transactions. There's much more to transactions than we can cover in this chapter, but the following examples will give you a foundation to extrapolate from to handle any combination of operations.

Try It Out: What Happens When the First Operation Fails

In this example, you'll try to insert an invalid (duplicate) customer and delete a deletable one.

1. Run sp_Trans_Test to add customer a and delete customer aa. The result should appear as in Figure 14-3.

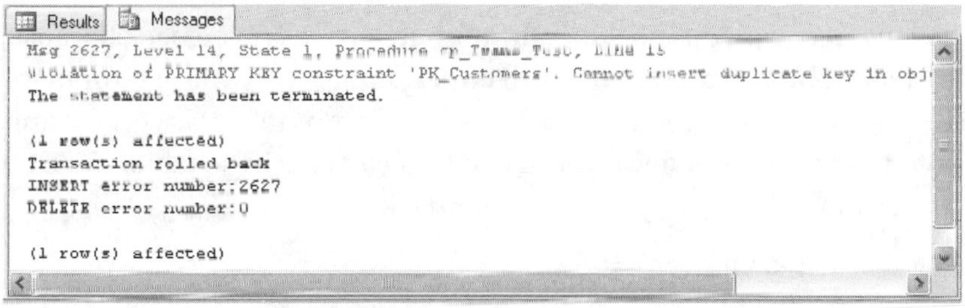

Figure 14-3. *Second operation rolled back*

2. In the Messages window, note that the transaction was rolled back because the INSERT failed and was terminated with error number 2627 (whose error message appears at the top of the window). The DELETE error number was 0, so it apparently executed successfully, but was rolled back. (If you check the table, you'll find aa is still a customer.)

How It Works

Since customer a already exists, SQL Server prevented the insertion of a duplicate, so the first operation failed. When the second statement in the transaction was executed, customer aa was deleted since it didn't have any child orders, but since @maxerr wasn't zero (it's 2627; see the Results window), you rolled back the transaction, undoing the deletion.

Try It Out: What Happens When the Second Operation Fails

In this example, you'll insert a valid new customer and try to delete an undeletable one.

1. Run sp_Trans_Test to add customer aaa and delete customer ALFKI. The result should appear as in Figure 14-4.

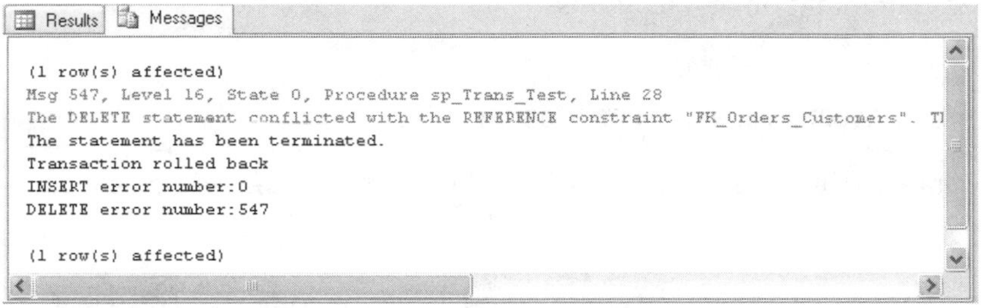

Figure 14-4. *First operation rolled back*

2. In the Messages window, note that the transaction was rolled back because the DELETE failed and was terminated with error number 547 (whose error message appears at the top of the window). The INSERT error number was 0, so it apparently executed successfully, but was rolled back. (If you check the table, you'll find aaa is not a customer.)

How It Works

Since customer aaa doesn't exist, SQL Server inserted the row, so the first operation succeeded. When the second statement in the transaction was executed, SQL Server prevented the deletion of customer ALFKI because it had child orders, but since @maxerr wasn't zero (it's 547; see the Results window), you rolled back the transaction, undoing the deletion.

Try It Out: What Happens When Both Operations Fail

In this example, you'll try to insert an invalid new customer and try to delete an undeletable one.

1. Run sp_Trans_Test to add customer a and delete customer ALFKI. The result should appear as in Figure 14-5.

2. In the Messages window, note that the transaction was rolled back (even though neither statement succeeded, so there was nothing to roll back) because @maxerr was 2627, returned for the INSERT. Error messages for both failing statements are displayed at the top of the window.

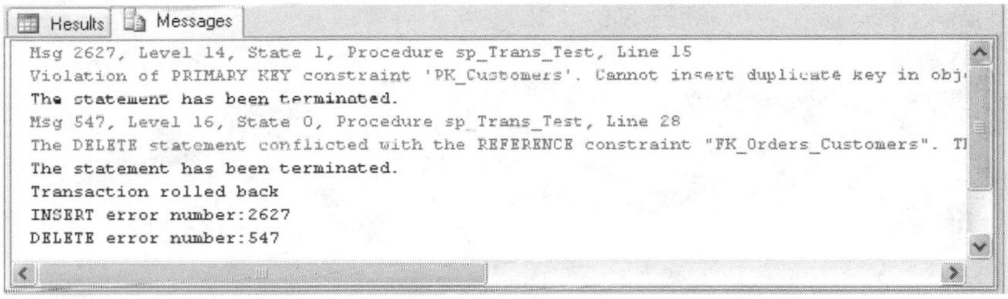

```
Results   Messages
Msg 2627, Level 14, State 1, Procedure sp_Trans_Test, Line 15
Violation of PRIMARY KEY constraint 'PK_Customers'. Cannot insert duplicate key in obj
The statement has been terminated.
Msg 547, Level 16, State 0, Procedure sp_Trans_Test, Line 28
The DELETE statement conflicted with the REFERENCE constraint "FK_Orders_Customers". Tl
The statement has been terminated.
Transaction rolled back
INSERT error number:2627
DELETE error number:547
```

Figure 14-5. *Both operations rolled back*

How It Works

By now, you should understand why both statements failed. This example proves that even when the first statement fails the second is executed (and in this case failed with error number 547), which our original example, where the error code was 0 when there were no rows to delete, didn't necessarily prove since the error number there may have come from the

```
set @maxerr = @inserr
```

immediately before the DELETE statement.

We've used rather straightforward but crude T-SQL to demonstrate transactions, primarily because we wanted to focus on the underlying operational dynamics, but we don't mean to suggest this is necessarily the best way to code transactions in T-SQL. Let's see a more C#-like alternative.

Try It Out: Coding a Transaction with the TRY...CATCH Construct

Let's code a transaction to both add a customer to and delete one from the Northwind Customers table. Customers has eleven columns, but only two, CustomerID and CompanyName, don't allow nulls, so we'll use just those columns for insertion. We'll also use arbitrary customer IDs to make it easy to find the rows we manipulate when viewing customers sorted by ID.

1. In SSMSE, create a stored procedure named sp_Trans_Try using the code in Listing 14-2. Note that you're using several new SQL statements for stored procedure programming. We don't explain the ones not involved in transactions, but their meaning and usage should be obvious.

Listing 14-2. sp_Trans_Try

```
create procedure sp_Trans_Try
    @newcustid nchar(5),
    @newconame nvarchar(40),
    @oldcustid nchar(5)
as
    declare @inserr int
    declare @delerr int
    declare @maxerr int

    set @maxerr = 0

    begin try
        begin transaction

        -- Add a customer
        insert into customers
        (
            customerid,
            companyname
        )
        values(@newcustid, @newconame)

        -- Save error number
        set @inserr = @@error
        if @inserr > @maxerr
            set @maxerr = @inserr

        -- Delete a customer
        delete from customers
        where
            customerid = @oldcustid

        -- Save error number
        set @delerr = @@error
        if @delerr > @maxerr
            set @maxerr = @delerr
```

```
    commit
    print 'Transaction committed'
end try
begin catch
        rollback
        print 'Transaction rolled back'
end catch

print 'INSERT error number:' + cast(@inserr as nvarchar(8))
print 'DELETE error number:' + cast(@delerr as nvarchar(8))

return @maxerr
```

2. Run the stored procedure from Object Explorer. When prompted, enter aaa for both @newcustid and @newconame and aa for @oldcustid. The Messages window (see Figure 14-6) is almost the same as Figure 14-1. The difference is that here we've actually deleted a row, for customer aa, so we see "1 row(s) affected" for the DELETE.

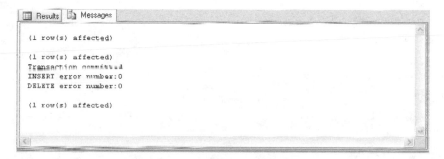

Figure 14-6. *Using TRY…CATCH with a transaction*

3. Look at the table with Object Explorer and you'll see that customer aaa has been inserted and customer aa deleted. (See Figure 14-7.)

CustomerID	CompanyName	ContactName	ContactTitle	Address	City
a	a	NULL	NULL	NULL	NULL
aaa	aaa	NULL	NULL	NULL	NULL
ALFKI	Alfreds Futterkiste	Maria Anders	Sales Represent…	Obere Str. 57	Berlin

Figure 14-7. *Rows inserted and deleted using TRY…CATCH*

How It Works

Most of the code remained the same. We left in the instrumentation, but we really don't need @maxerr, at least not to decide whether to roll back or commit, so the code is lengthier than it has to be.

The biggest changes were moving the statements, including COMMIT, into a TRY block:

```
begin try
   begin transaction

   -- Add a customer
   insert into customers
   (
      customerid,
      companyname
   )
   values(@newcustid, @newconame)

   -- Save error number
   set @inserr = @@error
   if @inserr > @maxerr
      set @maxerr = @inserr

   -- Delete a customer
   delete from customers
   where
      customerid = @oldcustid

   -- Save error number
   set @delerr = @@error
   if @delerr > @maxerr
      set @maxerr = @delerr

   commit
   print 'Transaction committed'
end try
```

and replacing the conditional logic for rolling back by moving ROLLBACK into a CATCH block:

```
begin catch
  rollback
  print 'Transaction rolled back'
end catch
```

Things work like in a C# try statement. In fact, unlike in `sp_Trans_Try` if you try to add a duplicate customer the DELETE is never executed, since the TRY block is exited as soon as the INSERT fails. Without further changes, the instrumentation will give deceptive results in this case, but we won't pursue that further since it's not part of transaction coding per se.

Now that you've seen how transactions work, you're ready to shift from T-SQL to C#!

Coding Transactions in ADO.NET

In ADO.NET, a transaction is an instance of a class that implements the interface `System.Data.IDbTransaction`. Like a data reader, a transaction has no constructor of its own but is created by calling another object's method—in this case, a connection's `BeginTransaction` method. Commands are associated with a specific transaction for a specific connection, and any SQL submitted by these commands is executed as part of the same transaction.

Try It Out: Working with ADO.NET Transactions

In this ADO.NET example, you'll code a C# equivalent of `sp_Trans Try`.

1. Create a new Windows Application project named `Chapter14`. When Solution Explorer opens, save the solution.

2. Rename the `Chapter14` project to `AdoNetTransactions` and `Program1.cs` to `AdoNetTransactions.cs`.

3. Change the Text property of `Form1` to `ADO.NET Transactions`.

4. Add three labels, three text boxes, and a button to the form as in Figure 14-8.

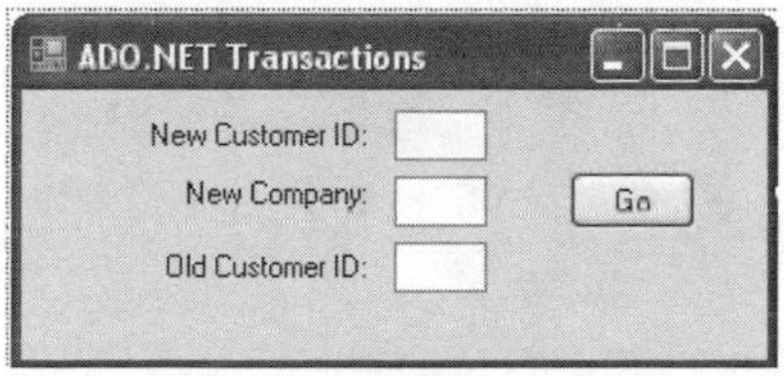

Figure 14-8. *ADO.NET Transactions form*

5. Add a using directive to Form1.cs:

```
using System.Data.SqlClient;
```

6. Insert the code in Listing 14-3 into the button's click event handler.

Listing 14-3. button1_Click()

```
SqlConnection conn = new SqlConnection(@"
    data source = .\sqlexpress;
    integrated security = true;
    database = Northwind
");

// INSERT statement
string sqlins = @"
    insert into customers
    (
        customerid,
        companyname
    )
    values(@newcustid, @newconame)
";

// DELETE statement
string sqldel = @"
    delete from customers
    where
        customerid = @oldcustid
";

// Open connection
conn.Open();

// Begin transaction
SqlTransaction sqltrans = conn.BeginTransaction();
```

```
try
{
    // create insert command
    SqlCommand cmdins = conn.CreateCommand();
    cmdins.CommandText = sqlins;
    cmdins.Transaction = sqltrans;
    cmdins.Parameters.Add("@newcustid", SqlDbType.NVarChar, 5);
    cmdins.Parameters.Add("@newconame", SqlDbType.NVarChar, 30);

    // create delete command
    SqlCommand cmddel = conn.CreateCommand();
    cmddel.CommandText = sqldel;
    cmddel.Transaction = sqltrans;
    cmddel.Parameters.Add("@oldcustid", SqlDbType.NVarChar, 5);

    // add customer
    cmdins.Parameters["@newcustid"].Value = textBox1.Text;
    cmdins.Parameters["@newconame"].Value = textBox2.Text;
    cmdins.ExecuteNonQuery();

    // delete customer
    cmddel.Parameters["@oldcustid"].Value = textBox3.Text;
    cmddel.ExecuteNonQuery();

    //Commit transaction
    sqltrans.Commit();

    // No exception, transaction committed, give message
    MessageBox.Show(
        "Transaction committed"
    );
}
catch (System.Data.SqlClient.SqlException  ex)
{
    //Roll back transaction
    sqltrans.Rollback();
```

```
        MessageBox.Show(
            "Transaction rolled back\n" + ex.Message,
            "Rollback Transaction"
        );
    }
    catch (System.Exception ex)
    {
        MessageBox.Show("System Error\n" + ex.Message, "Error");
    }
    finally
    {
    // Close connection
    conn.Close();
    }
```

7. Run the program with Ctrl+F5. Try the same kinds of insertions and deletions as you did with sp_Trans_Test, but use b, bb, and bbb, instead of a, aa, and aaa, for the new customers. You should see the same kind of results, but as with sp_Trans_Try, there can only be one error in any transaction.

How It Works

After you opened the connection, you created a transaction. Note that transactions are connection specific. You can't create a second transaction for the same connection before committing or rolling back the first one. Though the BeginTransaction method begins a transaction, the transaction itself performs no work until the first SQL is executed by a command.

```
    // Open connection
    conn.Open();

    // Begin transaction
    SqlTransaction sqltrans = conn.BeginTransaction();
```

■**Tip** BeginTransaction() is overloaded. You can give a transaction a name and specify its isolation level (see the next section, "Suggestions for Further Study"). We don't need either here, and you may not need them often.

You created separate commands for the INSERT and DELETE statements and associated them with the same transaction by setting their Transaction property to the same transaction, sqltrans.

```
// create insert command
SqlCommand cmdins = conn.CreateCommand();
cmdins.CommandText = sqlins;
cmdins.Transaction = sqltrans;
cmdins.Parameters.Add("@newcustid", SqlDbType.NVarChar, 5);
cmdins.Parameters.Add("@newconame", SqlDbType.NVarChar, 30);

// create delete command
SqlCommand cmddel = conn.CreateCommand();
cmddel.CommandText = sqldel;
cmddel.Transaction = sqltrans;
cmddel.Parameters.Add("@oldcustid", SqlDbType.NVarChar, 5);
```

Tip You could have used the same command object for both commands, but it really doesn't save you anything and it would prevent you from preparing the commands if the program were designed to do this.

You then assigned values to the parameters and executed the commands:

```
// add customer
cmdins.Parameters["@newcustid"].Value = textBox1.Text;
cmdins.Parameters["@newconame"].Value = textBox2.Text;
cmdins.ExecuteNonQuery();

// delete customer
cmddel.Parameters["@oldcustid"].Value = textBox3.Text;
cmddel.ExecuteNonQuery();
```

committing the transaction after the second command:

```
//Commit transaction
sqltrans.Commit();
```

or rolling it back in the database exception handler:

```
catch (System.Data.SqlClient.SqlException  ex)
{
   //Roll back transaction
   sqltrans.Rollback();
```

Suggestions for Further Study

You've seen only the tip of the transaction iceberg in this chapter. Though the basic techniques remain the same and you can write many real-world programs with what you've learned, you have a great deal more to learn about how both ADO.NET and SQL Server manage transactions. Some important topics include the following:

Isolation levels: These determine how a transaction is isolated from other concurrent transactions. SQL Server 2005 supports six isolation levels; the SQL standard itself defines four. The choice of which to use depends on what your program does and what kind of performance it seeks to achieve.

Nested transactions: Transactions can be nested. In general, commits and rollbacks are local to the nested transaction, but see BOL for specifics.

Distributed transactions: Transactions can affect more than one database on more than one server. The T-SQL BEGIN DISTRIBUTED TRANSACTION statement is used to start them.

Savepoints: Savepoints are defined by the SQL standard and supported by the T-SQL SAVE TRANSACTION statement.

Summary

This chapter covered the fundamentals of transactions, from concepts such as their ACID properties to hands-on coding of transactions in T-SQL and ADO.NET. There's much more to learn about transactions, but the techniques you practiced here are the basic ones for handling any transactional processing.

In the next chapter we'll look at the fundamentals of ADO.NET event handling.

■ ■ ■

Working with ADO.NET Events

ADO.NET objects (such as connections and datasets) can fire events when a property has changed. For example, you can make a connection that notifies you when it opens or closes. Similarly, you can create a dataset object that notifies you when a column value is changed or when a row is deleted.

In this chapter, we'll cover:

- What events and delegates are and how they're useful

- Different types of events supported by ADO.NET objects

- How to add and remove event handlers

Understanding Events and Delegates

An *event* is a class member (of the delegate type) that enables a class or an object to provide notifications by invoking methods on other objects that signal the occurrence of an action. The action could be a user interaction, such as a mouse click, or an operation carried out by a program. The object that triggers the event is the *event source*. The object that captures the event and responds to it is the *event consumer* (or *client*). The method that handles the event is the *event handler*.

The event source doesn't care what objects consume its events. The consumers give it delegates; that is, they give it a mapping to methods that the source will execute when the event occurs.

Delegates encapsulate an invocation list of one or more methods. A delegate is an object that can be sent to multiple sources, so a single delegate can handle multiple events. For example, a button-click event and a menu command–click event can both invoke the same delegate, which then calls a single method to handle these separate events the same way.

The binding mechanism used with delegates is dynamic; in other words, a delegate can be bound at runtime to any method whose signature matches that of the event handler. This feature allows you to set up or change the bound method depending on a condition and to attach an event handler dynamically to a control.

When an event is raised, the code within the event handler is executed. Each event handler provides two parameters that help handle the event correctly. The first parameter, the sender, provides a reference to the object that raised the event. The second parameter is an object specific to the event that's being handled. By referencing the object's properties (and sometimes its methods), you can obtain detailed information about the event. Typically, each event has an event handler with a different event-object type for the second parameter.

This event-handling process applies to all events in .NET. Consequently, ADO.NET objects, such as connections, data adapters, and datasets, all raise events that you can handle using the same process. We'll discuss the events raised by ADO.NET objects in detail throughout this chapter, but for now, let's get a feel for how all the different pieces of this process work.

Connections support two events: InfoMessage and StateChange. The declaration of the delegate that binds the StateChange event to an event handler looks like this:

```
public delegate void StateChangeEventHandler(
    object sender,
    StateChangeEventArgs e
);
```

The code to bind the StateChange event to an event handler named CnStateChange looks like this (note the += operator):

```
cn.StateChange += new StateChangeEventHandler(CnStateChange);
```

The event handler itself, which will execute after the event is raised, looks like this:

```
private void CnStateChange(object sender, StateChangeEventArgs ev)
{
    // Event handler code
}
```

Note the parameters of the event handler, which are the same as the parameters of the delegate declaration. The following sections cover all these in more detail. You'll now look at the syntax of adding and removing event handlers.

Adding and Removing Event Handlers

In C#, you specify a delegate by using the += operator. For example, you can bind the StateChange event of the connection object called cn to the CnStateChange method (which you write yourself) by activating a delegate called StateChangeEventHandler (which is provided for you by .NET). The StateChange event of the connection object fires whenever the connection state changes to open or closed:

```
cn.StateChange += new StateChangeEventHandler(CnStateChange);
```

Similarly, you can deactivate a delegate by removing it with the -= operator, as follows:

```
cn.StateChange -= new StateChangeEventHandler(CnStateChange);
```

Once deactivated, when the StateChange event fires, it won't be handled by the CnStateChange event handler. This process of activating and deactivating a delegate can take place as needed in code.

In this chapter, we'll discuss the events raised by ADO.NET objects and how to handle them. While events can be raised and handled by non-ADO.NET objects as well, this chapter pertains only to the ADO.NET objects.

Raising and Handling ADO.NET Events

You can handle the events raised by ADO.NET objects using appropriate delegates. These events are raised when a certain property of the object changes. Although these objects raise several events, we'll discuss only a few, because you can handle them all in the same fashion. You'll use the System.Data.SqlClient .NET data provider, but all data providers handle events in a similar way.

Working with Connection Object Events

The connection object has two events: StateChange and InfoMessage. Let's look at these in more detail.

Using the StateChange Event

The connection object raises the StateChange event when the state of the connection changes. The event handler receives a StateChangeEventArgs object, which you can examine for detailed information about the event. For example, it has OriginalState and CurrentState properties that you can access to find out the state of the connection object before and after a change.

Try It Out: Writing the Connection.StateChange Event

You'll now see how this event is handled. You'll open a connection to the Northwind data-base, retrieve one row from the Customers table, and close the connection. Then you'll write an event handler to notify you of when the connection state changes:

1. Create a new Windows Application project named Chapter15. When Solution Explorer opens, save the solution.

2. Rename the Chapter15 project AdoNetEvents.

3. Change the Text property of Form1 to ADO.NET Events.

4. Add four buttons, a label, and a list box to the form, as shown in Figure 15-1.

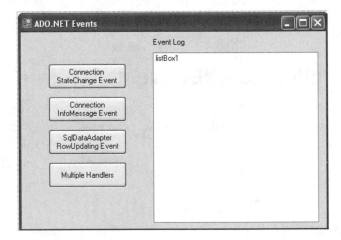

Figure 15-1. *ADO.NET Events form*

5. Add a using directive to Form1.cs for the System.Data.SqlClient namespace.

6. Insert the code in Listing 15-1 into the click event handler for the first button.

Listing 15-1. button1_Click()

```
// create connection
SqlConnection conn = new SqlConnection(@"
    data source = .\sqlexpress;
    integrated security = true;
    database = northwind
");
```

```
// create command
SqlCommand cmd = new SqlCommand();
cmd.CommandText = @"
   select top 1
      customerid,
      companyname
   from
      customers
";
cmd.Connection = conn;

// delegate the StateChange event to the ConnStateChange function
conn.StateChange += new StateChangeEventHandler(ConnStateChange);

try
{
   listBox1.Items.Clear();

   // open connection   ConnStateChange event will be fired
   conn.Open();

   // create data reader
   SqlDataReader dr = cmd.ExecuteReader();

   // display rows in list box
   while(dr.Read())
   {
      listBox1.Items.Add(dr.GetString(0) + "-" + dr.GetString(1));
   }
}
catch(SqlException e1)
{
   MessageBox.Show (e1.Message);
}
finally
{
   // close connection - ConnStateChange event will be fired
   conn.Close();
}
```

7. Add the method in Listing 15-2 to class Form1.cs.

Listing 15-2. ConnStateChange()

```
private void ConnStateChange(object sender, StateChangeEventArgs ev)
{
    // Event handler for the StateChange Event
    listBox1.Items.Add("-------------------------------");
    listBox1.Items.Add("Entering StateChange EventHandler");
    listBox1.Items.Add("Sender = " + sender.ToString());
    listBox1.Items.Add("Original State = " + ev.OriginalState.ToString());
    listBox1.Items.Add("Current State = " + ev.CurrentState.ToString());
    listBox1.Items.Add("Exiting StateChange EventHandler");
    listBox1.Items.Add("-------------------------------");
}
```

8. Build and run the solution with Ctrl+F5. Click the Connection StateChange Event button. You'll see the results in Figure 15-2.

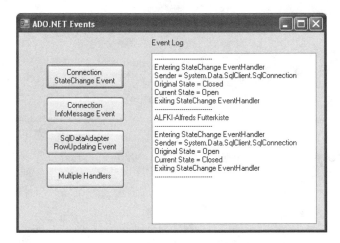

Figure 15-2. *Displaying StateChange Event information*

Notice the values of the Original State and Current State properties before and after the data displays. This example shows that as the connection state changes, the event handler takes over and handles the event.

How It Works

You use a query that selects one row from the Customers table:

```
// Create command
SqlCommand cmd = new SqlCommand();
cmd.CommandText = @"
    select top 1
        customerid,
        companyname
    from
        customers
";
cmd.Connection = conn;
```

Next, you specify the event handler for the StateChange event using the += operator:

```
// delegate the StateChange event to the ConnStateChange function
conn.StateChange += new StateChangeEventHandler(ConnStateChange);
```

The location in your code where you specify the event handler is important. In this case, since you want to capture the connection's StateChange event, you specify the delegate before you actually open the connection.

You then write the event handler. Earlier, you specified ConnStateChange as the name of the method that will handle the event. The StateChangeEventHandler delegate provides objects with information about the event: the sender object and the StateChangeEventArgs object. The StateChange event provides the delegate with these objects, and the delegate gives the event handler these objects so the event handler can handle the event appropriately. That's why the ConnStateChange event handler has the same parameters as the StateChangeEventHandler.

You display information each time the handler is called—that is, each time the connection undergoes a state change:

```
private void ConnStateChange(object sender, StateChangeEventArgs ev)
{
    // Event handler for the StateChange Event
    listBox1.Items.Add("------------------------------");
    listBox1.Items.Add("Entering StateChange EventHandler");
    listBox1.Items.Add("Sender = " + sender.ToString());
    listBox1.Items.Add("Original State = " + ev.OriginalState.ToString());
    listBox1.Items.Add("Current State = " + ev.CurrentState.ToString());
    listBox1.Items.Add("Exiting StateChange EventHandler");
    listBox1.Items.Add("------------------------------");
}
```

This makes it clear when the execution enters and leaves the event handler. You also see that the sender object is the connection. When the connection is opened, its current state is Open and its original state is Closed. When the connection is closed, the current state is Closed and the original state is Open.

This example runs pretty well, and you can see what's happening, but in a real-life application, why would users care to be notified if a connection is open or closed? All they need is to see the data. One way to use the StateChange event is to keep track of how many times connections are established and keep a running total. Based on this, you can charge users a fee per connection. (Of course, this is a rudimentary way of charging a fee, and you'll have to figure in other factors.) Another way to use this event would be to keep track of how much time a user has had a connection open and charge based on this.

Using the InfoMessage Event

The InfoMessage event is raised by the connection when the database gives out information messages. Information messages aren't error messages from the database. They're warning and informational messages issued by the database. In the case of SQL Server, any message with a severity of ten or less is considered informational and would be captured with the InfoMessage event.

The InfoMessage event handler receives an InfoMessageEventArgs object that contains a collection of the messages from the data source in its Errors collection property. The Error objects in this collection are of type SqlError and can be queried for information such as the number, the source, the message, and the exact line number in the stored procedure where this message originated from, among others. Let's run a query and a T-SQL PRINT statement. You'll capture this event and query the information in the Errors collection.

Try It Out: Writing the Connection.InfoMessage Event

To write the Connection.InfoMessage event, follow these steps:

1. Insert the code in Listing 15-3 into the click event handler for the second button.

Listing 15-3. button2_Click()

```
// create connection
SqlConnection conn = new SqlConnection(@"
    data source = .\sqlexpress;
    integrated security = true;
    database = northwind
");
```

```csharp
// delegate the InfoMessage event to the ConnInfoMessage method
conn.InfoMessage += new SqlInfoMessageEventHandler(ConnInfoMessage);

// delegate the StateChange event to the ConnStateChange function
conn.StateChange += new StateChangeEventHandler(ConnStateChange);

// create command
SqlCommand cmd = new SqlCommand();
cmd.CommandText = @"
    select top 2
        customerid
    from customers
";
cmd.Connection = conn;

try
{
    // clear list box
    listBox1.Items.Clear();

    // open connection
    conn.Open();

    // create data reader
    SqlDataReader rdr = cmd.ExecuteReader();

    while(rdr.Read())
    {
        listBox1.Items.Add(rdr.GetString(0));
    }

    rdr.Close();

    // execute a PRINT statement
    cmd.CommandText = @"
        print 'Get CustomerId for all customers'
    ";
    cmd.ExecuteNonQuery();
}
catch(SqlException ex)
```

```
        {
            MessageBox.Show (ex.Message);
        }
        finally
        {
            // close connection
            conn.Close();
        }
```

2. Add the method in Listing 15-4 to class Form1.cs.

Listing 15-4. ConnInfoMessage()

```
    private void ConnInfoMessage(object sender, SqlInfoMessageEventArgs ev)
    {
        foreach (SqlError err in ev.Errors)
        {
            listBox1.Items.Add("-----------------------------");
            listBox1.Items.Add("Entering InfoMessage Event Handler");
            listBox1.Items.Add("Source- " + err.Source);
            listBox1.Items.Add("State- " + err.State);
            listBox1.Items.Add("Number- " + err.Number);
            listBox1.Items.Add("Procedure- " + err.Procedure);
            listBox1.Items.Add("Server- " + err.Server);
            listBox1.Items.Add("Message- " + err.Message);
            listBox1.Items.Add("Exiting InfoMessage Event Handler");
            listBox1.Items.Add("-----------------------------");
        }
    }
```

3. Build and run the solution with Ctrl+F5. Click the Connection InfoMessage Event button. You'll see the results shown in Figure 15-3. Scroll down to see how all the information is displayed.

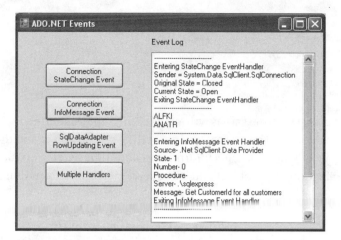

Figure 15-3. *Displaying InfoMessage Event information*

How It Works

After creating a connection object, you specify the CnInfoMessage function as the EventHandler for the InfoMessage event:

```
// delegate the InfoMessage event to the ConnInfoMessage method
conn.InfoMessage += new SqlInfoMessageEventHandler(ConnInfoMessage);
```

You also captured the StateChange event by using the same EventHandler you used before.

```
// delegate the StateChange event to the ConnStateChange function
conn.StateChange += new StateChangeEventHandler(ConnStateChange);
```

Then you execute a query, get the CustomerIds of two employees, and add them to the list box:

```
// create command
SqlCommand cmd = new SqlCommand();
cmd.CommandText = @"
    select top 2
        customerid
    from customers
";
```

Then you execute a PRINT statement against the database. You use the ExecuteNonQuery method of the command object, since the PRINT statement doesn't return any rows:

```
          // execute a PRINT statement
          cmd.CommandText = @"
             print 'Get CustomerId for all customers'
          ";
          cmd.ExecuteNonQuery();
```

The EventHandler method connInfoMessage is written with the same signature as the delegate SqlInfoMessageEventHandler. The two arguments are the sender object and the SqlInfoMessageEventArgs object, which contains information about the event. You then loop through the Errors collection of the object and list several pieces of information about the message itself:

```
      private void ConnInfoMessage(object sender, SqlInfoMessageEventArgs ev)
      {
          foreach (SqlError err in ev.Errors)
          {
              listBox1.Items.Add("------------------------------");
              listBox1.Items.Add("Entering InfoMessage Event Handler");
              listBox1.Items.Add("Source- " + err.Source);
              listBox1.Items.Add("State- " + err.State);
              listBox1.Items.Add("Number- " + err.Number);
              listBox1.Items.Add("Procedure- " + err.Procedure);
              listBox1.Items.Add("Server- " + err.Server);
              listBox1.Items.Add("Message- " + err.Message);
              listBox1.Items.Add("Exiting InfoMessage Event Handler");
              listBox1.Items.Add("------------------------------");
          }
      }
```

Working with RowUpdate Events

So far, you've seen the connection events. ADO.NET supports a wide variety of other events for the purpose of aiding in data validation. For example, a data adapter serves as a bridge between a dataset and a database. When the data adapter is ready to update the changes in the dataset, it raises predefined events. You can code handlers for these events to find more information about the status of the update. Table 15-1 lists some of the common events raised when data is manipulated in ADO.NET objects. The table presents the object that raises the event, the event name, and the name of the delegate. The "Remarks" column describes the EventArgs object received by the event handler. The object received by the event handler itself has several properties you can use to take appropriate action.

Table 15-1. *Common ADO.NET Events*

Object	Event	Delegate	Remarks
SqlDataAdapter	RowUpdating	SqlRowUpdatingEventHandler	Raised before the row is updated in the database. The event handler receives a SqlRowUpdatingEventArgs object.
SqlDataAdapter	RowUpdated	SqlRowUpdatedEventHandler	Raised after a row is updated in the database. The event handler receives a SqlRowUpdatedEventArgs object.
SqlDataAdapter	FillError	FillErrorEventHandler	Raised when the Fill method is called. The event handler receives a FillErrorEventArgs object.
DataRow	ColumnChanging	DataColumnChangeEventHandler	Raised when the data in a data column is changing. The handler receives a DataColumnChangeEventArgs object.
DataRow	ColumnChanged	DataColumnChangeEventHandler	Raised after a value has been changed for the specified data column in a data row. The handler receives a DataColumnChangedEventArgs object.
DataTable	RowChanging	DataRowChangeEventHandler	Raised when a data row is changing. The event handler receives a DataChangeEventArgs object.
DataTable	RowChanged	DataRowChangeEventHandler	Raised after a data row has changed. The event handler receives a DataChangeEventArgs object.
DataTable	RowDeleting	DataRowChangeEventHandler	Raised before a data row is deleted. The event handler receives a DataRowChangeEventArgs object.
DataTable	RowDeleted	DataRowChangeEventHandler	Raised after a data row is deleted. The event handler receives a DataRowChangeEventArgs object.

Try It Out: Using RowUpdating and RowUpdated Events

Let's experiment with the SQL Server data adapter's RowUpdating and RowUpdated events; in this example, you'll see how they're raised and handled when a value in a dataset changes:

1. Insert the code in Listing 15-5 into the click event handler for the third button.

Listing 15-5. button3_Click()

```
// clear list box
listBox1.Items.Clear();

// create connection
SqlConnection conn = new SqlConnection(@"
    data source = .\sqlexpress;
    integrated security = true;
    database = northwind
");

try
{
    // open connection
    conn.Open();

    // create data adapter
    SqlDataAdapter da = new SqlDataAdapter(
        @"
        select
            *
        from
            Customers
        ",
        conn
    );

    // build command
    SqlCommandBuilder cb = new SqlCommandBuilder(da);

    // create and fill dataset (select only first row)
    DataSet ds = new DataSet();
    da.Fill(ds, 0, 1, "Customers");

    // add handlers
    da.RowUpdating += new SqlRowUpdatingEventHandler(OnRowUpdating);
    da.RowUpdated += new SqlRowUpdatedEventHandler(OnRowUpdated);
```

```
        // modify dataset
        DataTable dt = ds.Tables["Customers"];
        dt.Rows[0][1] = "The Volcano Corporation";

        // update - this operation fires two events (RowUpdating/RowUpdated)
        da.Update(ds, "Customers");

        // remove handlers
        da.RowUpdating -= new SqlRowUpdatingEventHandler(OnRowUpdating);
        da.RowUpdated -= new SqlRowUpdatedEventHandler(OnRowUpdated);
    }
    catch (SqlException ex)
    {
        MessageBox.Show(ex.Message);
    }
    finally
    {
        // close connection
        conn.Close();
    }
```

2. Add the method in Listing 15-6 to class Form1 to handle the RowUpdating event.

Listing 15-6. *Handling the* RowUpdating *Event*

```
private void OnRowUpdating(object sender, SqlRowUpdatingEventArgs e)
{
    DisplayEventArgs(e);
}
```

3. Add the method in Listing 15-7 to class Form1 to handle the RowUpdated event.

Listing 15-7. *Handling the* RowUpdated *Event*

```
private void OnRowUpdated(object sender, SqlRowUpdatedEventArgs e)
{
    DisplayEventArgs(e);
}
```

4. Add the overloaded DisplayEventArgs methods in Listing 15-8 to class Form1.

Listing 15-8. *Displaying Event Arguments*

```
private void DisplayEventArgs(SqlRowUpdatingEventArgs args)
{
    listBox1.Items.Add("OnRowUpdating event");
    if (args.Status != UpdateStatus.Continue)
        listBox1.Items.Add("RowStatus = " + args.Status.ToString());
}


private void DisplayEventArgs(SqlRowUpdatedEventArgs args)
{
    listBox1.Items.Add("OnRowUpdated event");
    listBox1.Items.Add("Records Affected = " + args.RecordsAffected);
}
```

5. Build and run the solution with Ctrl+F5. Click the SqlDataAdapter RowUpdating
   Event button. You'll see the results shown in Figure 15-4.

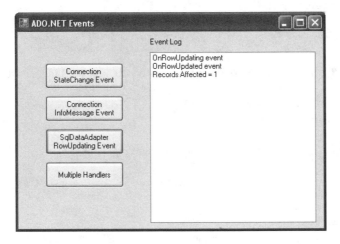

Figure 15-4. *Displaying RowUpdating and RowUpdated Event information*

6. Click the button again. You'll see the results shown in Figure 15-5.

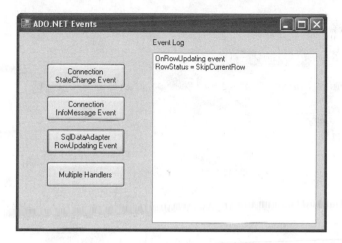

Figure 15-5. *Displaying only RowUpdating Event information*

How It Works

Note that the first time the button is clicked, the RowUpdating and RowUpdated events fire. But the second time, the RowUpdated event doesn't fire, and the RowStatus is SkipCurrentRow.

What you've essentially done in this example is retrieve one row from the Customers table, update it to get the RowUpdating and RowUpdated events to fire, and handle the events. You create and initialize a data adapter and a command builder:

```
// create data adapter
SqlDataAdapter da = new SqlDataAdapter(
    @"
    select
        *
    from
        Customers
    ",
    conn
);

// build command
SqlCommandBuilder cb = new SqlCommandBuilder(da);
```

Then you create a dataset and use the Fill method to fill it with one row of data:

```
// create and fill dataset (select only first row)
DataSet ds = new DataSet();
da.Fill(ds, 0, 1, "Customers");
```

Then you add handlers for the RowUpdating and RowUpdated events using the += operator:

```
// add handlers
da.RowUpdating += new SqlRowUpdatingEventHandler(OnRowUpdating);
da.RowUpdated += new SqlRowUpdatedEventHandler(OnRowUpdated);
```

You then modify the dataset. You change the name of the company to "The Volcano Corporation":

```
// modify dataset
DataTable dt = ds.Tables["Customers"];
dt.Rows[0][1] = "The Volcano Corporation";
```

You then update the database by sending the dataset changes to it. At that moment, the RowUpdating event and the RowUpdated event fire:

```
// update - this operation fires two events (RowUpdating/RowUpdated)
da.Update(ds, "Customers");
```

Finally, you remove the handlers. It isn't necessary in this example, but we've shown it for demonstration purposes. As mentioned earlier in the chapter, the location in code where handlers are added and removed is important and will affect whether events are handled, even if event handlers are present. Notice that you use the -= operator to remove the handlers:

```
// remove handlers
da.RowUpdating -= new SqlRowUpdatingEventHandler(OnRowUpdating);
da.RowUpdated -= new SqlRowUpdatedEventHandler(OnRowUpdated);
```

Both the OnRowUpdating and OnRowUpdated event handlers call a method named DisplayEventArgs. The OnRowUpdating event handler receives the SqlRowUpdatingEventArgs object, and the OnRowUpdated event handler receives the SqlRowUpdatedEventArgs object. As these two events are different, the delegates of these events pass slightly different information to the handler:

```
private void OnRowUpdating(object sender, SqlRowUpdatingEventArgs e)
{
    DisplayEventArgs(e);
}

private void OnRowUpdated(object sender, SqlRowUpdatedEventArgs e)
{
    DisplayEventArgs(e);
}
```

The overloaded DisplayEventArgs method adds an item to the list box to indicate that the executing code has entered it. It also uses the argument passed to it and checks Status. Status is an enumeration of type UpdateStatus. If Status isn't UpdateStatus. Continue, the status is written to the list box. When a row is in the process of being updated, if a change has been made to the row, the status of the row will be marked as Continue and the RowUpdated event will fire for the row. If the status isn't UpdateStatus. Continue, then the RowUpdated event won't fire:

```
private void DisplayEventArgs(SqlRowUpdatingEventArgs args)
{
    listBox1.Items.Add("OnRowUpdating event");
    if (args.Status != UpdateStatus.Continue)
        listBox1.Items.Add("RowStatus - " + args.Status.ToString());
}
```

If the row can be updated, the RowUpdated event will fire, which will be handled by the OnRowUpdated event handler, which in turn will pass the execution to the version of the DisplayEventArgs method that takes the SqlRowUpdatedEventArgs object as the parameter. This object carries with it information about how many rows were updated in the RecordsAffected property, which is displayed in the list box:

```
private void DisplayEventArgs(SqlRowUpdatedEventArgs args)
{
    listBox1.Items.Add("OnRowUpdated event");
    listBox1.Items.Add("Records Affected = " + args.RecordsAffected);
}
```

The first time the button is clicked, the company name changes to "The Volcano Corporation." This raises both the RowUpdating and the RowUpdated events. The second time the button is clicked, since the company name is already "The Volcano Corporation," only the RowUpdating event is raised, and the row's UpdateStatus is marked as SkipCurrentRow. So the RowUpdated event doesn't fire.

Working with Multiple Handlers

It's also possible to have the same event call multiple handlers. You can do this in two ways. You can individually bind the event to two different event handlers, or you can use a *multicast delegate*, where you specify a list of event handlers, and, when the event is fired, all the listed handlers will be invoked successively. You'll use the first alternative in the following example.

Try It Out: Using Multiple Handlers for the Same Event

Follow these steps:

1. Insert the code in Listing 15-9 into the click event handler for the fourth button.

Listing 15-9. `button4_Click()`

```
// create connection
SqlConnection conn = new SqlConnection(@"
    data source = .\sqlexpress;
    integrated security = true;
    database = northwind
");

// delegate the StateChange event to two handlers
conn.StateChange += new StateChangeEventHandler(ConnStateChange);
conn.StateChange += new StateChangeEventHandler(ConnStateChange2);

// create command
SqlCommand cmd = new SqlCommand();
cmd.CommandText = "SELECT TOP 1 CustomerId, CompanyName FROM Customers";
cmd.Connection = conn;

try
{
    listBox1.Items.Clear();
    // open connection
    conn.Open();
    // create data reader
    SqlDataReader dr = cmd.ExecuteReader();

    while(dr.Read())
```

```
        {
            listBox1.Items.Add(dr.GetString(0) + "-" + dr.GetString(1));
        }
    }
    catch(SqlException ex)
    {
        MessageBox.Show (ex.Message);
    }
    finally
    {
        // close connection
        conn.Close();
    }
}
```

2. Add the code in Listing 15-10 to class Form1 as a second event handler for the
   StateChange event.

Listing 15-10. *Alternate Handler for the* StateChange *Event*

```
private void ConnStateChange2(object sender, StateChangeEventArgs ev)
{
    listBox1.Items.Add("--------- --------------------");
    listBox1.Items.Add("Entering Second StateChange EventHandler");
    listBox1.Items.Add("Sender = " + sender.ToString());
    listBox1.Items.Add("Original State = " + ev.OriginalState.ToString());
    listBox1.Items.Add("Current State = " + ev.CurrentState.ToString());
    listBox1.Items.Add("Exiting Second StateChange EventHandler");
    listBox1.Items.Add("------ --------------------");
}
```

3. Build and run the solution with Ctrl+F5. Click the Multiple Handlers button. You'll
   see the results shown in Figure 15-6.

Observe that the event log in Figure 15-6 shows that the first StateChange event handler was invoked and then the second StateChange event handler was invoked. You can code these two handlers to perform different actions, of course.

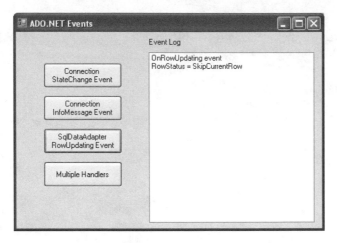

Figure 15-6. *Multiple state change event handlers*

How It Works

You separately bind the StateChange event to two different handlers:

```
// delegate the StateChange event to two handlers
conn.StateChange += new StateChangeEventHandler(ConnStateChange);
conn.StateChange += new StateChangeEventHandler(ConnStateChange2);
```

Notice that in the second instance, you bind it to the CnStateChange2 method, which is the same as CnStateChange except for its enter and exit messages:

```
private void ConnStateChange2(object sender, StateChangeEventArgs ev)
{
    listBox1.Items.Add("------------------------------");
    listBox1.Items.Add("Entering Second StateChange EventHandler");
    listBox1.Items.Add("Sender = " + sender.ToString());
    listBox1.Items.Add("Original State = " + ev.OriginalState.ToString());
    listBox1.Items.Add("Current State = " + ev.CurrentState.ToString());
    listBox1.Items.Add("Exiting Second StateChange EventHandler");
    listBox1.Items.Add("------------------------------");
}
```

Summary

In this chapter, we covered the basics of handling ADO.NET events. You saw what events are and how to use delegates to bind them to event handlers. Specifically, you saw the following:

- That a connection's StateChange event fires when the state changes from Open to Closed or from Closed to Open. You wrote an event handler for this event using the StateChangeEventHandler delegate. In the process, you saw that the signature of the event handler must be the same as the signature of the delegate.

- That a connection's InfoMessage event fires when the database returns informational messages that aren't errors. You also saw that you can bind any number of events to their respective event handlers from within the same function.

- How to use a data adapter's RowUpdating and RowUpdated events to determine the status of a row before and after it's updated.

- How to bind the same event to more than one event handler. This results in each event handler being called and executed.

In the next chapter, you'll see how to store and retrieve binary and text data.

Working with Text and Binary Data

Some kinds of data have special formats, are very large, or vary greatly in size. In this chapter, you'll learn techniques for working with text and binary data, including the following:

- What data types to use

- Loading, retrieving, and displaying image data

- Working with headers in binary data

- Working with data too large to fit easily into memory

- Retrieving and storing text data

We'll also present the T-SQL for creating a table in the tempdb database, which is intended to hold any temporary table. We'll start by covering what data types support these kinds of data.

Understanding SQL Server Text and Binary Data Types

SQL Server provides the types CHAR, NCHAR, VARCHAR, NVARCHAR, BINARY, and VARBINARY for working with reasonably small text and binary data. You can use these with text (character) data up to a maximum of 8,000 bytes (4,000 bytes for Unicode data, NCHAR, and NVARCHAR, which use 2 bytes per character).

For larger data, which SQL Server 2005 calls *large-value data types*, you should use the VARCHAR(MAX), NVARCHAR(MAX), and VARBINARY(MAX) data types. VARCHAR(MAX) is for non-Unicode text, NVARCHAR(MAX) is for Unicode text, and VARBINARY(MAX) is for images and other binary data.

Warning In SQL Server 2000, large data was stored in NTEXT, TEXT, and IMAGE data types. These data types are deprecated and will likely be removed in the future. If you work with legacy applications, you should consider converting NTEXT, TEXT, and IMAGE to NVARCHAR(MAX), VARCHAR(MAX), and VARBINARY(MAX), respectively. However, the System.Data.SqlDbType enumeration does not yet include members for these data types, so we use VARCHAR(MAX) and VARBINARY(MAX) for column data types but Text and Image when specifying data types for command parameters.

An alternative to using these data types is to not store the data itself in the database but instead define a column containing a path that points to where the data is actually stored. This can be more efficient for accessing large amounts of data, and it can save resources on the database server by transferring the demand to a file server. It does require more complicated coordination and has the potential for database and data files to get out of sync. We won't use this technique in this chapter.

Tip Since SSE databases cannot exceed 4GB, this technique may be your only alternative for very large text and image data.

Within a C# program, binary data types map to an array of bytes (byte[]), and character data types map to strings or character arrays (char[]).

Note DB2, MySQL, Oracle, and the SQL standard call such data types *large objects* (LOBs); specifically, they're binary large objects (BLOBs) and character large objects (CLOBs). But, as with many database terms, whether BLOB was originally an acronym for anything is debatable. Needless to say, it has always implied a data type that can handle large amounts of (amorphous) data, and SQL Server documentation uses BLOB as a generic term for large data and data types.

Storing Images in a Database

Let's start by creating a database table for storing images and then loading some images into it. We'll use small images but use VARBINARY(MAX) to store them. We'll use images in C:\Program Files\Microsoft.NET\SDK\v2.0\QuickStart\aspnet\samples\monitoring\tracing\Images.

Try It Out: Loading Image Binary Data from Files

In this example, you'll write a program that creates a database table and then stores milk carton images in it.

1. Create a new Console Application project named Chapter16. When Solution Explorer opens, save the solution.

2. Rename the Chapter16 project LoadImages. Rename Program.cs to LoadImages.cs, and replace its code with the code in Listing 16-1.

Listing 16-1 LoadImages.cs

```
using System;
using System.Data;
using System.Data.SqlClient;
using System.IO;

namespace LoadImages
{
    class LoadImages
    {
        string imageFileLocation =
            @"C:\Program Files\Microsoft.NET\SDK\v2.0\QuickStart\"
            + @"aspnet\samples\monitoring\tracing\Images\";

        string imageFilePrefix = "milk";
        int numberImageFiles = 8;
        string imageFileType = ".gif";
        int maxImageSize = 10000;
        SqlConnection conn = null;
        SqlCommand cmd = null;

        static void Main()
        {
            LoadImages loader = new LoadImages();
```

```
try
{
    // Open connection
    loader.OpenConnection();
    // Create command
    loader.CreateCommand();
    // Create table
    loader.CreateImageTable();
    // Prepare insert
    loader.PrepareInsertImages();
    // Insert images
    int i;
    for (i = 1; i <= loader.numberImageFiles; i++)
    {
        loader.ExecuteInsertImages(i);
    }
}
catch (SqlException ex)
{
    Console.WriteLine(ex.ToString());
}
finally
{
    loader.CloseConnection();
}
}

void OpenConnection()
{
    // Create connection
    conn = new SqlConnection(@"
        server = .\sqlexpress;
        integrated security = true;
        database = tempdb
    ");
    // Open connection
    conn.Open();
}
```

```csharp
void CloseConnection()
{
    // close connection
    conn.Close();
    Console.WriteLine("Connection Closed.");
}

void CreateCommand()
{
    cmd = new SqlCommand();
    cmd.Connection = conn;
}

void ExecuteCommand(string cmdText)
{
    int cmdResult;
    cmd.CommandText = cmdText;
    Console.WriteLine("Executing command:");
    Console.WriteLine(cmd.CommandText);
    cmdResult = cmd.ExecuteNonQuery();
    Console.WriteLine("ExecuteNonQuery returns {0}.", cmdResult);
}

void CreateImageTable()
{
    ExecuteCommand(@"
        create table imagetable
        (
            imagefile nvarchar(20),
            imagedata varbinary(max)
        )
    ");
}

void PrepareInsertImages()
{
    cmd.CommandText = @"
        insert into imagetable
        values (@imagefile, @imagedata)
    ";
```

```
        cmd.Parameters.Add("@imagefile", SqlDbType.NVarChar, 20);
        cmd.Parameters.Add("@imagedata", SqlDbType.Image, 1000000);

        cmd.Prepare();
    }

    void ExecuteInsertImages(int imageFileNumber)
    {
        string imageFileName = null;
        byte[] imageImageData = null;

        imageFileName =
            imageFilePrefix + imageFileNumber.ToString() + imageFileType;
        imageImageData =
            LoadImageFile(imageFileName, imageFileLocation, maxImageSize);

        cmd.Parameters["@imagefile"].Value = imageFileName;
        cmd.Parameters["@imagedata"].Value = imageImageData;

        ExecuteCommand(cmd.CommandText);
    }

    byte[] LoadImageFile(
        string fileName,
        string fileLocation,
        int maxImageSize
    )
    {
        byte[] imagebytes = null;
        string fullpath = fileLocation + fileName;
        Console.WriteLine("Loading File:");
        Console.WriteLine(fullpath);
        FileStream fs = new FileStream(fullpath, FileMode.Open, FileAccess.Read);
        BinaryReader br = new BinaryReader(fs);
        imagebytes = br.ReadBytes(maxImageSize);

        Console.WriteLine(
            "Imagebytes has length {0} bytes.",
            imagebytes.GetLength(0)
        );
```

```
        return imagebytes;
    }
  }
}
```

3. Run the program with Ctrl+F5. You should see the output in Figure 16-1. It shows the information for loading the last two images, the operations performed, their statuses, and the size of each of the eight images.

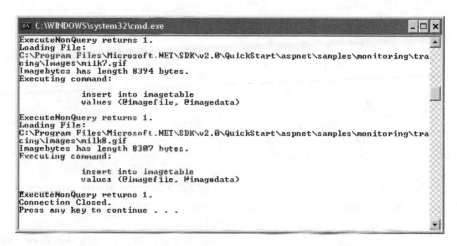

Figure 16-1. *Loading image data*

How It Works

In the Main method you did three major things. You called an instance method to create a table to hold images:

```
// Create table
loader.CreateImageTable();
```

You called an instance method to prepare a command (yes, you finally prepared a command, since you expected to run it multiple times) to insert images:

```
// Prepare insert
loader.PrepareInsertImages();
```

You then looped through the image files and inserted them:

```
// Insert images
int i;
for (i = 1; i <= loader.numberImageFiles; i++)
{
    loader.ExecuteInsertImages(i);
}
```

Note that you connected to tempdb, the temporary database that's re-created when SQL Server starts:

```
// Create connection
conn = new SqlConnection(@"
    server = .\sqlexpress;
    integrated security = true;
    database = tempdb
");
// Open connection
conn.Open();
```

The tables in this database are temporary; that is, they're always deleted when SQL Server stops. This is ideal for these examples and many other situations, but don't use tempdb for any data that needs to persist permanently.

When you created the table, a simple one containing the image filename and the image, you used the VARBINARY(MAX) data type for the imagedata column:

```
void CreateImageTable()
{
    ExecuteCommand(@"
        create table imagetable
        (
            imagefile nvarchar(20),
            imagedata varbinary(max)
        )
    ");
}
```

but when you configured the INSERT command, you used the Image member of the SqlDbType enumeration, since there is no member for the VARBINARY(MAX) data type. You specified lengths for both variable-length data types, since you can't prepare a command unless you do. You prepared the command:

```
void PrepareInsertImages()
{
    cmd.CommandText = @"
        insert into imagetable
        values (@imagefile, @imagedata)
    ";
    cmd.Parameters.Add("@imagefile", SqlDbType.NVarChar, 20);
    cmd.Parameters.Add("@imagedata", SqlDbType.Image, 1000000);

    cmd.Prepare();
}
```

The ExecuteInsertImages method accepts an integer to use as a suffix for the image filename, calls LoadImageFile to get a byte array containing the image, assigns the filename and image to their corresponding command parameters, and then executes the command to insert the image:

```
void ExecuteInsertImages(int imageFileNumber)
{
    string imageFileName = null;
    byte[] imageImageData = null;

    imageFileName =
        imageFilePrefix + imageFileNumber.ToString() + imageFileType;
    imageImageData =
        LoadImageFile(imageFileName, imageFileLocation, maxImageSize);

    cmd.Parameters["@imagefile"].Value = imageFileName;
    cmd.Parameters["@imagedata"].Value = imageImageData;

    ExecuteCommand(cmd.CommandText);
}
```

The LoadImageFile method reads the image file, displays the name of and the number of bytes in the file, and returns the image as a byte array:

```
byte[] LoadImageFile(
    string fileName,
    string fileLocation,
    int maxImageSize
)
```

```
    {
      byte[] imagebytes = null;
      string fullpath = fileLocation + fileName;
      Console.WriteLine("Loading File:");
      Console.WriteLine(fullpath);
      FileStream fs = new FileStream(fullpath, FileMode.Open, FileAccess.Read);
      BinaryReader br = new BinaryReader(fs);
      imagebytes = br.ReadBytes(maxImageSize);

      Console.WriteLine(
        "Imagebytes has length {0} bytes.",
        imagebytes.GetLength(0)
      );

      return imagebytes;
    }
  }
```

Rerunning the Program

Since the program always creates the `imagetable` table, you must cycle (stop and restart) SSE before rerunning the program, to remove the table by re-creating an empty tempdb database. You'll see how to avoid this problem in "Working with Text Data" later in this chapter.

Retrieving Images from a Database

Now that you've stored some images, let's retrieve and display them with a Windows application.

Try It Out: Displaying Stored Images

To display your stored images:

1. Add a Windows Application project named `DisplayImages` to your solution. Rename `Form1.cs` to `DisplayImages.cs`.

2. Add a text box, a button, and a picture box control to the form and set its `Text` property to `Display Images` as in Figure 16-2.

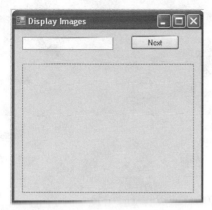

Figure 16-2. *DisplayImages form*

3. Add a new class named Images to the project. Replace the code in Images.cs with the code in Listing 16-2.

Listing 16-2. Images.cs

```
using System;
using System.Data;
using System.Data.SqlClient;
using System.Drawing;
using System.IO;

namespace DisplayImages
{
    public class Images
    {
        string imageFilename = null;
        byte[] imageBytes = null;

        SqlConnection imageConnection = null;
        SqlCommand imageCommand = null;
        SqlDataReader imageReader = null;
```

```csharp
// Constructor
public Images()
{
    imageConnection = new SqlConnection(@"
        data source = .\sqlexpress;
        integrated security = true;
        initial catalog = tempdb;
    ");

    imageCommand = new SqlCommand(
        @"
        select
            imagefile,
            imagedata
        from
            imagetable
        ",
        imageConnection
    );

    // Open connection and create data reader
    imageConnection.Open();
    imageReader = imageCommand.ExecuteReader();
}

public Bitmap GetImage()
{
    MemoryStream ms = new MemoryStream(imageBytes);
    Bitmap bmap = new Bitmap(ms);

    return bmap;
}

public string GetFilename()
{
    return imageFilename;
}
```

```csharp
    public bool GetRow()
    {
        if (imageReader.Read())
        {
            imageFilename = (string) imageReader.GetValue(0);
            imageBytes = (byte[]) imageReader.GetValue(1);

            return true;
        }
        else
        {
            return false;
        }
    }

    public void EndImages()
    {
        // Close the reader and the connection.
        imageReader.Close();
        imageConnection.Close();
    }
  }
}
```

4. Insert an instance variable (as in the bold code shown here) of type Images into
   DisplayImagesDesigner.cs:

```csharp
private System.Windows.Forms.TextBox textBox1;
private System.Windows.Forms.Button button1;
private System.Windows.Forms.PictureBox pictureBox1;
private Images images;
```

5. Insert the code in Listing 16-3 into DisplayImages.cs after the call to
   InitializeComponent() in the constructor.

Listing 16-3. *Initialize Images Display in* DisplayImages *Constructor*

```
images = new Images();

if (images.GetRow())
{
   this.textBox1.Text = images.GetFilename();
   this.pictureBox1.Image = (Image)images.GetImage();
}
else
{
   this.textBox1.Text = "DONE";
   this.pictureBox1.Image = null;
}
```

6. Insert the code in Listing 16-3 (*except for the first line*) into the button1_Click event handler.

7. Insert the highlighted line shown here into the Dispose method of DisplayImages in DisplayImages.Designer.cs:

```
images.endImages();
if (disposing && (components != null))
{
   components.Dispose();
}
base.Dispose(disposing);
```

8. Make it the startup project and run it with Ctrl+F5. You should see the output in Figure 16-3. Click Next to see all the milk carton images in succession; when the last is reached, the word DONE will appear in the text box. Since you didn't add an Exit button, just close the window to exit.

Figure 16-3. *Displaying images*

How It Works

You declared a type, Images, to access the database and provide methods for the form
components to easily get and display images. In its constructor, you connected to the
database and created a data reader to handle the result set of a query that retrieves all
the images you stored earlier.

```
// Constructor
public Images()
{
   imageConnection = new SqlConnection(@"
     data source = .\sqlexpress;
     integrated security = true;
     initial catalog = tempdb;
   ");

   imageCommand = new SqlCommand(
     @"
     select
        imagefile,
        imagedata
     from
        imagetable
     ",
     imageConnection
   );
```

```
    // Open connection and create data reader
    imageConnection.Open();
    imageReader = imageCommand.ExecuteReader();
}
```

When the form was initialized, the new code created an instance of Images, looked for an image with GetRow(), and, if one was found, assigned the filename and image to the text box and picture box with the GetFilename and GetImage methods, respectively.

```
images = new Images();

if (images.GetRow())
{
    this.textBox1.Text = images.GetFilename();
    this.pictureBox1.Image = (Image)images.GetImage();
}
else
{
    this.textBox1.Text = "DONE";
    this.pictureBox1.Image = null;
}
```

You used the same if statement in the Next button's click event handler to look for the next image. If none was found, you displayed the word DONE in the text box.

You called the endImages method when the form terminated to close the connection. (Had you used a dataset instead of a data reader, you could have closed the connection in the Images instance immediately after the images were retrieved, which would be a good exercise for you to attempt.)

```
protected override void Dispose(bool disposing)
{
    images.endImages();
    if (disposing && (components != null))
    {
        components.Dispose();
    }
    base.Dispose(disposing);
}
```

The image is returned from the database as an array of bytes. The PictureBox control Image property can be a Bitmap, Icon, or Metafile (all derived classes of Image). Bitmap supports a variety of formats, including BMP, GIF, and JPG. The getImage method, shown here, returns a Bitmap object:

```
public Bitmap GetImage()
{
    MemoryStream ms = new MemoryStream(imageBytes);
    Bitmap bmap = new Bitmap(ms);

    return bmap;
}
```

Bitmap's constructor doesn't accept a byte array, but it will accept a MemoryStream (which is effectively an in-memory representation of a file), and MemoryStream has a constructor that accepts a byte array. So, you create a memory stream from the byte array and then create a bitmap from the memory stream.

Working with Text Data

Handling text is similar to handling images except for the data type used for the database column.

Try It Out: Loading Text Data from a File

Follow these steps:

1. Add a C# Console Application project named LoadText to the solution.

2. Rename Program.cs to LoadText.cs, and replace the code with that in Listing 16-4.

Listing 16-4. LoadText.cs

```
using System;
using System.Data;
using System.Data.SqlClient;
using System.Data.SqlTypes;
using System.IO;
namespace LoadText
{
    class LoadText
    {
        static string fileName =
            @"c:\bcs2005db\examples\chapter16\loadtext\loadtext.cs";
```

```csharp
    SqlConnection conn = null;
    SqlCommand cmd = null;

    static void Main()
    {
        LoadText loader = new LoadText();
        try
        {
            // Get text file
            loader.GetTextFile(fileName);
            // Open connection
            loader.OpenConnection();
            // Create command
            loader.CreateCommand();
            // Create table
            loader.CreateTextTable();
            // Prepare insert command
            loader.PrepareInsertTextFile();
            // Load text file
            loader.ExecuteInsertTextFile(fileName);
            Console.WriteLine(
                "Loaded {0} into texttable.", fileName
            );
        }
        catch (SqlException ex)
        {
            Console.WriteLine(ex.ToString());
        }
        finally
        {
            loader.CloseConnection();
        }
    }

    void CreateTextTable()
    {
        ExecuteCommand(@"
            if exists
```

```
        (
            select
                *
            from
                information_schema.tables
            where
                table_name = 'texttable'
        )
        drop table texttable
    ");

    ExecuteCommand(@"
        create table texttable
        (
            textfile varchar(255),
            textdata varchar(max)
        )
    ");
}

void OpenConnection()
{
    // Create connection
    conn = new SqlConnection(@"
        data source = .\sqlexpress;
        integrated security = true;
        initial catalog = tempdb;
    ");

    // Open connection
    conn.Open();
}

void CloseConnection()
{
    // Close connection
    conn.Close();
}
```

```
void CreateCommand()
{
   cmd = new SqlCommand();
   cmd.Connection = conn;
}

void ExecuteCommand(string commandText)
{
   int commandResult;
   cmd.CommandText = commandText;
   Console.WriteLine("Executing command:");
   Console.WriteLine(cmd.CommandText);
   commandResult = cmd.ExecuteNonQuery();
   Console.WriteLine("ExecuteNonQuery returns {0}.", commandResult);
}
void PrepareInsertTextFile()
{
   cmd.CommandText = @"
      insert into texttable
      values (@textfile, @textdata)
   ";
   cmd.Parameters.Add("@textfile", SqlDbType.NVarChar, 30);
   cmd.Parameters.Add("@textdata", SqlDbType.Text, 1000000);
}

void ExecuteInsertTextFile(string textFile)
{
   string textData = GetTextFile(textFile);
   cmd.Parameters["@textfile"].Value = textFile;
   cmd.Parameters["@textdata"].Value = textData;
   ExecuteCommand(cmd.CommandText);
}

string GetTextFile(string textFile)
{
   string textBytes = null;
   Console.WriteLine("Loading File: " + textFile);

   FileStream fs = new FileStream(textFile, FileMode.Open, FileAccess.Read);
   StreamReader sr = new StreamReader(fs);
   textBytes = sr.ReadToEnd();
```

```
        Console.WriteLine("TextBytes has length {0} bytes.",
            textBytes.Length);

        return textBytes;
    }
  }
}
```

3. Make the project the startup project, and run it with Ctrl+F5. You should see the results in Figure 16-4.

Figure 16-4. *Loading a text file into a table*

How It Works

You simply loaded the source code for the LoadText program:

```
static string fileName =
    @"c:\bcs2005db\examples\chapter16\loadtext\loadtext.cs";
```

into a table:

```
cmd.CommandText = @"
    insert into texttable
    values (@textfile, @textdata)
";
cmd.Parameters.Add("@textfile", SqlDbType.NVarChar, 30);
cmd.Parameters.Add("@textdata", SqlDbType.Text, 1000000);
```

that you created in the temporary database:

```
ExecuteCommand(@"
    if exists
      (
        select
            *
        from
            information_schema.tables
        where
            table_name = 'texttable'
      )
      drop table texttable
");

ExecuteCommand(@"
    create table texttable
      (
        textfile varchar(255),
        textdata varchar(max)
      )
");
```

Note that you first checked to see if the table existed. If it did, you dropped it so you could re-create it.

■Note The `information_schema.tables` *view* (a named query) is compatible with the SQL standard INFORMATION_SCHEMA view of the same name. It limits the tables you can see to the ones you can access. Microsoft recommends you use the new *catalog views* to get database metadata in SQL Server 2005, and SQL Server itself uses them internally. The catalog view for this query would be `sys.tables` and the column name would be `name`. We've used the INFORMATION SCHEMA view here because you may still see it often.

Instead of the `BinaryReader` you used for images, `GetTextFile` used a `StreamReader` (derived from `System.IO.TextReader`) to read the contents of the file into a `string`:

```
string GetTextFile(string textFile)
{
    string textBytes = null;
    Console.WriteLine("Loading File: " + textFile);

    FileStream fs = new FileStream(textFile, FileMode.Open, FileAccess.Read);
    StreamReader sr = new StreamReader(fs);
    textBytes = sr.ReadToEnd();

    Console.WriteLine("TextBytes has length {0} bytes.",
        textBytes.Length);

    return textBytes;
}
```

Otherwise, the processing logic is basically the same as you've seen many times throughout the book: open a connection, access a database, and then close the connection.

Now let's retrieve the text you just stored.

Retrieving Data from Text Columns

Retrieving data from TEXT columns is just like retrieving it from the smaller character data types. You'll now write a simple console program to see how this works.

Try It Out: Retrieving Text Data

Follow these steps:

1. Add a C# Console Application project named `RetrieveText` to the solution.

2. Rename `Program.cs` to `RetrieveText.cs`, and replace the code with that in Listing 16-5.

Listing 16-5. RetrieveText.cs

```csharp
using System;
using System.Data;
using System.Data.SqlClient;

namespace RetrieveText
{
   public class RetrieveText
   {
      string textFile = null;
      char[] textChars = null;
      SqlConnection conn = null;
      SqlCommand cmd = null;
      SqlDataReader dr = null;

      public RetrieveText()
      {
         // Create connection
         conn = new SqlConnection(@"
            data source = (local)\netsdk;
            integrated security = sspi;
            initial catalog = tempdb;
         ");

         // Create command
         cmd = new SqlCommand(@"
            select
               textfile,
               textdata
            from
               texttable
         ", conn);

         // Open connection
         conn.Open();

         // Create data reader
         dr = cmd.ExecuteReader();
      }
```

```
public bool GetRow()
{
    long textSize;
    int bufferSize = 100;
    long charsRead;
    textChars = new Char[bufferSize];

    if (dr.Read())
    {
        // Get file name
        textFile = dr.GetString(0);
        Console.WriteLine("      start of file:");
        Console.WriteLine(textFile);
        textSize = dr.GetChars(1, 0, null, 0, 0);
        Console.WriteLine("--- size of text: {0} characters -----",
            textSize);
        Console.WriteLine("--- first 100 characters in text -----");
        charsRead = dr.GetChars(1, 0, textChars, 0, 100);
        Console.WriteLine(new String(textChars));
        Console.WriteLine("--- last 100 characters in text -----");
        charsRead = dr.GetChars(1, textSize - 100, textChars, 0, 100);
        Console.WriteLine(new String(textChars));

        return true;
    }
    else
    {
        return false;
    }
}

public void endRetrieval()
{
    // Close the reader and the connection.
    dr.Close();
    conn.Close();
}
```

```csharp
static void Main()
{
    RetrieveText rt = null;
    try
    {
        rt = new RetrieveText ();

        while (rt.GetRow() == true)
        {
            Console.WriteLine("----- end of file:");
            Console.WriteLine(rt.textFile);
            Console.WriteLine("======================================");
        }
    }
    catch (SqlException ex)
    {
        Console.WriteLine(ex.ToString());
    }
    finally
    {
        rt.endRetrieval();
    }
}
```

3. Make it the startup project and run it with Ctrl+F5. You should see the result in Figure 16-5.

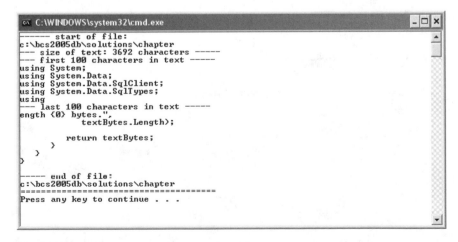

Figure 16-5. *Retrieving text from a table*

How It Works

After querying the database:

```
// Create command
cmd = new SqlCommand(@"
    select
        textfile,
        textdata
    from
        texttable
", conn);

// Open connection
conn.Open();

// Create data reader
dr = cmd.ExecuteReader();
```

you looped through the result set (but here there was only one row), got the filename from the table with GetString(), and printed it to show which file was displayed. You then called GetChars() with a null character array to get the size of the VARCHAR(MAX) column:

```
if (dr.Read())
{
    // Get file name
    textFile = dr.GetString(0);
    Console.WriteLine("------ start of file:");
    Console.WriteLine(textFile);
    textSize = dr.GetChars(1, 0, null, 0, 0);
    Console.WriteLine("--- size of text: {0} characters -----",
        textSize);
    Console.WriteLine("--- first 100 characters in text -----");
    charsRead = dr.GetChars(1, 0, textChars, 0, 100);
    Console.WriteLine(new String(textChars));
    Console.WriteLine("--- last 100 characters in text -----");
    charsRead = dr.GetChars(1, textSize - 100, textChars, 0, 100);
    Console.WriteLine(new String(textChars));
```

```
        return true;
    }
    else
    {
        return false;
    }
```

Rather than print the whole file, you displayed the first 100 bytes, using `GetChars()` to extract a substring. You did the same thing with the last 100 characters.

Otherwise, this program is like any other that retrieves and displays database character data.

Summary

In this chapter, you practiced storing and retrieving binary and text data using data types for large objects. There's more to learn about large objects, particularly about issues that affect performance, but you've now seen the fundamental ADO.NET techniques.

In the next chapter we'll look at another special kind of object (which can be as large as the objects we discussed here): the XML document. You'll see how SQL Server supports it with the XML data type.

■ ■ ■

Using XML

XML and its related technologies are major foundations of both the Internet and .NET. How much about XML you need to know depends on what kind of programming you do, and you may not need to know anything about it. However, you'll be doing yourself a disservice if you don't learn at least something about XML, and the more you know about it, the more valuable you can be to a database programming team. Our goal here is to introduce you to the most essential XML concepts and terminology and the most basic techniques for using XML with SQL Server. This will enable you to handle the most common programming tasks and to quickly learn more about XML as the need arises.

In this chapter, we'll cover:

- What XML is

- How to generate XML from tables with T-SQL's TO XML clause

- How to query XML documents with T-SQL's OPENXML function

- How to store and retrieve XML documents using the xml data type

What Is XML?

Extensible Markup Language (XML) is a *metalanguage*. A metalanguage isn't used for programming but rather for defining other languages, and the languages XML defines are known as *markup languages*. Markup is exactly what it implies, a means of "marking up" something. You create XML *documents* by marking up data—that is, by enclosing data between *start tags* and *end tags*. The *elements* you define by your tags (and your choice of tags is arbitrary) form a *hierarchy*, so XML documents organize data into parent-child relationships. XML documents are text documents readable by both humans and computers.

> ■**Note** In essence, each XML document is an instance of a language defined by the XML elements used in the document. The specific language may or may not have been explicitly defined, but professional use of XML demands carefully planning one's XML *vocabulary* and specifying its definition in a *schema* that can be used to validate that documents adhere to both the syntax and semantics of a vocabulary. The XML Schema definition language (usually referred to as XSD) is the language for defining XML vocabularies.

The World Wide Web Consortium (W3C) developed XML in 1996. Intended to support a wide variety of applications, XML was used by the W3C to create Extensible HTML (XHTML), an XML vocabulary. Since 1996, the W3C has developed a variety of other XML-oriented technologies, including Extensible Stylesheet Language (XSL), which provides the same kind of facility for XHTML that Cascading Style Sheets (CSS) does for HTML, and XSL Transformations (XSLT), which is a language for transforming XML documents into other XML documents.

The list goes on and on, and the complexity of the languages that you can use to process XML documents grows with it. Of passing interest to us is XML Path Language (XPath), used by XSLT to access parts of an XML document. We use a few XPath expressions throughout this chapter, but you won't need to learn anything about XPath to use them.

> ■**Note** XML Query Language (XQuery) is an extension of XPath designed to simplify retrieving information from XML documents. It is also used occasionally in SQL Server XML technologies, but we won't use it here.

Fortunately, XML itself and XML documents are the things you'll work with most of the time. They aren't hard to understand.

Understanding XML Documents

An XML document could be a physical file on a computer, a data stream over a network (in theory, formatted so a human could read it, but in practice, often in compressed binary form), or just a string in memory. It has to be complete in itself, however, and even without a schema, it must obey certain rules.

The most fundamental rule is that XML documents must be *well formed*. At its simplest, this means that overlapping elements aren't allowed, so you must close all *child* elements before the end tag of their *parent* element. For example, this XML document

```
<states>
    <state>
        <name>Delaware</name>
        <city>Dover</city>
        <city>Wilmington</city>
    </state>
</states>
```

is well formed. It has a *root* (or *document*) element, states, delimited by a start tag, <states>, and an end tag, </states>. The root element is the parent of the state element, which is in turn the parent of a name element and two city elements. An XML document can have only one root element.

Elements may have *attributes*. For example, the document could have been written as

```
<states>
    <state name="Delaware">
        <city>Dover</city>
        <city>Wilmington</city>
    </state>
</states>
```

and retained the same information, replacing the name element, that occurs only once, with a name attribute and changing the *content* of the original element (Delaware) into the *value* of the attribute ("Delaware"). An element may have any number of attributes, but it may not have duplicate attributes, so the city elements weren't candidates for replacement.

Elements may have content (text data or other elements), or they may be *empty*. For example, if you want (just for the sake of argument) to keep track of how many states are in the document, you could use an empty element to do it:

```
<states>
    <controlinfo count="1"/>
    <state name="Delaware">
        <city>Dover</city>
        <city>Wilmington</city>
    </state>
</states>
```

The empty element, controlinfo, has one attribute, count, but no content. Note that it isn't delimited by start and end tags, but exists within an *empty element tag* (that starts with < and ends with />).

An alternative syntax for empty elements, using start and end tags, is also valid:

```
<controlinfo count="1"></controlinfo>
```

Many programs that generate XML use this form.

■**Note** Though it's easy to design XML documents, designing them well is as much a challenge as designing a database. Many experienced XML designers disagree over the best use of attributes and even whether attributes should be used at all (and without attributes, empty elements have virtually no use). While elements may in some ways map more ideally to relational data, this doesn't mean that attributes have no place in XML design. After all, XML isn't intended to (and in principle, can't) conform to the relational model of data. In fact, you'll see that a "pure" element-only design can be more difficult to work with in T-SQL.

Understanding the XML Declaration

In addition to elements and attributes, XML documents can have other parts, but most of them are important only if you really need to delve deeply into XML. Though it is optional, the *XML declaration* is one part that should be included in an XML document to precisely conform to the W3C recommendation. If used, it must occur before the root element in an XML document.

The XML declaration is similar in format to an element, but it has question marks immediately next to the angle brackets. It always has an attribute named version; currently, this has two possible values: "1.0" and "1.1". (A couple other attributes are defined but aren't required.) So, the simplest form of an XML declaration is:

```
<?xml version="1.0" ?>
```

XML has other aspects, but this is all you need to get started. In fact, this may be all you'll ever need to be quite effective. As you'll see, we don't use any XML declarations (or even more important things such as XML schemas and namespaces) for our XML documents, yet our small examples work well, are representative of fundamental XML processing, and could be scaled up to much larger XML documents.

Using FOR XML

Near the end of Chapter 8, in "Using Datasets and XML," we showed how to extract data from a dataset, convert it into XML, and write it to a file with the dataset's WriteXml method. Here, we'll convert database data into XML with T-SQL's FOR XML clause.

■Note In addition to WriteXml(), there are many other ADO.NET methods, including ReadXml(), that you can use to do the same kinds of things (as well as others) that we do in this chapter with T-SQL. But, there are a lot of other ways a C# programmer can handle XML too, so we had to draw the line somewhere. We believe that a T-SQL perspective is the best for starting out and that by using T-SQL, you'll get a real hands-on feeling for XML processing that will make it easy for you to use ADO.NET XML features if you choose to.

The FOR XML clause has four *modes*:

- RAW

- AUTO

- EXPLICIT

- PATH

We'll use the first two in examples to show how to generate XML with a query.

■Note EXPLICIT mode is rather complicated. PATH mode is intended to make things a bit easier, at least for those familiar with XPath. For detailed explanations of how to use all the FOR XML modes, see Chapter 14 of Joseph Sack's *SQL Server 2005 T-SQL Recipes* (Berkeley, CA: Apress, 2005)

Try It Out: Creating Some Sample Data

To give you something reasonably easy to work with, let's create some straightforward sample data:

1. In SSMSE, create and populate two tables with the T-SQL in Listing 17-1. You should see the results shown in Figure 17-1.

■Note You'll get error messages for the two DROP statements the first time you run them because the tables don't exist yet, but as you learned in Chapter 14, the rest of the statements will nonetheless run. Also, we haven't defined primary or foreign keys because our data is trivial, we know it already has entity and referential integrity, and we aren't going to update it. We could have used tempdb instead of Northwind for this chapter, but by using Northwind, the tables will stay around for you to play with even if you shut down SSE.

Listing 17-1. *Creating Sample Tables*

```
use northwind
go

drop table xmlstate;

drop table xmlcity;
go

create table xmlstate
(
    abbr char(2),
    name varchar(20)
)
;

create table xmlcity
(
    sabbr char(2),
    name varchar(20)
)
;
go

insert into xmlstate values('CA', 'California');
insert into xmlstate values('DE', 'Delaware');

insert into xmlcity values('CA', 'Berkeley');
insert into xmlcity values('CA', 'Los Angeles');
insert into xmlcity values('CA', 'Wilmington');
insert into xmlcity values('DE', 'Newark');
insert into xmlcity values('DE', 'Wilmington');
go

select
    s.abbr,
    s.name,
    c.name
```

```
from
  xmlstate s
  inner join
  xmlcity c
  on
  s.abbr = c.sabbr
;
```

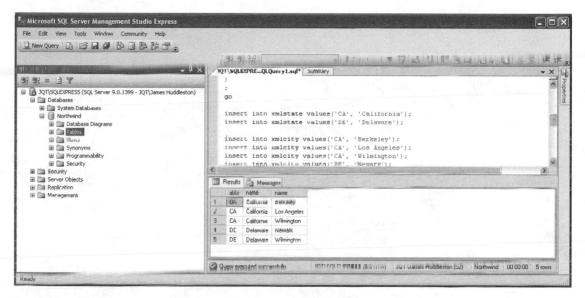

Figure 17-1. *Sample state and city data*

How It Works

You drop (or at least try to drop) two tables, re-create them, and insert two states and five cities. You then run a query to prove everything worked as planned.

You design things so that both tables are in third normal form, and they are, but admittedly, the xmlcity table could well use another column, such as a city abbreviation column, to form a composite primary key with sabbr. (Which only goes to show that 3NF doesn't necessarily mean a table is optimally designed.)

You'd eventually like to see an XML document that looks like this

```
<states>
   <state>
      <abbr>CA</abbr>
      <name>California</name>
      <city>Berkeley</city>
      <city>Los Angeles</city>
      <city>Wilmington</city>
   </state>
   <state>
      <abbr>CA</abbr>
      <name>Delaware</name>
      <city>Newark</city>
      <city>Wilmington</city>
   </state>
</states>
```

or like this

```
<states>
   <state abbr="CA" name="California">
      <city name="Berkeley"/>
      <city name="Los Angeles"/>
      <city name="Wilmington"/>
   </state>
   <state abbr="DE" name="Delaware">
      <city name="Newark"/>
      <city name="Wilmington"/>
   </state>
</states>
```

or some other XML document format that accurately represents the same data and relationships as the tables.

Try It Out: Using FOR XML RAW

Let's extract the states and their cities as XML with the RAW mode of the FOR XML clause:

1. Run the query in Listing 17-2. Click on the displayed row, and you should see the results shown in Figure 17-2.

Listing 17-2. *Querying with* FOR XML RAW

```
select
    s.abbr abbr,
    s.name sname,
    c.name cname
from
    xmlstate s
    inner join
    xmlcity c
    on
    s.abbr = c.sabbr
for xml raw
```

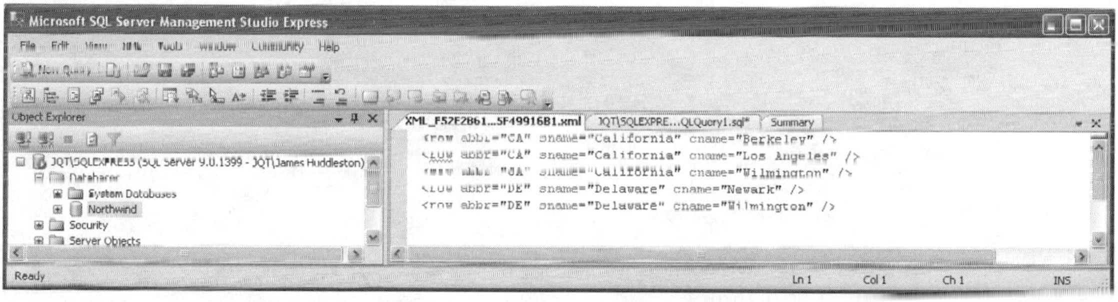

Figure 17-2. *Using FOR XML RAW*

How It Works

RAW mode produces very "raw" XML. It turns each row in the result set into an XML row empty element and uses an attribute for each of the column values, using the alias names we specified in the query as the attribute names. It produces a string composed of all the elements.

RAW mode doesn't produce an XML document, since it has as many root elements (raw) as there are rows in the result set, and an XML document can have only one root element. However, you can use the ROOT directive to specify the root element, as in

```
for xml raw, root('states')
```

and we'll use ROOT in the next example.

Try It Out: Using FOR XML AUTO

Let's try the AUTO mode of FOR XML:

1. Run the query in Listing 17-3. Click on the displayed row, and you should see the results shown in Figure 17-3.

Listing 17-3. *Querying with* FOR XML AUTO

```
select
    s.abbr abbr,
    s.name sname,
    c.name cname
from
    xmlstate s
    inner join
    xmlcity c
    on
    s.abbr = c.sabbr
for xml auto, root('states')
```

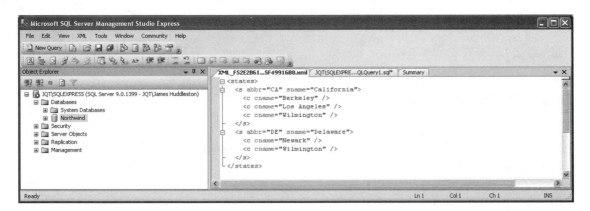

Figure 17-3. *Using FOR XML AUTO*

How It Works

AUTO mode is an improvement over RAW mode, but not quite enough to get us to the XML we'd like to see. However, by representing the parent-child relationship between states and cities, it does get us appreciably nearer.

It turns the rows into a hierarchy, recognizing the foreign-key relationship between the tables, which it generates s elements for, and their cities, which it generates c elements for. Like RAW, it uses attributes for all column values, and the c elements are empty elements, but the ROOT directive does give the states root element you want.

Try It Out: Using FOR XML AUTO Again

Let's try getting a bit closer with AUTO mode:

1. Run the query in Listing 17-4. Click on the row, and you should see the results shown in Figure 17-4.

Listing 17-4. *Querying with* FOR XML AUTO *Again*

```
select
    state.abbr abbr,
    state.name sname,
    city.name cname
from
    xmlstate state
    inner join
    xmlcity city
    on
    state.abbr = city.sabbr
for xml auto, root('states')
```

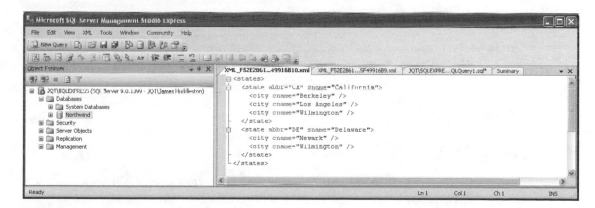

Figure 17-4. *Using FOR XML AUTO again*

How It Works

By changing the correlation names for the tables to the element names you want, AUTO generates the desired elements. The SQL isn't quite as elegant, but you've basically matched the format of the second XML document:

```
<states>
   <state abbr="CA" name="California">
      <city name="Berkeley"/>
      <city name="Los Angeles"/>
      <city name="Wilmington"/>
   </state>
   <state abbr="DE" name="Delaware">
      <city name="Newark"/>
      <city name="Wilmington"/>
   </state>
</states></states>
```

It is possible to produce both XML documents in their precise formats, but not with RAW or AUTO modes (not with a single query, that is, but you can with a bit more knowledge of T-SQL and some ingenuity). Either the PATH or EXPLICIT modes can do it, but explaining how to do it would take almost a chapter in itself and would not necessarily be worth your reading.

Teaching yourself about other the options for RAW and AUTO modes is probably your best next step. They can take you a long way. Now that you've seen how easy it is to use SSMSE to experiment with FOR XML and you have a small, well-defined problem to work on, you're ready to completely solve it on your own, if you care to.

■**Tip** As we said to open this chapter, how much XML you need to know depends on what you need to do with it. Even the rawest XML that RAW produces may (often) be enough.

Using OPENXML

So far, you've written data in XML format. Now we'll cover how to read XML documents and use them in queries. T-SQL provides the OPENXML function to do this. With OPENXML, you can use a *parsed* XML document like a table in a query. Parsing is the process of converting elements and attributes into *nodes* in a *Document Object Model* (DOM) tree, so element contents and attribute values can be accessed easily.

T-SQL provides a stored procedure, sp_xml_preparedocument, to parse XML documents. OPENXML works with the in-memory DOM tree that sp_xml_preparedocument produces.

■**Tip** You can use another stored procedure, sp_xml_removedocument, to free the DOM tree from memory. We don't need to do this for our simple examples.

Since you need to parse an XML document with sp_xml_preparedocument before you can use it with OPENXML, you'll use the XML document that FOR XML AUTO substantially matched, since it's the kind of XML design that T-SQL handles most easily

```
<states>
    <state abbr="CA" name="California">
        <city name="Berkeley"/>
        <city name="Los Angeles"/>
        <city name="Wilmington"/>
    </state>
    <state abbr="DE" name="Delaware">
        <city name="Newark"/>
        <city name="Wilmington"/>
    </state>
</states>
```

and which we provide in the states.xml file.

Try It Out: Using OPENXML

In Figure 17-1, you displayed the state and city to check that you'd loaded the tables. The XML document in states.xml accurately represents this data, so you want to see if you can query it instead of the tables and get the same results:

1. Create a stored procedure named xml2tbl in the Northwind database with the T-SQL in Listing 17-5.

Listing 17-5. *Creating the* xml2tbl *Stored Procedure*

```
use northwind
go

create procedure xml2tbl
    @xdoc xml
as
    declare @xdocp int

    exec sp_xml_preparedocument @xdocp output, @xdoc

    select
        sabbr,
        sname,
        cname
    from
        openxml(
            @xdocp,
            '/states/state/city',
            0
        )
    with
    (
        sabbr char(2)      '../@abbr',
        sname varchar(20) '../@name',
        cname varchar(20) '@name'
    )
```

2. Replace the code in the edit window with that in Listing 17-6, which provides the XML document and runs the query. You should see the results shown in Figure 17-5, and they should be the same results as in Figure 17-1.

Listing 17-6. *Running the* xml2tbl *Stored Procedure*

```
declare @xdoc xml

set @xdoc = '
<states>
    <state abbr="CA" name="California">
```

```
      <city name="Berkeley"/>
      <city name="Los Angeles"/>
      <city name="Wilmington"/>
   </state>
   <state abbr="DE" name="Delaware">
      <city name="Newark"/>
      <city name="Wilmington"/>
   </state>
</states>
'

exec xml2tbl @xdoc
```

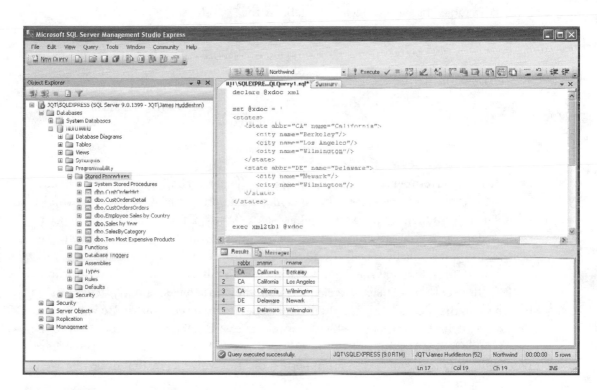

Figure 17-5. *Displaying states.xml data*

How It Works

You create a stored procedure because you need to do a couple things together: parse the XML document, then query the parsed version. The procedure has one input parameter, @xdoc, for the XML document it will process:

```
create procedure xml2tbl
   @xdoc xml
as
```

You declare a local variable, @xdocp, to hold the pointer to the memory buffer where the parsed XML will be put by sp_xml_preparedocument. Then you call that stored procedure, passing it the XML document as the second argument:

```
declare @xdocp int
```

```
exec sp_xml_preparedocument @xdocp output, @xdoc
```

You then execute a query, whose FROM and WITH clauses enable you to use the parsed XML like a table. Instead of specifying a table in the FROM clause, you call the OPENXML function

```
from
   openxml(
      @xdocp,
      '/states/state/city',
      0
   )
```

passing it three arguments: the pointer (@xdocp)to the parsed XML document, an XPath expression ('/states/state/city') that specifies what part of the DOM hierarchy you intend to access (all of it), and a flag (0) that tells OPENXML what kind of mapping to use to retrieve data from the DOM tree. The default mapping is *attribute-centric*, vs. *element-centric*, and you explicitly specify the equivalent of the default.

In the WITH clause, you specify the *schema* for the table OPENXML would return. You declare three columns (sabbr, sname, and cname), their data types, and XPath expressions for where in the hierarchy to find them. Since all data is stored as attribute values, you prefix the attribute names in the XPath expressions with @. Since cname comes from the lowest node in the hierarchy (city), you simply specify the attribute name. The other two columns come from city's parent node (state), so you specify that node relative to the city node with ../:

```
with
(
   sabbr char(2)     '../@abbr',
   sname varchar(20) '../@name',
   cname varchar(20) '@name'
)
```

The WITH clause is optional. If it's not used, OPENXML will produce an *edge table* whose contents can be used like any table in a query. Edge tables provide a fine-grained view of an XML document. We won't go into details here, but we'll show you in the next example what the edge table for states.xml looks like.

You then test the procedure in a convenient way, declaring a local variable, @xdoc, assigning the text of the XML document to it, and passing it to xml2tbl (you could have read the XML document from states.xml, but the T-SQL for that is beyond the scope of this book):

```
declare @xdoc xml

set @xdoc = '
<states>
    <state abbr="CA" name="California">
        <city name="Berkeley"/>
        <city name="Los Angeles"/>
        <city name="Wilmington"/>
    </state>
    <state abbr="DE" name="Delaware">
        <city name="Newark"/>
        <city name="Wilmington"/>
    </state>
</states>
'

exec xml2tbl @xdoc
```

Try It Out: Generating an Edge Table

To produce an edge table for states.xml:

1. Create a stored procedure named xml2edge in the Northwind database with the T-SQL in Listing 17-7.

Listing 17-7. *Creating the* xml2edge *Stored Procedure*

```
use northwind
go
```

```
create procedure xml2edge
  @xdoc xml
as
  declare @xdocp int

  exec sp_xml_preparedocument @xdocp output, @xdoc

  select
    *
  from
    openxml(
      @xdocp,
      '/states/state/city',
      0
    )
```

2. Run it and you should see the results shown in Figure 17-6.

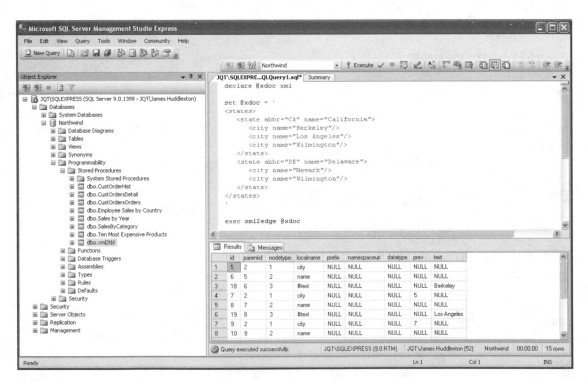

Figure 17-6. *The edge table for states.xml*

How It Works

You remove the WITH clause from the query in xml2tbl, so an edge table is produced by OPENXML. You change the select list to display all the columns in the result set.

Now that you know what columns are in an edge table, you might want to modify the query in xml2edge to play around with the edge table. If you rely heavily on OPENXML in your work, you may find edge tables quite valuable. If you don't, you may never see one again.

Using the XML Data Type

SQL Server 2005 has a new data type, xml, that is designed not just for holding XML documents (which are essentially characters strings and can be stored in any character column big enough to hold them) but for processing XML documents. When we discussed parsing an XML document into a DOM tree, we didn't mention that once it's parsed, the XML document can be updated. You can change element contents and attribute values, and you can add and remove element occurrences to and from the hierarchy.

We won't update XML documents here, but the xml data type provides methods to do it. It is a very different kind of SQL Server data type, and describing how to exploit it would take a book of its own—maybe more than one. Our focus here will be on what every database programmer needs to know: how to use the xml type to store and retrieve XML documents.

Note There are so many ways to process XML documents (even in ADO.NET and with SQLXML, a support package for SQL Server 2000) that only time will tell if incorporating such features into a SQL Server data type was worth the effort. Because XML is such an important technology, being able to process XML documents purely in T-SQL does offer many possibilities, but right now it's unclear how much more about the xml data type you'll ever need to know. At any rate, this chapter will give you what you need to know to start experimenting with it.

In the following examples, you'll use the two XML documents you were trying to produce in "Using FOR XML." The first thing you'll do is create a table in which to store them.

Try It Out: Creating a Table to Store XML

To create a table to hold XML documents:

    1. In SSMSE, run the T-SQL in Listing 17-8.

Listing 17-8. *Creating the* xmltest *Table*

```
use northwind
go

create table xmltest
(
    xid  int not null primary key,
    xdoc xml not null
)
```

How It Works

It works just as you expected. Though we've said the xml data type is different from other SQL Server data types, columns of xml type are defined just like any other columns. (But they can't be used in primary keys.)

    Now, you'll insert your XML documents into xmltest and query it to see that they were stored.

Try It Out: Storing and Retrieving XML Documents

To insert your XML documents:

    1. Replace the code in the SQL edit window with that in Listing 17-9.

Listing 17-9. *Inserting XML Documents into* xmltest

```
insert into xmltest
values(
1,
'
```

```
<states>
    <state>
        <abbr>CA</abbr>
        <name>California</name>
        <city>Berkeley</city>
        <city>Los Angeles</city>
        <city>Wilmington</city>
    </state>
    <state>
        <abbr>DE</abbr>
        <name>Delaware</name>
        <city>Newark</city>
        <city>Wilmington</city>
    </state>
</states>
'
)
;


insert into xmltest
values(
2,
'
<states>
    <state abbr="CA" name="California">
        <city name="Berkeley"/>
        <city name="Los Angeles"/>
        <city name="Wilmington"/>
    </state>
    <state abbr="DE" name="Delaware">
        <city name="Newark"/>
        <city name="Wilmington"/>
    </state>
</states>
'
)
```

2. Run the two INSERT statements, then display the table with select * from xmltest.
   You see the two rows displayed. Click on the xdoc column in the first row, and you
   should see the XML shown in Figure 17-7.

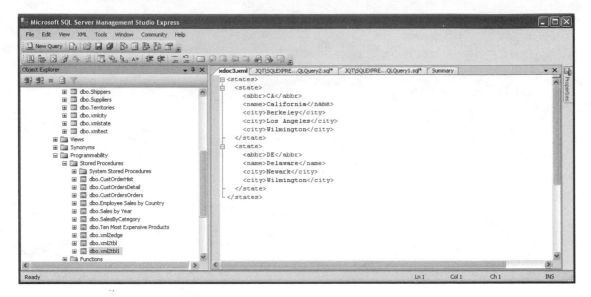

Figure 17-7. *Viewing an XML document*

How It Works

It works the same way all INSERTs work. You simply provide the primary keys as integers and the XML documents as strings. The query works just as expected too.

Now that you have some XML documents in a database, let's see how OPENXML handles them.

Try It Out: Using OPENXML with XML Columns

To use OPENXML with the second XML document in xmltest:

1. Run the code in Listing 17-10. You should see the results shown in Figure 17-8.

Listing 17-10. *Using OPENXML with* xmltest

```
declare @xdoc xml

    select
        @xdoc = xdoc
    from
        xmltest
    where
        xid = 2

exec xml2tbl @xdoc
```

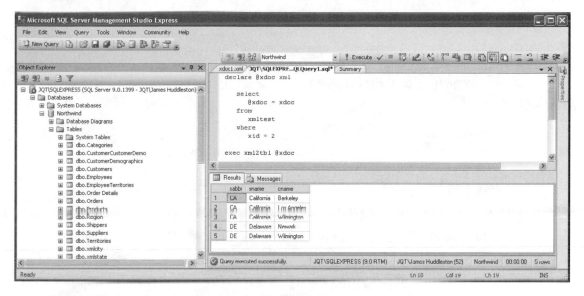

Figure 17-8. *Retrieving XML data as columns with OPENXML*

2. Now change the xid value to 1 in the WHERE clause and rerun the code. You should see the results shown in Figure 17-9. Hmmm. What happened? You get five rows, as expected, but all the values are NULL.

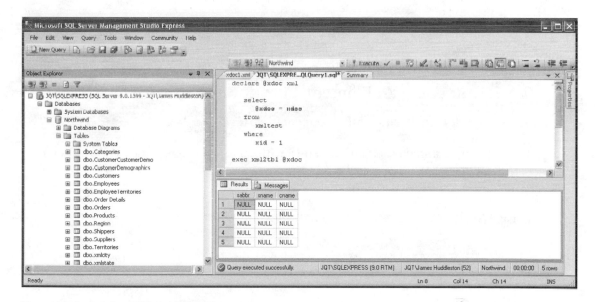

Figure 17-9. *Getting only NULL values*

How It Works

Unlike in Listing 17-6, where you hard-coded the XML document, this time you retrieve it from the database with a query. Since you expect a single value in the result set, you simply assign it to the local variable in the select list, so you can later pass it to xml2tbl:

```
select
    @xdoc = xdoc
from
    xmltest
where
    xid = 2
```

OPENXML works fine for the attribute-centric second XML document, but it returns only NULLs for the element-centric first one. This makes sense, since the schema you define in the WITH clause in xml2tbl

```
with
(
    sabbr char(2)       '../@abbr',
    sname varchar(20) '../@name',
    cname varchar(20) '@name'
)
```

isn't appropriate for the first XML document. Let's see how to make OPENXML correctly handle the element-centric XML document.

Try It Out: Using an Element-Centric Schema with OPENXML

To use OPENXML with the first XML document in xmltest:

1. Create a stored procedure, xml2tbl1, with the T-SQL in Listing 17-11. You should see the results shown in Figure 17-8.

Listing 17-11. *Creating the* xml2tbl1 *Stored Procedure*

```
use northwind
go

create procedure xml2tbl1
    @xdoc xml
as
    declare @xdocp int
```

```
exec sp_xml_preparedocument @xdocp output, @xdoc

select
    sabbr,
    sname,
    cname
from
    openxml(
        @xdocp,
        '/states/state/city',
        2
    )
with
(
    sabbr char(2)     '../abbr',
    sname varchar(20) '../name',
    cname varchar(20) '.'
)
```

2. Now change the query that returned NULLs to call xml2tbl1. You should see the results shown in Figure 17-10.

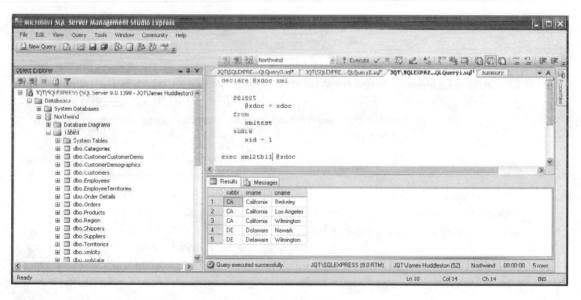

Figure 17-10. *Using OPENXML with element-centric XML*

How It Works

Schemas define the format of XML documents, so they have to match the format of whatever XML document you retrieve from the database. Since you aren't going after attributes, you change the flag from 0 to 2 in the call to OPENXML:

```
from
    openxml(
        @xdocp,
        '/states/state/city',
        2
    )
```

You also change the XPath expressions in the WITH clause to reference element rather than attribute names by removing the @ prefixes for the first two columns. Finally, you change the XPath expression for the third column to simply '.' since this means to retrieve the content for the element at the bottom level of the hierarchy, the city element, as you specified in the OPENXML call:

```
with
(
    sabbr char(2)     '../abbr',
    sname varchar(20) '../name',
    cname varchar(20) '.'
)
```

Well, that's enough XML for now. There's so much more you can learn about it, but very little we think we should try to teach you here. We believe that what we've covered in this chapter is exactly what you most need to get started with a firm conceptual foundation that will make it easy to pursue further study of the huge and complex (and often very confusing) world of XML.

■**Tip** Throughout this book, we've tried to provide balanced coverage of both T-SQL and ADO.NET, because each is essential to C# database programmers. However, T-SQL is by far the more important tool, and we hope we've introduced you to it in a clear and comfortable way. For more on the XML data type (as well as many, many other T-SQL topics), please see Michael Coles's *Pro T-SQL 2005 Programmer's Guide* (Berkeley, CA: Apress, 2007). It is simply the best book we've ever read on T-SQL, and you're now ready to read it with the same pleasure we do.

Summary

This chapter covered the fundamentals of XML that every C# programmer needs to know. It also showed you how to use the most frequently used T-SQL features for extracting XML from tables and querying XML documents like tables. Finally, we discussed the xml data type and gave you some practice using it.

How much more you need to know about XML or T-SQL and ADO.NET facilities for using XML documents depends on what you need to do. For many, this chapter may be all you ever really need to know and understand. For those who do more sophisticated XML processing, you now have a strong foundation for experimenting on your own.

This completes our coverage of C# 2005 database programming with ADO.NET 2.0. Our next (and final) chapter will preview the changes to database programming that are coming in C# 3.0 and ADO.NET 3.0.

CHAPTER 18

∎∎∎

Introducing LINQ

ADO.NET 2.0 is a mature (but still growing) data access API that has considerably more power than we've covered in this introductory book. It's reasonably straightforward to use and lets us simulate the same kinds of data structures and relationships that exist in relational databases.

However, we don't interact with data in datasets or data tables in the same way we do with data in database tables. The difference between the relational model of data and the object-oriented model of programming is considerable, and ADO.NET does relatively little to reduce the impedance between the two models.

But the future is quite promising. Microsoft is adding a general-purpose query capability, called LINQ (Language-Integrated Query), to .NET. LINQ provides a single declarative query facility for any kind of data source, including relational data, XML, and in-memory data structures.

▌Note Though it's called Language-Integrated *Query*, LINQ can be used to update database data. We'll only cover simple queries here, to give you your first taste of LINQ, but LINQ is a general-purpose facility for accessing data. In many respects, it's the future of ADO.NET. For a concise but comprehensive introduction to LINQ, see Fabio Claudio Ferracchiati's *LINQ for Visual C# 2005* (Apress, 2006).

In this chapter we'll cover:

- What LINQ is

- Installing LINQ

- Using LINQ to SQL

- Using LINQ to DataSet

What Is LINQ?

LINQ is a combination of namespaces and C# 3.0 (yes, we mean 3.0, not 2.0 or 2005) language enhancements. Through the *very* clever use of generics and other powerful new features of .NET 2.0 and using some functional programming techniques (like those natively available in F#), LINQ provides a high-level abstraction of virtually any data and emulates the query operations of the relational model. The LINQ Project seems to be just the beginning of many other future dramatic enhancements to .NET and .NET languages.

■**Note** Throughout this book we've called the C# language *C# 2005* because *Visual C# 2005* is the name of the compiler Microsoft provides with .NET 2.0. Internally, Microsoft calls the language *C# 2.0*. Likewise, we've called SQL Server *SQL Server 2005* because that's the name of the product, though it's internally version 9.0. Currently, the only name for the next version of C# is C# 3.0, so that's why we've changed nomenclature.

These operations are coded using LINQ's *standard query operators* (SQO), which are implemented as methods in class Sequence in the System.Query namespace. You can call the SQO methods directly, but C# 3.0 provides syntax that is much more elegant. You just code C# and the compiler transforms your code into the appropriate method calls.

■**Tip** The source code for System.Query.Sequence.cs is provided in the LINQ download.

LINQ has three major components:

- LINQ to Objects

- LINQ to ADO.NET, which includes

    - LINQ to DataSet (originally called LINQ over DataSet)

    - LINQ to Entities

    - LINQ to SQL (originally called DLinq)

- LINQ to XML (originally called XLinq)

LINQ to Objects deals with in-memory data. Any class that implements the IEnumerable<T> interface (in the System.Collections.Generic namespace) can be queried with SQO.

LINQ to ADO.NET deals with data from external sources, basically anything ADO.NET can connect to. Any class that implements IEnumerable<T> or IQueryable<T> (in the System.Query namespace) can be queried with SQO.

LINQ to XML is a comprehensive API for in-memory XML programming. Like the rest of LINQ, it includes SQO, and it can also be used in concert with LINQ to ADO.NET, but its primary purpose is to unify and simplify the kinds of things that disparate XML tools, like XQuery, XPath, and XSLT, are typically used to do.

In this chapter we'll preview LINQ to SQL and LINQ to DataSet, since they're most closely related to the C# database programming we've covered in this book.

■**Note** LINQ to Entities will bring LINQ to the ADO.NET Entity Framework, which combines an Entity Data Model with an extended version of SQL (eSQL) in yet another effort to address the data-object impedance issue. Since the Entity Framework is an ADO.NET 3.0 feature, we won't cover LINQ to Entities here

---

Installing LINQ

Installing LINQ doesn't replace any .NET 2.0 assemblies, but it does change our VCSE development environment, adding some new project types that support LINQ and use the C# 3.0 compiler (as you'll see later in Figure 18-7).

The May 2006 LINQ CTP (Community Technology Preview) can be downloaded from the LINQ Project home page, http://msdn.microsoft.com/data/ref/linq/. Go there and click Microsoft Visual Studio Code Name "Orcas" - LINQ CTP (May 2006), which will take you to the download page. It's small enough to just run the download if you have a reasonably fast Internet connection, but we save it to c:\bcs2005db\install.

To install LINQ:

1. Run LINQ Preview (May 2006).msi, which starts the LINQ installation process. When the Welcome window appears (see Figure 18-1), click Next.

2. When the License Agreement window appears (see Figure 18-2), click the I Agree radio button and when the Next button is enabled, click it.

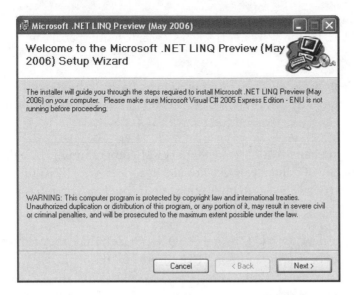

Figure 18-1. *LINQ installation Welcome window*

Figure 18-2. *LINQ License Agreement window*

3. When the Update C# Language Service for LINQ window appears (see Figure 18-3), click the Update C# Language Service radio button and click Next.

4. When the Confirm Installation window appears (see Figure 18-4), click Next.

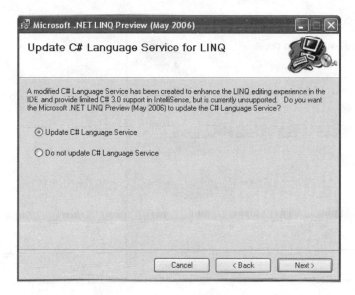

Figure 18-3. *Update C# Language Service for LINQ window*

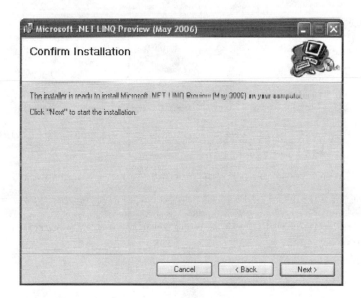

Figure 18-4. *LINQ Confirm Installation window*

5. A progress window appears (see Figure 18-5). When the Next button is enabled, click it.

6. When the Installation Complete window appears (see Figure 18-6), click Close. LINQ is now installed, and you'll find a lot of useful things in C:\Program Files\ LINQ Preview. (We recommend you look at ReadMe for C#.htm.)

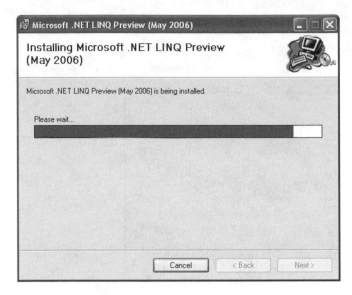

Figure 18-5. *LINQ insallation progress window*

Figure 18-6. *LINQ Installation Complete window*

7. Open VCSE and create a new project. You should see the four new templates for LINQ shown in Figure 18-7. Select LINQ Console Application, change the project name to Chapter18, and click OK.

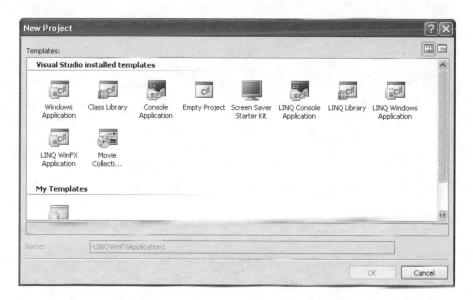

Figure 18-7. *VCSE New Project window with LINQ templates*

8. A message box will alert you to your use of an unsupported version of C# 3.0 (see Figure 18-8). Don't worry, it works well enough for this chapter (in fact, it works quite stably). Click OK.

Figure 18-8. *Unsupported version of C# 3.0 message box*

9. In Solution Explorer, expand the References node. Note the four new assemblies (System.Data.DLinq, System.Data.Extensions, System.Query, and System.Xml.XLinq) VCSE automatically provides (see Figure 18-9).

10. Double-click Program.cs. Note the three new namespaces (System.Query, System.Xml.XLinq, and System.Data.DLinq) VCSE automatically provides using directives for (see Figure 18-10). Save the solution. We're ready to do some LINQ database programming.

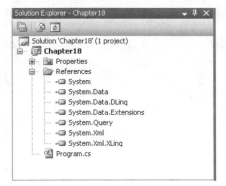

Figure 18-9. *LINQ references*

```
Program.cs  Start Page
Chapter18.Program                              Main(string[] args)
 1  using System;
 2  using System.Collections.Generic;
 3  using System.Text;
 4  using System.Query;
 5  using System.Xml.XLinq;
 6  using System.Data.DLinq;
 7
 8  namespace Chapter18
 9  {
10      class Program
11      {
12          static void Main(string[] args)
13          {
14          }
15      }
16  }
17
```

Figure 18-10. *LINQ references*

Using LINQ to SQL

LINQ to SQL is a facility for managing and accessing relational data as objects. It's logically similar to ADO.NET in some ways but views data from a more abstract perspective that simplifies many operations. It connects to a database, converts LINQ constructs into SQL, submits the SQL, transforms results into objects, and can even track changes and automatically request database updates.

A simple LINQ query requires three things:

- An entity class

- A data context

- A LINQ query

Try It Out: Coding a Simple LINQ to SQL Query

Let's use LINQ to SQL to retrieve all customers from the Northwind Customers table.

1. Rename the Chapter18 project in the Chapter18 solution to LinqToSql, then rename Program.cs to LinqToSql.cs. Replace the code in LinqToSql.cs with the code in Listing 18-1.

Listing 18-1. LinqToSql.cs

```csharp
using System;
using System.Collections.Generic;
using System.Text;
using System.Query;
using System.Xml.XLinq;
using System.Data.DLinq;

namespace Chapter18
{
    [Table]
    public class Customers
    {
        [Column(Id=true)]
        public string customerId;
        [Column]
        public string companyName;
        [Column]
        public string city;
        [Column]
        public string country;
    }

    class LinqToSql
    {
        static void Main(string[] args)
        {
            // connection string
            string connString = @"
                server = .\sqlexpress;
                integrated security = true;
                database = northwind
            ";
```

```
        // create data context
        DataContext db = new DataContext(connString);

        // create typed table
        Table<Customers> customers = db.GetTable<Customers>();

        // query database
        var custs =
            from c in customers
            select
                c
        ;

        // display customers
        foreach (var c  in custs)
            Console.WriteLine(
                "{0} {1} {2} {3}",
                c.customerId,
                c.companyName,
                c.city,
                c.country
            );
    }
  }
}
```

2. Run the program with Ctrl+F5 and you should see results as in Figure 18-11 (which displays the last ten rows).

Figure 18-11. *Retrieving customer data with LINQ to SQL*

How It Works

You defined an *entity class*, Customers:

```
[Table]
public class Customers
{
    [Column(Id=true)]
    public string customerId;
    [Column]
    public string companyName;
    [Column]
    public string country;
}
```

Entity classes provide objects in which LINQ stores data from data sources. They're like any other C# class, but LINQ defines attributes that tell it how to use the class.

The [Table] attribute marks the class as an entity class and has an optional Name property that can be used to give the name of a table, which defaults to the class name. That's why you named the class Customers rather than Customer. A more typical approach would be

```
[Table(Name="Customers")]
public class Customer
```

and then you'd have to change the typed table definition to

```
Table<Customer> customers = db.GetTable<Customer>();
```

to be consistent.

The [Column] attribute marks a field as one that will hold data from a table. You can declare fields in an entity class that don't map to table columns, and LINQ will just ignore them, but those decorated with the [Column] attribute must be of types compatible with the table columns they map to. The [Column] attribute also has an optional Name property that can be used to specify a specific column and defaults the column name to the field name. (Note that since SQL Server table and column names aren't case sensitive, the default names do not have to be identical in case to the names used in the database.)

You used the Id property in the [Column] attribute for the first field:

```
[Column(Id=true)]
public string customerId;
```

because CustomerID is the primary key of the Customers table. LINQ will deduce whatever it can about a column, but you need to tell it explicitly that a column is part of a primary key.

Note that you made only four of the eleven columns in the Customers table available to LINQ.

Tip SQLMetal is a tool that comes with LINQ that can generate entity class declarations from a SQL Server database. It's described in section 6.3 of the DLinq Overview for CSharp Developers.doc file, which comes with LINQ and is the basic documentation for LINQ to SQL.

You created a data context:

```
// create data context
DataContext db = new DataContext(connString);
```

A data context does what an ADO.NET connection does, but it also does things that a data provider handles. It not only manages the connection to a data source, but also translates LINQ requests (expressed in SQO) into SQL, passes the SQL to the database server, and creates objects from the result set.

You created a *typed table*:

```
// create typed table
Table<Customers> customers = db.GetTable<Customers>();
```

A typed table is a collection (of type System.Data.Dlinq.Table<T>) whose elements are of a specific type. The GetTable method of the data context specifies the data context to access and where to put the results. Here, you got all the rows (but only four columns) from the Customers table and the data context created an object for each row in the customers typed table.

Tip Data contexts can be *strongly typed*, and that's the recommended way to use them, but we intentionally didn't do that so we'd have to explicitly create a typed table and show you how to load it. See DLinq Overview for CSharp Developers.doc, section 2.2, to learn how to define a strongly typed data context.

You declared a C# 3.0 *implicitly typed local variable*, cust s, of type var:

```
// query database
var custs =
```

An implicitly typed local variable is just what its name implies. When C# sees the var type, it infers the type of the local variable based on the type of the expression in the initializer to the right of the = sign.

You initialized the local variable with a *query expression*:

```
from c in customers
select
    c
;
```

A query expression is composed of a from clause and a *query body*. We've used the simplest form of the from clause and query body here. This from clause declares an iteration variable, c, to be used to iterate over the result of the expression, customers—that is, over the typed table we earlier created and loaded. A query body must include a select or groupby clause, which may be preceded by a where or an orderby clause.

Your select clause was the most primitive possible:

```
select
    c
```

and, like a SQL SELECT *, gets all columns, so the variable custs is implicitly typed to handle a collection of objects that contain all the fields in the Customers class.

Note As we mentioned earlier in "What Is LINQ?" C# translates query expressions into calls to SQO methods. In fact, C# can also translate parts of query expressions into *extension methods*, which enable you to code custom methods for use with LINQ objects. This is far beyond the scope of this book, but it's a functional programming feature that you can use to great advantage.

Finally, you looped through the custs collection and displayed each customer. Except for the use of the var type in the foreach statement, this was just C# 2.0.

```
// display customers
foreach (var c  in custs)
    Console.WriteLine(
        "{0} {1} {2}",
        c.customerId,
        c.companyName,
        c.country
    );
```

Despite the new C# features and terminology, what you did should feel familiar. Once you get the hang of it, it's an appealing alternative for coding queries. You basically coded a query expression instead of SQL to populate a collection that you could iterate through with a foreach statement. However, you provided a connection string, but didn't explicitly open or close a connection. Further, no command, data reader, or indexer was required. You didn't even need the System.Data or System.Data.SqlClient namespaces to access SQL Server.

Pretty cool.

Try It Out: Using the where Clause

Let's modify LinqToSql.cs to retrieve only customers in the United States.

1. Add the following two bold lines to LinqToSql.cs:

```
// query database
var custs =
    from c in customers
    where
        c.country == "USA"
    select
        c
;
```

2. Rerun the program with Ctrl+F5 and you should see results as in Figure 18-12.

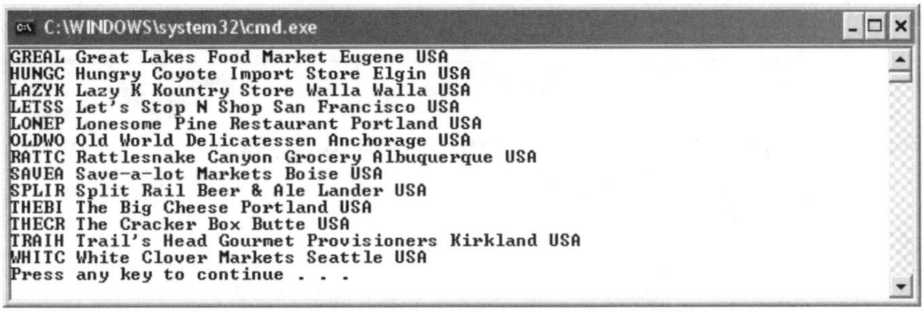

```
C:\WINDOWS\system32\cmd.exe
GREAL Great Lakes Food Market Eugene USA
HUNGC Hungry Coyote Import Store Elgin USA
LAZYK Lazy K Kountry Store Walla Walla USA
LETSS Let's Stop N Shop San Francisco USA
LONEP Lonesome Pine Restaurant Portland USA
OLDWO Old World Delicatessen Anchorage USA
RATTC Rattlesnake Canyon Grocery Albuquerque USA
SAVEA Save-a-lot Markets Boise USA
SPLIR Split Rail Beer & Ale Lander USA
THEBI The Big Cheese Portland USA
THECR The Cracker Box Butte USA
TRAIH Trail's Head Gourmet Provisioners Kirkland USA
WHITC White Clover Markets Seattle USA
Press any key to continue . . .
```

Figure 18-12. *Retrieving only US customers with a where clause*

How It Works

You simply used a C# 3.0 where clause to limit the rows selected:

```
where
    c.country == "USA"
```

It was just like a SQL WHERE clause, except for using == and "USA" instead of = and 'USA', since you coded C#, not SQL.

Try It Out: Using the orderby Clause

Let's modify LinqToSql.cs to sort US customers by city.

1. Add the following two bold lines to your revised LinqToSql.cs:

    ```
    // query database
    var custs =
        from c in customers
        where
            c.country == "USA"
        orderby
            c.city
        select
            c
    ;
    ```

2. Replace the foreach statement that displays the results with the following line of code. Add a reference for the ObjectDumper.dll assembly to the project. The assembly is in the C:\Program Files\LINQ Preview\Bin folder.

    ```
    ObjectDumper.Write(custs);
    ```

3. Rerun the program with Ctrl+F5 and you should see results as in Figure 18-13.

4. Add the keyword descending to the orderby clause:

    ```
    orderby
        c.city descending
    ```

5. Rerun the program with Ctrl+F5 and you should see results as in Figure 18-14.

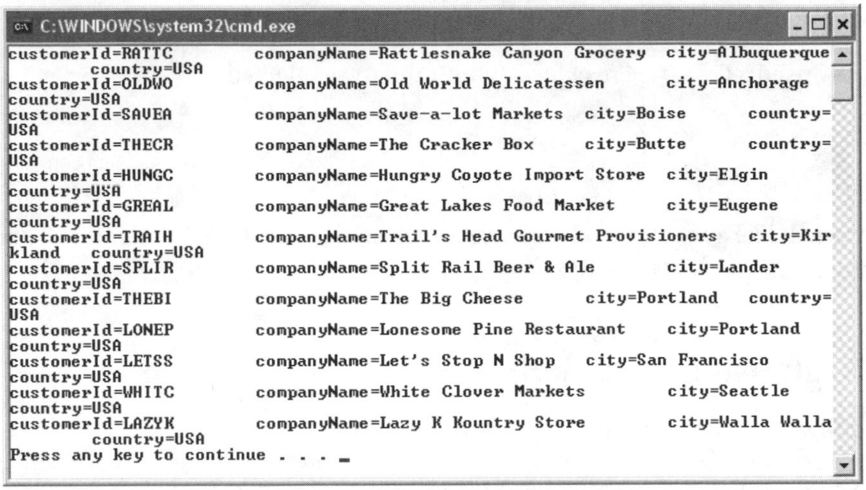

Figure 18-13. *Displaying US customers sorted by city with ObjectDumper*

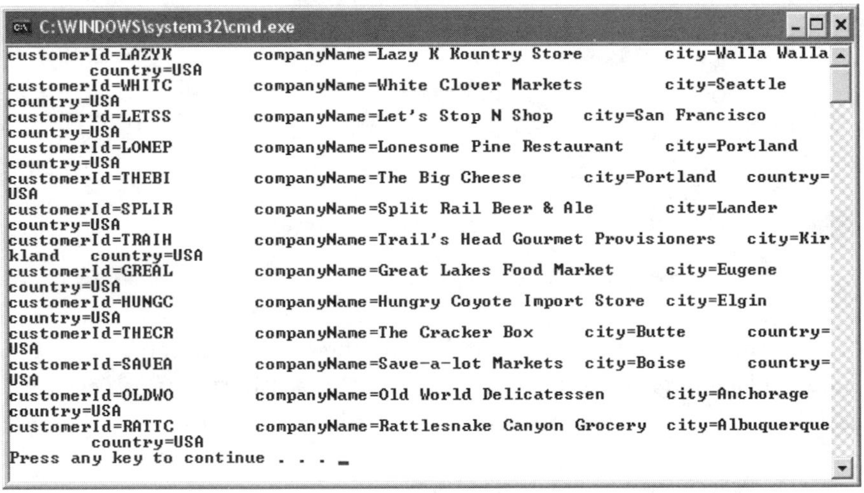

Figure 18-14. *Displaying US customers sorted descending by city*

How It Works

You simply used a C# 3.0 orderby clause to sort rows by city:

```
orderby
    c.city
```

Then you used the *ordering direction indicator,* descending (the default is ascending), to sort rows in reverse order:

```
orderby
    c.city descending
```

■**Tip** The new C# 3.0 features are specified in `CSharp 3.0 Specification.doc`, which comes with LINQ.

You used a utility method provided by LINQ, `ObjectDumper.Write()`, to display the result:

```
ObjectDumper.Write(custs);
```

`ObjectDumper.Write()` is a very convenient tool for playing around with LINQ in console programs. It displays all the fields in an object as fieldname=value pairs. The field names defaulted to the field names in the `Customers` class. (You'll see how to provide your own in the next section.) Its source code comes with LINQ in `ObjectDumper.cs`.

We've only scratched the surface of LINQ to SQL. Remember, SQO emulates relational operations. You can join database tables and nest queries. Just as with ADO.NET and SQL, you can update a database and call stored procedures and user-defined functions. You can even control (to some extent) what parts of a query expression will execute locally or on the database server. You can do a lot more than that too. C# 3.0 query expressions can be much more elaborate, yet still elegant, and can be extraordinarily powerful.

And that's with just the May 2005 CTP. The final release will be even richer.

Using LINQ to DataSet

ADO.NET datasets and data tables are rather sophisticated objects. How much of this sophistication you typically need is debatable (and ADO.NET 2.0 recognizes this by making data tables more independent of datasets for almost all uses).

As we saw in Chapter 8, navigating data tables is an iterative process through collections of rows and columns. It sure would be nice to make this not only more convenient but more powerful. It would be nice to use LINQ to Objects to query these collections. Unfortunately, neither `DataTable` nor `DataSet` implements either `IEnumerable<T>` or `IQueryable<T>`. Fortunately, there's LINQ to DataSet.

LINQ to DataSet lets us use the standard query operators and some operators that are specific to datasets and data tables. It treats data tables as enumerations of `DataRow` objects.

It doesn't care how data gets into a dataset. We could use a data adapter, as we did in Chapter 8, but since we've just seen how to use LINQ to SQL, let's use that.

Try It Out: Coding a Simple LINQ to DataSet Query

We'll modify the LinqToSql.cs code in Listing 18-1 to load a data table, then we'll use LINQ to DataSet against the table.

1. Add a LINQ Console Application project named LinqToDataSet to the Chapter18 solution. Rename Program.cs to LinqToDataSet.cs.

2. Replace the code in LinqToDataSet.cs with the code in Listing 18-2.

Listing 18-2. LinqToDataSet.cs

```
using System;
using System.Collections.Generic;
using System.Text;
using System.Query;
using System.Xml.XLinq;
using System.Data.DLinq;
using System.Data;

namespace Chapter18
{

    [Table]
    public class Customers
    {
        [Column(Id=true)]
        public string customerId;
        [Column]
        public string companyName;
        [Column]
        public string city;
        [Column]
        public string country;
    }

    class LinqToDataSet
    {
        static void Main(string[] args)
```

```
    {
        // connection string
        string connString = @"
            server = .\sqlexpress;
            integrated security = true;
            database = northwind
        ";

        // create data context
        DataContext db = new DataContext(connString);

        // create typed table
        Table<Customers> customers = db.GetTable<Customers>();

        // create dataset
        DataSet ds = new DataSet();

        // load typed table into data set
        ds.Tables.Add(customers.ToDataTable());

        // query data table
        var custs =
            from c in ds.Tables[0].ToQueryable()
            select new {
                cid = c.Field<string>("customerid"),
                co  = c.Field<string>("companyname")
            }
        ;

        ObjectDumper.Write(custs);
    }
  }
}
```

3. Make it the startup project and run it with Ctrl+F5. You should see the results in Figure 18-15.

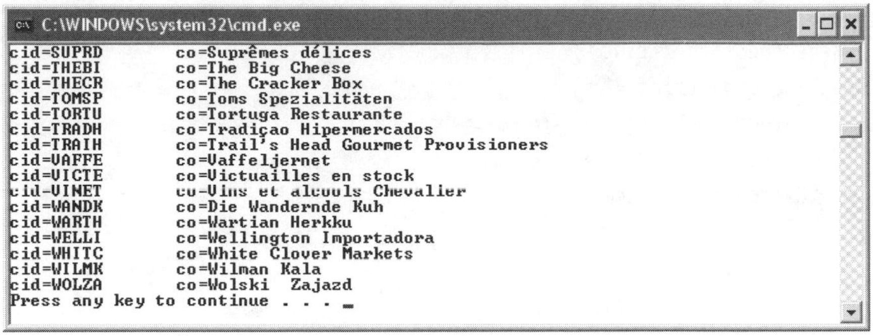

Figure 18-15. *Using LINQ to DataSet against a data table*

How It Works

Up through creating a typed table, the only thing that changed was

```
using System.Data;
```

to make the DataSet type available by simple name.

Since you wanted to store customer data in a dataset rather than leave it in a typed table, you added

```
// create dataset
DataSet ds = new DataSet();
```

to create a DataSet object and then added

```
// load typed table into data set
ds.Tables.Add(customers.ToDataTable());
```

to create a new data table in the dataset. You called the ToDataTable method on the typed table, customers, to convert the typed table into a DataTable object that could be stored in a dataset.

Note that since you used LINQ to SQL, no SqlClient operations were necessary.

You changed the query in a couple ways. First, you changed the expression in the from clause from a typed table to the data table you wanted to access:

```
from c in ds.Tables[0].ToQueryable()
```

and then you did something rather different in the select clause, to get only two columns from the data table:

```
select new {
    cid = c.Field<string>("customerid"),
    co  = c.Field<string>("companyname")
}
```

Regarding the from clause, the DataTable class doesn't implement the IEnumerable<T> or IQueryable<T> interface, but calling ToQueryable() on a data table makes it available to LINQ queries. You could have declared an implicitly typed local variable, like

```
var custq = ds.Tables[0].ToQueryable();
```

and then used custq in the from clause, but we've done it this way to demonstrate that the expression after the in keyword can be any expression that evaluates to an object LINQ can query.

Regarding the select clause, you used an *anonymous object initializer* (the block following the new keyword) to create an object of an *anonymous type*. The members of an anonymous type are properties inferred from the initializer, so this anonymous type had two members:

```
cid = c.Field<string>("customerid"),
co  = c.Field<string>("companyname")
```

The first member was named cid and was of type string, and its value came from the customerId column in the data table. The second member was named co and was of type string, and its value came from the companyName column in the data table. You needed to call the Field<T> method for each member to tell LINQ what type to use for the member, since you were accessing an untyped dataset.

Try It Out: Using LINQ to DataSet with a Typed Dataset

As we promised back at the end of Chapter 8, we'll use a typed dataset and show you how to create one. Our purpose is to show how a query expression can be simplified when using a typed dataset. You'll first create a typed table in VCSE and then modify the LinqToDataSet.cs code in Listing 18-2 to use it.

1. Add a LINQ Console Application project named LinqToTyped to the Chapter18 solution. Rename Program.cs to LinqToTyped.cs.

2. Right-click the project, click Add, then click New Item.... The window in Figure 18-16 appears.

3. Click the DataSet icon, change the name from DataSet1.xsd to TypedCustomers.xsd, then click Add. An edit window for TypedCustomers.xsd opens, as in Figure 18-17.

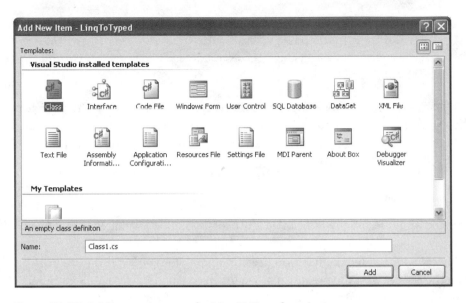

Figure 18-16. *Adding an item to the LinqToTyped project*

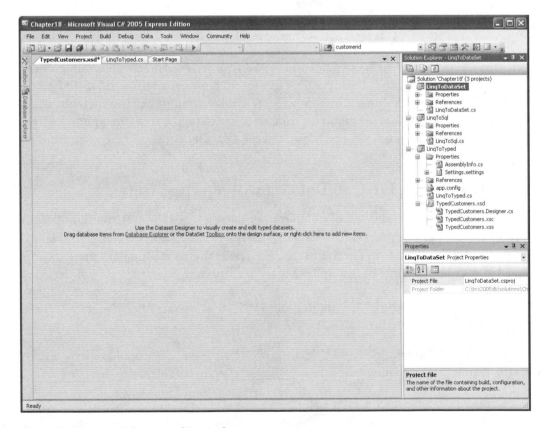

Figure 18-17. *Typed dataset edit window*

4. From Database Explorer, drag the Customers table onto the edit window. You'll see the screen in Figure 18-18. Notice that the CustomerID column is marked as the primary key (with a key icon). You now have a typed dataset with one table in it.

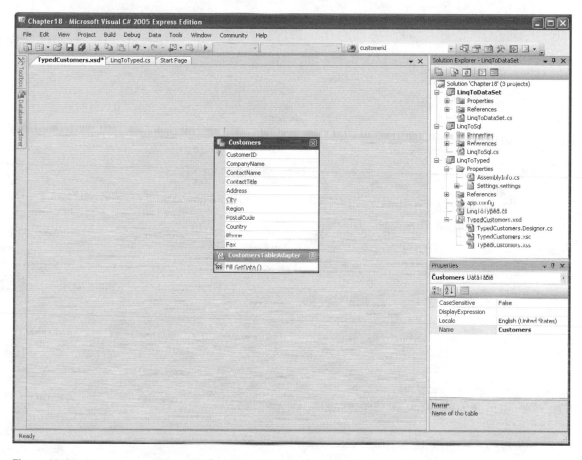

Figure 18-18. *Customers table added to TypedCustomer.xsd*

■**Note** Typed datasets can have as many tables and the same kind of relationships as untyped tables, and VCSE lets you create such things visually, but we only need the Customers table, so that's all we'll cover here.

---

5. Replace the code in LinqToTyped.cs with the code in Listing 18-3.

Listing 18-3. LinqToTyped.cs

```csharp
using System;
using System.Collections.Generic;
using System.Text;
using System.Query;
using System.Xml.XLinq;
using System.Data.DLinq;
using System.Data;
using System.Data.SqlClient;
using LinqToTyped;

namespace Chapter18
{
    class LinqToTyped
    {
        static void Main(string[] args)
        {
            // connection string
            string connString = @"
                server = .\sqlexpress;
                integrated security = true;
                database = northwind
            ";

            // create connection
            SqlConnection conn = new SqlConnection(connString);

            // create dataset
            TypedCustomers ds = new TypedCustomers();

            // create data adapter
            SqlDataAdapter da = new SqlDataAdapter(@"
                select
                    *
                from
                    customers
                ",
                conn
            );
```

```
    // fill data table
    da.Fill(ds, "Customers");

    // query data table
    var custs =
        from c in ds.Customers
        where
            c.Country == "USA"
        select new {
            c.CustomerID,
            c.CompanyName
        }
    ;

    ObjectDumper.Write(custs);
    }
  }
}
```

6. Run the code with Ctrl+F5 and you should see the results in Figure 18-19.

Figure 18-19. *Using LINQ to DataSet against a data table*

How It Works

You're using a typed dataset, so you can't just add a new data table to it as you did for the untyped dataset in LinqToDataSet. Instead of using LINQ to SQL to access the database, you filled the Customers data table with a data adapter (and you added a using directive for System.Data.SqlClient because you now need to use SqlConnection and SqlDataAdapter).

```
        // create connection
        SqlConnection conn = new SqlConnection(connString);

        // create dataset
        TypedCustomers ds = new TypedCustomers();

        // create data adapter
        SqlDataAdapter da = new SqlDataAdapter(@"
           select
              *
           from
              customers
           ",
           conn
        );

        // fill data table
        da.Fill(ds, "Customers");
```

Because you used a typed dataset, you were able simplify both the `from`

```
        from c in ds.Customers
```

and `select`

```
        select new {
           c.CustomerID,
           c.CompanyName
```

clauses in your query expression, by referring to the table and column names simply by
name, without having to explicitly make the data table queryable or specify the column
types.

■**Warning** Table and column names in typed datasets are case sensitive.

You simplified the anonymous object initializer even further, omitting the member
identifiers. The data table column names were used by default.

This concludes our introduction to LINQ, but it should be only the beginning of your
playing with LINQ. Just as query expressions provide an attractive C# 3.0 programming
alternative but do not supersede or deprecate traditional C# coding, LINQ to ADO.NET

offers an attractive alternative to using some ADO.NET 2.0 features but does not make them obsolete. You can use whatever techniques you prefer. There's no doubt, though, that the LINQ Project's perspective is Microsoft's on the direction ADO.NET and .NET languages should take.

■**Note** The underlying LINQ implementation relies on some powerful functional programming techniques, and C# 3.0's implicit and anonymous typing (among other things) are borrowed from functional programming. If you want to know more about the power of functional programming in .NET, read *Foundations of F#* by Robert Pickering or *Expert F#* by Don Syme (the inventor of F#), Adam Granicz, and Antonio Cisternino, both published by Apress in 2007.

Summary

In this chapter, we covered the essentials of using LINQ for simple queries. We introduced you to two of LINQ to ADO.NET's main components, LINQ to SQL and LINQ to DataSet. We discussed several new features of C# 3.0 that support using LINQ. We also showed you how to create a typed dataset.

With LINQ, database programming in C# takes another interesting and powerful turn, and with LINQ we bring our book to a close. Thanks for reading and best of luck in your database programming!

Index

You Need the Companion eBook

Your purchase of this book entitles you to buy the companion PDF-version eBook for only $10. Take the weightless companion with you anywhere.

We believe this Apress title will prove so indispensable that you'll want to carry it with you everywhere, which is why we are offering the companion eBook (in PDF format) for $10 to customers who purchase this book now. Convenient and fully searchable, the PDF version of any content-rich, page-heavy Apress book makes a valuable addition to your programming library. You can easily find and copy code—or perform examples by quickly toggling between instructions and the application. Even simultaneously tackling a donut, diet soda, and complex code becomes simplified with hands-free eBooks!

Once you purchase your book, getting the $10 companion eBook is simple:

❶ Visit **www.apress.com/promo/tendollars/**.

❷ Complete a basic registration form to receive a randomly generated question about this title.

❸ Answer the question correctly in 60 seconds, and you will receive a promotional code to redeem for the $10.00 eBook.

2560 Ninth Street • Suite 219 • Berkeley, CA 94710

eBookshop

THE EXPERT'S VOICE™

Offer valid through 4/30/2007.